A NOBLE FEAST

English Silver from the Jerome and Rita Gans Collection

at the Virginia Museum of Fine Arts

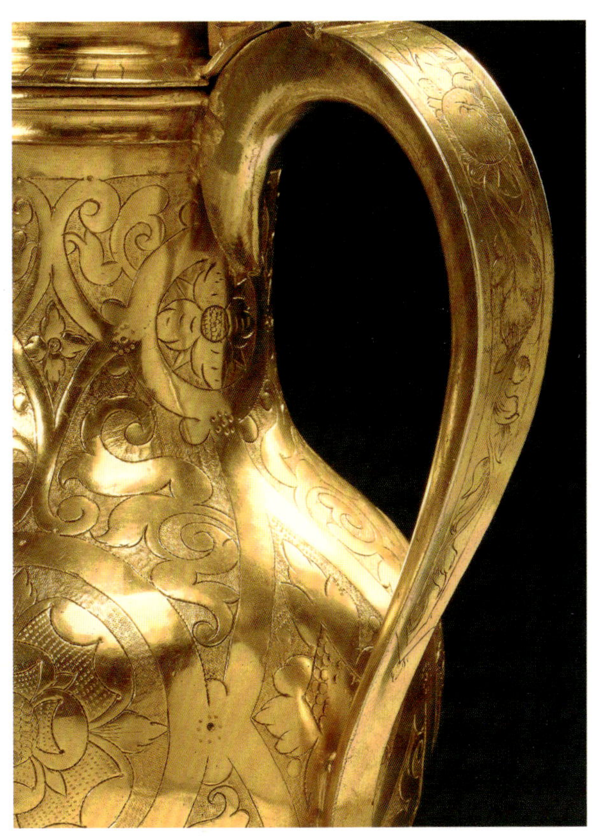

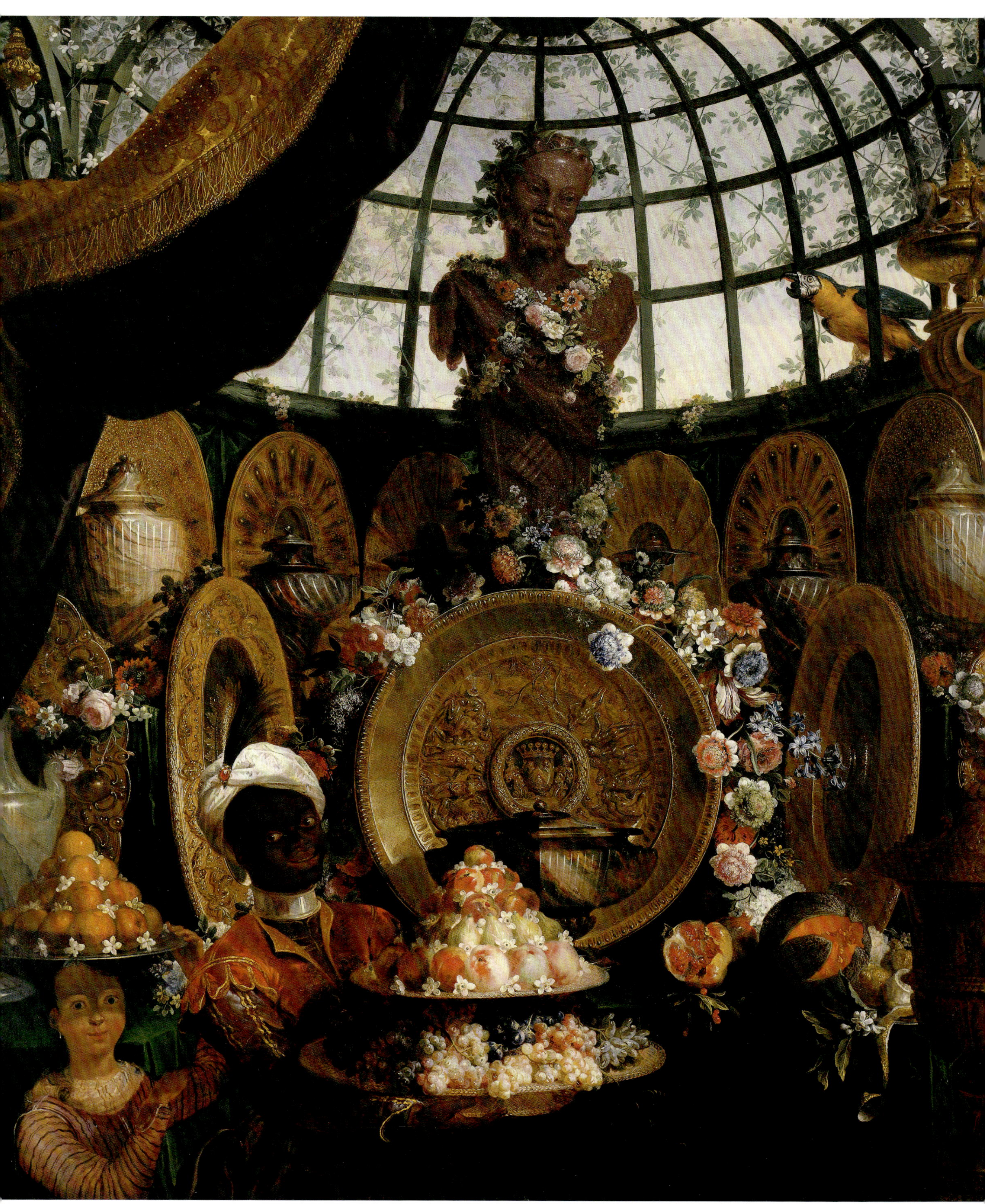

A NOBLE FEAST

English Silver from the Jerome and Rita Gans Collection at the Virginia Museum of Fine Arts

by Christopher Hartop
with a preface by Ellenor Alcorn
and two *entremets* by Philippa Glanville

VIRGINIA MUSEUM OF FINE ARTS
Richmond, Virginia
in association with
JOHN ADAMSON
Cambridge, England

Published to mark the opening of the new Silver Gallery
at the Virginia Museum of Fine Arts, February 27, 2007

Edited and produced by John Adamson

Co-published by
Virginia Museum of Fine Arts
200 N. Boulevard
Richmond, Virginia, 23220-4007
and
John Adamson
90 Hertford Street
Cambridge CB4 3AQ, England

Distributed by University of Virginia Press,
Charlottesville and London

First published 2007

Copyediting by Monica S. Rumsey, Richmond, Virginia
Designed by Design4Science Ltd., London, England
Printed on Burgo Larius 170 gsm matt by Conti Tipocolor, Florence, Italy

Frontispiece: Jean-Baptiste Blin de Fontenay (1653–1715), *Buffet under a Trellis*, oil on canvas, c. 1700. Magnificent silver-gilt dishes and salvers create an impression of profusion in this still life depicting the components of a "banquet," or elegant dessert of exotic fruits, sweetmeats, and spiced sweet wines, which was often served in a garden. *Virginia Museum of Fine Arts, Museum Purchase, The Adolph D. and Wilkins C. Williams Fund.*

Library of Congress Cataloging-in-Publication Data
Virginia Museum of Fine Arts
The Jerome and Rita Gans collection of English silver at the Virginia Museum of Fine Arts / by Christopher Hartop ; with a preface by Ellenor Alcorn and two entremets by Philippa Glanville. -- 1st ed.
p. cm.
Includes bibliographical references.
ISBN 978-0-917046-83-4 (alk. paper)
1. Silverwork—England—Exhibitions. 2. Gans, Jerome—Art collections—Exhibitions. 3. Gans, Rita—Art collections—Exhibitions. 4. Silverwork—Private collections—Virginia—Richmond—Exhibitions. 5. Virginia Museum of Fine Arts—Exhibitions. I. Hartop, Christopher. II. Title.
NK7143.V57 2007
739.2'30942074755451--dc22
2007002516

CONTENTS

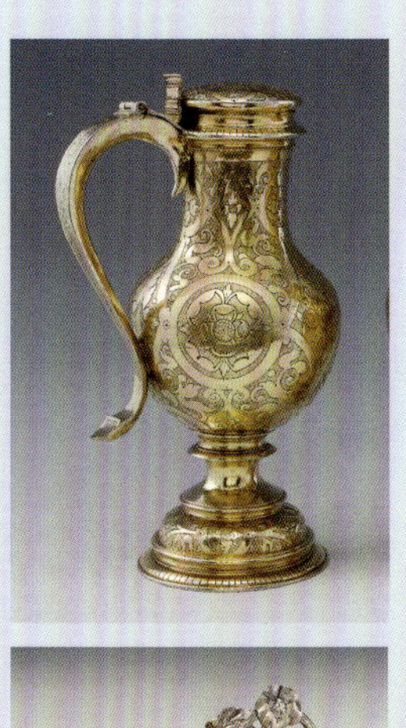
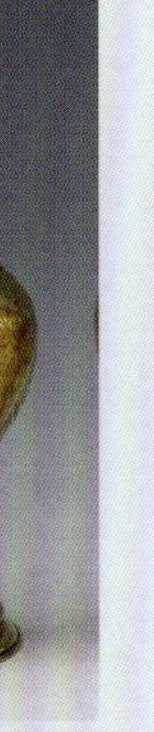
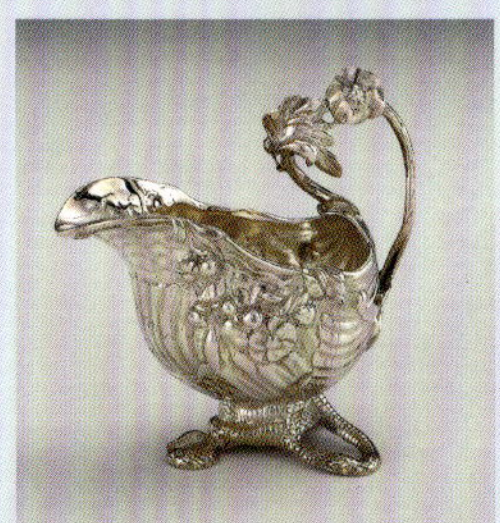
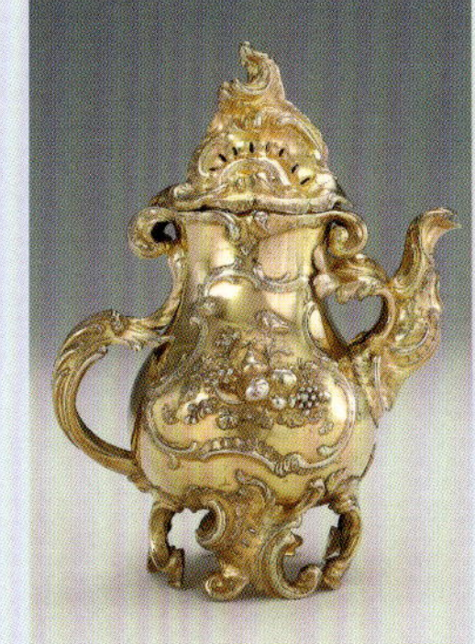

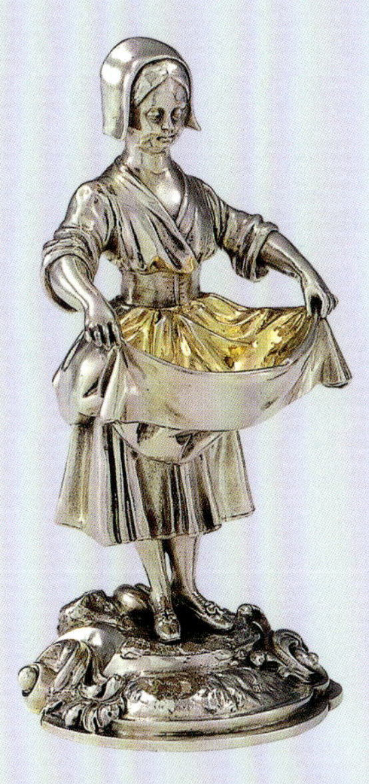

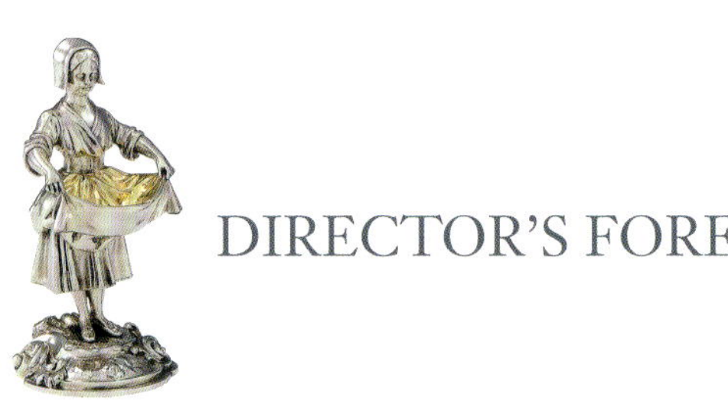

DIRECTOR'S FOREWORD

Since the eighteenth century, Southern homes have possessed the finest English silver, crafted in a great tradition of style and workmanship that dates back to the Middle Ages. It is therefore especially fitting that the Virginia Museum of Fine Arts, through the munificence of Mrs. Rita Gans, should have become the home of one of the most celebrated English silver collections in America. In 1987, with the loan of some seventy-eight pieces from their collection, Rita Gans and her late husband, Jerome, became generous supporters of the museum. In 1997, what had begun as a loan was made a gift and, since then, the Gans Collection displayed at Richmond has grown steadily, with further donations by Rita in 1999 and 2001. In 2006 she gave the museum sixteen more objects. Now, with this new gift, the Gans Collection at VMFA extends from a Henry VII chalice of about 1500 to a whimsical Chinese-inspired jug of 1878.

In addition to these generous gifts of silver, Rita has also supported a number of educational initiatives at the VMFA. In 2004, for instance, she underwrote a major symposium at the museum on English rococo silver, which attracted curators, researchers, and collectors from all over the United States and Europe. Eight distinguished speakers offered not only a wealth of new material, but also new insights. Their papers were published, also thanks to her support, by the Silver Society in 2006. The year 2007 has seen the opening of the new Gans Gallery and its innovative display of the entire collection at Richmond, which this book, *A Noble Feast*, celebrates.

Rita's dynamic personality is legendary, and I learned about her generosity to the museum long before arriving to assume the position of Director. She is completely committed to sharing her enthusiasm for silver with the Richmond audience, and she has formed lasting attachments to our staff. This happy relationship between the Gans Collection and the VMFA could not have happened without the enthusiastic and unstinting support given to the museum by Rita's brother Leon Horowitz and Carl Leonard, as well as by Rita herself.

At the Virginia Museum of Fine Arts, we are grateful to Mitchell Merling, Paul Mellon Curator and Curator of European Art; Richard Woodward, Senior Associate Director for Architecture and Design; and Lee Anne Hurt, Assistant to the Director, for providing their expertise, leadership, and assistance during the reinstallation of *Noble Silver: The Jerome and Rita Gans Collection of English Silver at the Virginia Museum of Fine Arts* and the publication of this catalogue. Kathy Gillis, Conservator of Objects, and her entire department have ensured that the silver is in excellent condition. Katherine Wetzel, Chief Collections Photographer, has provided beautiful photographs of the VMFA collection of silver. Lisa Hancock, Head Registrar, and Susan Turbeville, Assistant Registrar for Operations, were an invaluable source of knowledge during the writing of this thoroughly comprehensive study of English silver at VMFA. Finally, we owe special thanks to Suzanne Freeman, Publications Manager; Rosalie West, Editor-in-Chief; Sarah Lavicka, Chief Graphic Designer; and Monica Rumsey, Copyeditor, who have worked diligently with the author and the publisher of this book to help create a truly delightful publication.

This catalogue draws the entire Gans Collection together for the first time in print. Written by Christopher Hartop, the noted British silver scholar, it includes his entertaining and erudite essay on the history of eating and drinking in England from the seventeenth to the nineteenth century, richly illustrated by works from the Gans Collection. Philippa Glanville, formerly chief curator of metalwork, silver, and jewelry at the Victoria and Albert Museum, who has lectured at the Virginia Museum of Fine Arts on many occasions, penned two culinary interludes, aptly named *entremets*, or side dishes, looking at the pervasive French influence on the arts of the table in England.

Over the years, a number of silver scholars have researched and documented the Gans Collection for the VMFA. The museum's own decorative arts curator, Joseph Bliss, authored the first catalogue of the original seventy-eight objects in 1992. The British silver scholar John Culme prepared two supplements to that catalogue, featuring additional donations in 1999 and 2001. Since 2003, Ellenor Alcorn, for twenty years a curator at the Museum of Fine Arts, Boston, has been the Consulting Curator for the Gans Collection at VMFA. In this capacity she has overseen, with flair and meticulous attention to detail, the arrangement and installation of the new Gans Gallery. To this new catalogue, Ms. Alcorn has contributed a fascinating verbal portrait of Jerome and Rita Gans as collectors. This new scholarship has been expertly produced by John Adamson, whose Cambridge publishing firm so deftly assembled these fine texts into a meaningful and elegant whole.

We hope you will enjoy this feast in honor of the silversmith's art, and will soon visit the collection in person to savor it in all its shining glory.

Alex Nyerges
Director, Virginia Museum of Fine Arts
Richmond

ACKNOWLEDGMENTS

For Jerry and Rita Gans one of the most pleasurable aspects of collecting was the opportunity for friendship it offered. Many of those friends, in museums and the antique silver trade, have been of inestimable help in preparing this new survey of the collection. Thanks are especially due to David Beasley, Vanessa Brett, Harry Charteris, Eileen Goodway, Alain Gruber, Colin Levene, Martin Levene, Tim Martin, Jessie McNab, Lucy Morton, Tessa Murdoch, Anthony Phillips, Rosemary Ransome Wallis, John Martin Robinson, Timothy Schroder, Kevin Tierney, Steve Tucker, John Ward, and Harry Williams-Bulkeley. The Duke of Norfolk has kindly given permission for the Rundell, Bridge & Rundell bills of the 12th Duke to be quoted.

Ellenor Alcorn has been most generous in sharing her extensive knowledge and wisdom and I am grateful for the many discussions we have had on English silver. Philippa Glanville has, as always, been a source of inspiration. The work on the Gans Collection done by Joseph Bliss, John Culme, and John Davis has laid the foundations for much of the checklist in this book. I also wish to acknowledge the debt I owe to the published work of James Lomax and Barbara Ketcham Wheaton on dining, and of Timothy Schroder on silver.

Once again, it has been a pleasure to work with John Adamson, whose professionalism in editing and producing this book has been the mainstay of the project. Chris Jones in London has applied her customary flair in creating an elegant, eye-catching design, while in printing the book the team at Conti Tipocolor in Florence has shown its outstanding eye for quality and craftsmanship.

I am grateful for the friendship of Rita Gans and that of Leon Horowitz and Carl Leonard, which has resulted in many happy hours looking at and talking about silver in various places in Britain and America, always in the company of my wife, Juliet, to whom I dedicate this book.

Christopher Hartop

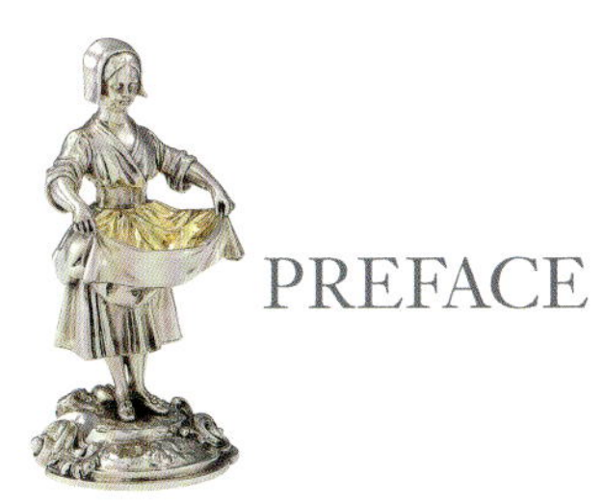

PREFACE

The Jerome and Rita Gans Collection of English Silver directly reflects the ebullient couple responsible for assembling it. The 102 pieces featured in this catalogue, ranging in date from the late seventeenth to the late nineteenth century, are vigorous, surprising examples of their kind. This is not a collection of teapots, tankards, or toast racks; it is unconventional in the best sense. The voluptuous soup tureen by Robert Garrard (cat. no. 77) and the quirky and whimsical Victorian salts (cat. nos. 95–98) do have their place in the history of the decorative arts, but they also represent the adventurous, energetic spirit of a remarkable couple. When the Gans Collection was given to the Virginia Museum of Fine Arts in 1997 the museum became, overnight, one of the most important repositories of English silver in America.

Jerry and Rita Gans, both New Yorkers, began buying silver in the 1970s. Rita, a mathematician, explains with characteristic candor that they became collectors by sheer accident. She and her husband were furnishing a new house on Long Island. Shopping one day with her brother, Leon Horowitz, she spotted a pair of John Hunt wine coolers, and, thinking of a bare spot in the corner of the dining room, asked the price. It was a considerable sum—equal, she says, to the price of a Levittown house at the time—so she decided to discuss it with her husband. That was the beginning of a long and stimulating enthusiasm that the couple shared with each other, and through their generosity to the Virginia Museum of Fine Arts, with the public at large.

Americans have had a long and passionate attachment to English silver. In the early years of the twentieth century most of them favored the austere, undecorated silver of the reigns of Queen Anne or George I. By the 1950s, a few, like the Memphis collectors Lillian and Morrie Moss, were more daring, favoring sculptural pieces in the rococo style or the monumental classicism of Paul Storr and his contemporaries. When the Moss collection was sold in the 1970s, Jerry and Rita took notice. They traveled to Los Angeles, where the silver dealer David Orgell had arranged the collection in his dramatically lit gallery. "We were like kids in a candy store," Rita recalls.

As their interest became more focused, Jerry and Rita Gans began to make annual trips to London. Many of the silver dealers then in business have since disappeared from the scene, but in the 1970s and 1980s there were at least a dozen sources for antique silver of high quality. There was also spirited competition among a small group of serious collectors for choice pieces. Jerry and Rita also bought at auction on both sides of the Atlantic, where they enjoyed the theater of the auction room. They pursued the pieces they loved, never intending to form a didactic collection. Jerry, an engineer whose business designed and manufactured power plants, was interested in the technical side of the silversmiths' trade. He also loved the histories associated with the objects, fixing in particular on the adventurous admiral who patronized Paul de Lamerie, George Anson. Rita responded more to the formal qualities of a piece. "I love a piece that talks to me, that has a vitality or simplicity about it," she says. A new purchase would sit, sometimes for weeks, on the desk in the middle of the room, where Jerry could absorb every detail of its design and construction, before placing it on a shelf with the rest of the collection.

Serendipity also governed the disposition of the collection. As their interest in silver became more serious, Jerry and Rita visited museums to strengthen their knowledge. It was a disappointing experience since, although a surprising number of American museums own English silver, few had galleries of any size devoted to it. Eager to share their enthusiasm, they decided to set out in search of a potential home for their collection. They were attracted to the Virginia Museum of Fine Arts' collection of Fabergé and they were impressed on their first visit. Unannounced ("we were two brash New Yorkers," Rita recalls), they made their way to the office of then-director Paul Perrot, who promised to visit them in New York. Some weeks went by with no call from Virginia, and Jerry picked up the phone, preparing to chide Mr. Perrot for his inertia. Perrot was delighted to receive the call, explaining that the note on which he had written their contact information had been laundered with his shirt. The collection was installed in the museum's Evans Court in 1988. At the opening, John Davis, Curator of Metalwork at Colonial Williamsburg, gave a lecture. It was the first time Jerry and Rita had seen their collection seriously interpreted for the public, and it confirmed their conviction that silver, with its rich forms and historical associations, could be a powerful enticement for museum-goers.

Following Jerry's death in 1996, Rita declared that her collecting days were over. She became interested in the educational component of the gallery, and supported an innovative discovery area where children and adults could explore the relationship of antique silver to modern life. She encouraged scholarship in the field through her support of publications and symposia, at the VMFA and elsewhere. Encouraged by her brother Leon and Carl Leonard, she did not forego the pleasures of collecting very long, however. In 1999 she added eight pieces to the museum's holdings, and in 2001 she offered the rosewater dish and pair of ewers by Benjamin Pyne (cat. no. 5), perhaps the finest examples of silver of the period in America.

The publication of this book coincides with the opening of a new gallery devoted to the Gans Collection and it also marks Rita's gift of a further sixteen pieces to the museum. This group, which includes the Drury-Lowe tureen (cat. no. 15) and the pair of livery pots (cat. no. 2), adds considerable depth and richness to the collection. The Jerome and Rita Gans Collection will doubtless be the subject of serious study for future generations, and schoolchildren and their parents will puzzle over the unfamiliar forms and unimaginable lifestyles that they represent. Most immediately, however, all will be fascinated by the joyful exuberance of the objects, a quality that perfectly describes Jerry and Rita Gans.

Ellenor Alcorn
Gans Curator, Virginia Museum of Fine Arts, Richmond

1. Nicolas Bonnart (1636–1718), *Elegant people dining*. Decorated pies and roasts take up almost all of the tabletop at this dinner *à la française* from the early eighteenth century. *Musée des arts et traditions populaires, Paris. Photo: Réunion des Musées Nationaux/H. Jézéquel.*

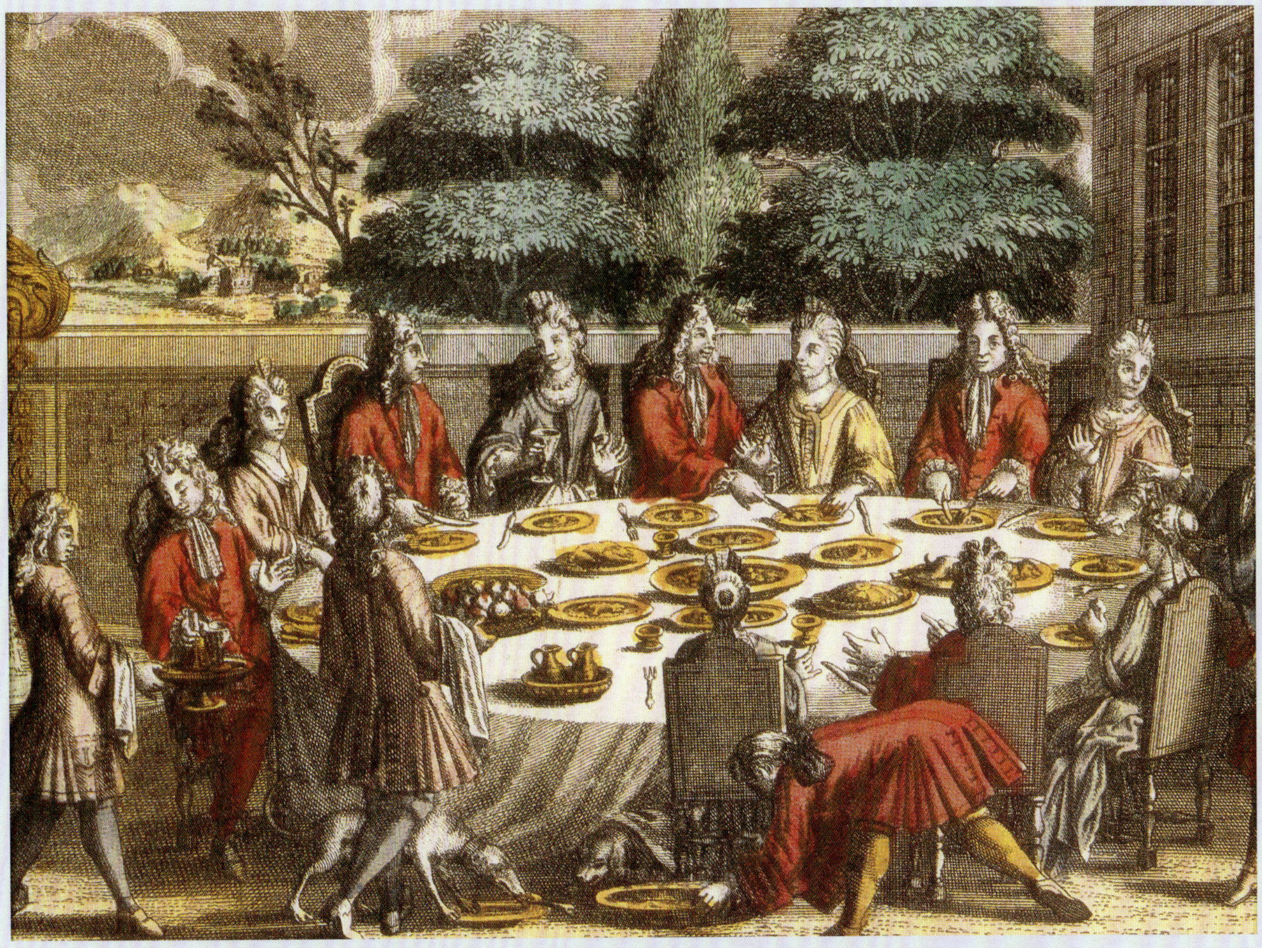

EATING AND DRINKING IN ENGLAND

1600–1900

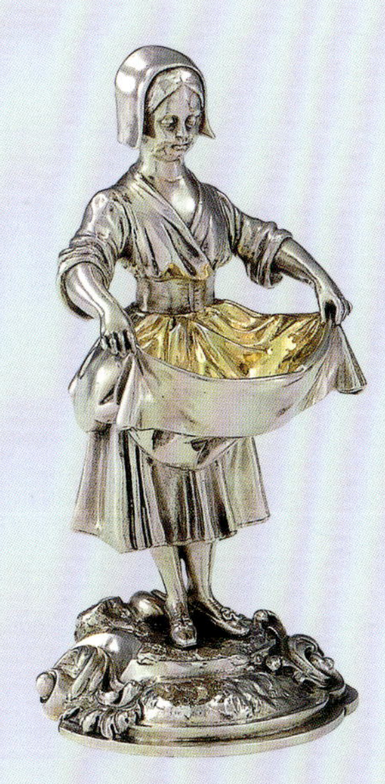

Hors d'œuvre

Show me another pleasure like dinner, which comes every day and lasts an hour.

Prince de Talleyrand (1754–1838)

It was not until well into the seventeenth century that French cuisine acquired its reputation for unparalleled excellence. Before then, the quality and freshness of English food, particularly its meat, had been held in high regard across continental Europe, and the hazards of eating in French inns had been well known to English travelers. So little time has lapsed since English cooking stooped to its nadir in the twentieth century, when England was among the first nations to sacrifice its cooking on the altar of convenience, that it is hard to believe that English food could ever have enjoyed a great reputation. In spite of the undisputed supremacy of French cookery during the seventeenth and eighteenth centuries, the Roast Beef of Old England, as celebrated by the artist William Hogarth in his picture *Calais Gate*, remained close to the hearts of English men and women.

This is the story of eating and drinking in England as told through its silver. At the same time, it is the story of the English people's love–hate relationship with French cooking and French wine, which was played out against a backdrop of intermittent war between the two nations. While the great Duke of Marlborough led the allied armies against the French at the beginning of the eighteenth century, the English aristocracy continued to speak French, dress in the latest French fashions, and employ French cooks. Things had changed little a hundred years later, for even as Nelson and Wellington sought to contain Napoleon's depredations in Europe, it was considered *de rigueur* for a fashionable aristocratic household in England to have a French chef and, lower down the social scale, bills of fare were written in French; even English cookery writers named their dishes in French. This approach was also reflected in silver; patrons at the end of the seventeenth century had vessels wrought in "French fashion" and, in the 1720s, Francophiles like the 4th Earl of Chesterfield ordered copies of newfangled French vessels such as wine coolers and soup tureens from London silversmiths. "The English are boobies," he famously declared to his son, and advised him to imitate the French in all things.

It would be a mistake, however, to see all English cookery, and the silver that was used to serve it, as emulating the French. Many English looked suspiciously at French sauces and assumed, often quite rightly, that they covered up the bad quality of the ingredients, while in silver the "native" traditions in technique and style were pervasive through all the social classes that possessed and used it. The Jerome and Rita Gans Collection is rich in silver both in the English and French styles, with a wealth of examples of the type of silver used by the aristocracy as well as by those whom Daniel Defoe dubbed "the middling sort." It therefore provides an elegant opportunity to tell the story of eating and drinking in England from the sixteenth to the nineteenth century through its silverware.

2. Frontispiece from Eliza Smith, *The Compleat Housewife: or, Accomplish'd Gentlewoman's Companion*, 1753, engraving. The superior quality of the ingredients in English cooking was proudly proclaimed by its advocates, who denigrated the "kickshaws" and sauces of French cuisine. *Private Collection*.

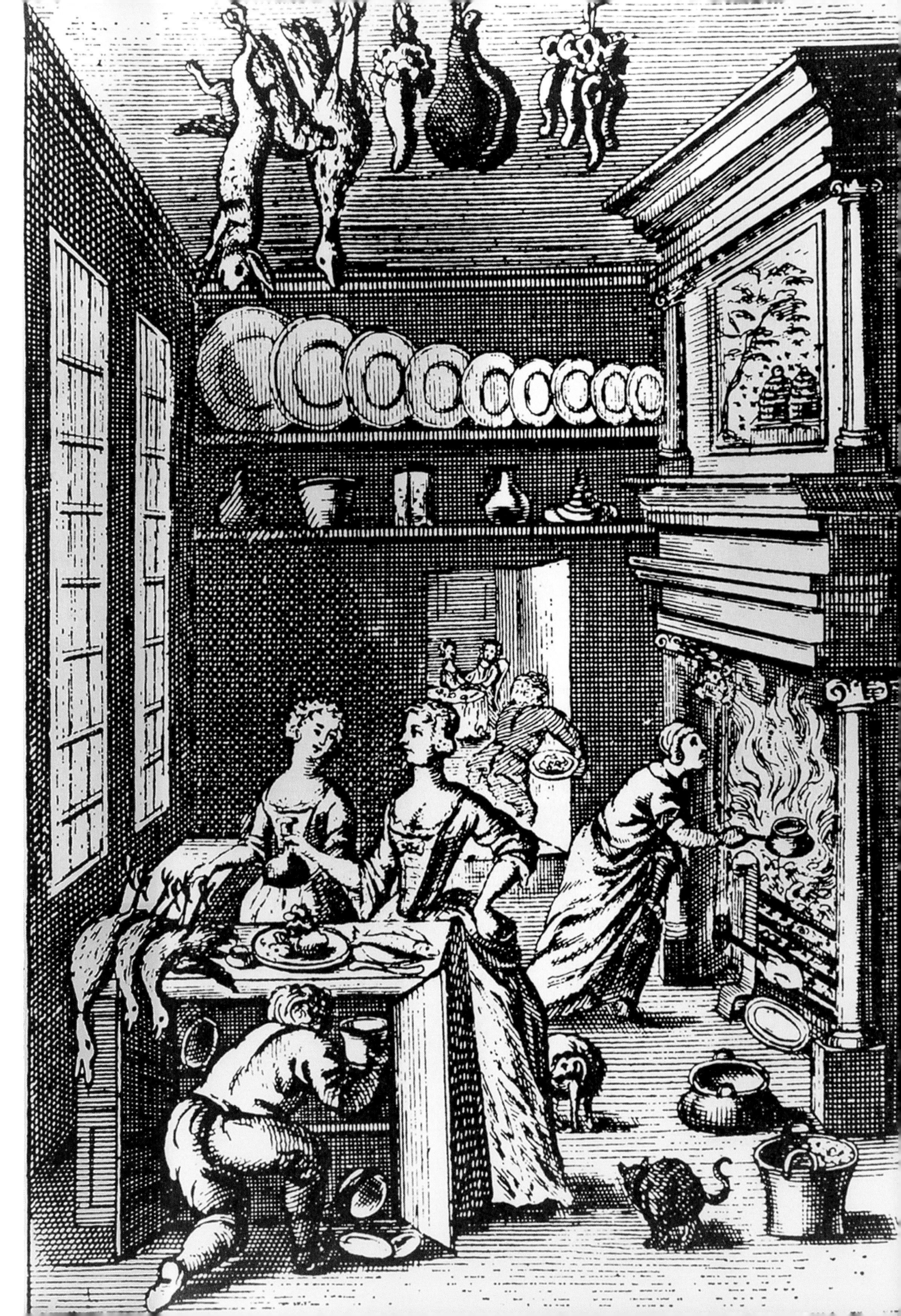

From Renaissance Magnificence to Enlightened Elegance

The Spaniard eats, the German drinks, and the English exceed in both.

Thomas Muffet, *Healths Improvement*, 1655

Silver has been the material of choice for eating and drinking—at least for those who could afford it—since time immemorial. During the period 1660 to 1900 it became accessible to more and more people, as growing prosperity broadened the consumer base, and supplies of the raw material increased. Attractive and malleable, silver does not stain easily and, most importantly, it is aseptic. In the Middle Ages, when virtually all eating and drinking vessels were communal, its purity was highly prized, even though its owners may not have understood the scientific reasons behind this. As important was the fact that silver was also currency, and could be melted down to provide cash at short notice. Just as easily, it could also be recycled into something more up-to-date, making it all the more remarkable that any silverware from an earlier age has survived the vicissitudes of later centuries. Of even greater impact than the upheavals caused by the Civil War in the seventeenth century, changes of fashion in eating and drinking between 1600 and 1700 led to the destruction of vast quantities of obsolete silver. As the ornate pies and tarts, and decorated roasts which covered the table in the reign of Elizabeth gave way to wetter dishes like *fricassées* and *ragoûts*, heavy silver platters and dishes were melted down to make new, deeper vessels.

In the sixteenth century, the quantities of silver and silver gilt found in the houses of the aristocracy, gentry and merchants were remarked upon by both foreign visitors and English commentators. William Harrison, in his *Description of England* of 1587, wrote: "Certes in noblemen's houses it is not rare to see abundance of arras, rich hangings of tapestry, silver vessels and so much other plate as may furnish sundry cupboards to the sum oftentimes of a thousand or two thousand pounds at the least ... likewise in the houses of knights, gentlemen, merchantmen and some other wealthy citizens, it is not reason to behold generally their great provision of tapestry Turkey work, pewter, brass, fine linen and thereto costly cupboards of plate, worth five or six hundred or a thousand pounds to be deemed by estimation."

These "cupboards of plate" were the tiered sideboards which were a regular feature of halls and parlors. Here were displayed the lavish cups and covers, tankards, and other drinking vessels that showed the wealth and status of the host. On the table itself there was far less room for display pieces, for the food—elaborately decorated pies and roasts, took up virtually all of the space available. A roast swan might be sewn up in its feathers, or a bacon pie might be fashioned to look like a boar's head. Apart from the serving platters needed for the many dishes that made up each course, the only other silver on the table was a costly salt, often heavily adorned and incorporating exotic materials such as rock crystal, set near the host. Only when the fashionable hour for dinner became later in the eighteenth century were candlesticks and candelabra needed on the dining table.

Drink was also served from these "cupboards" for, as the traveler and writer Fynes Moryson observed in 1617, "Neither use they to set drinke on the Table for which no roome is left, but the Cuppes and Glasses are served in upon a side Table, drinke being offered to none

3. Pair of livery pots, silver gilt, London, 1602/03, maker's mark *TE in monogram, pellet below*. "Livery," meaning allocation, included the daily allowance of drink given to all retainers in a noble household. Although by the early seventeenth century the custom of the lord dining in the hall with his entire household had all but died out, flagons such as these retained the name "livery" pots.
Cat. no. 2

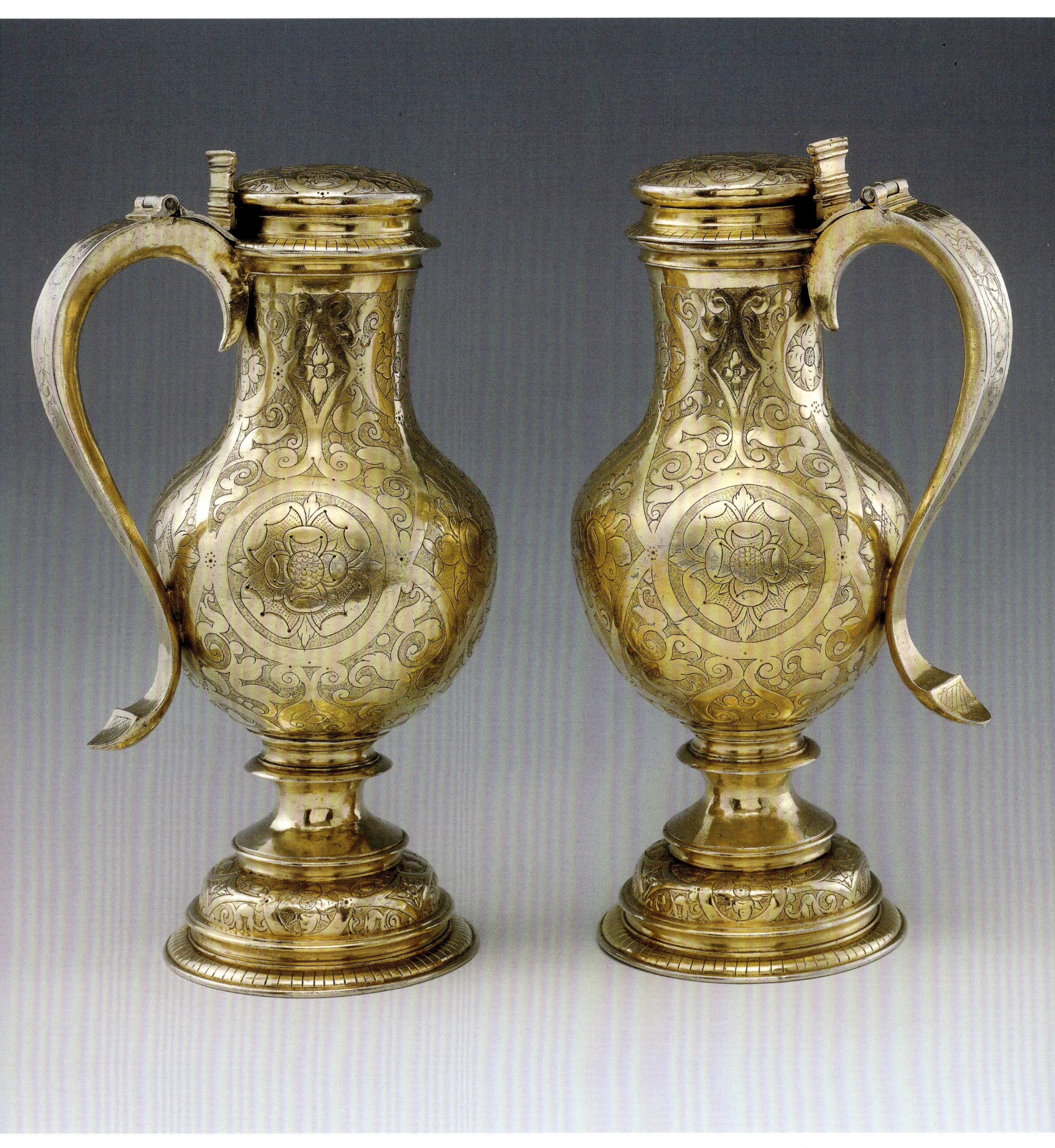

till they call for it." This custom, of calling for drink and then toasting your dining companion, persisted in England until well into the nineteenth century. The magnificent silver-gilt livery pots in figure 3 are a precious survival of this custom. The term "livery" comes from the old French word *livrée* meaning allocation, or what servants or retainers received from their lord as clothing, food, and drink. When a medieval nobleman dined in state with his entire household, large pots such as these were used to decant wine from the casks held in the cellar and were placed on the sideboard or buffet in the great hall.

The original owner of the two Gans livery pots is not known, but he was clearly a man of substance with a large household. The pots, with their continuous decoration of engraved stylized foliage and Tudor roses, are of a type common in silver, and copied in pewter and brass, from 1570 to 1620. But already noblemen had started to dine in private, with their families and friends, far away from the communal bustle of the great hall where their household, retainers, and workers all dined together. As a result, the plate used in the great hall gradually became less ornamental and more functional.

Some of the rare surviving examples of this type of vessel owe their existence to having been given to churches for use as flagons to serve communion wine, sometime after they began to look old-fashioned on the display buffet. In 1631 Lady Savile gave to Eton College chapel a pair of flagons from 1598/99 "to the intent that they may be employed always to the holding of wine for the Holy Sacrement [*sic*] only and not to any other purpose." Five similar flagons are in the Kremlin in Moscow, brought to Russia as gifts for the tsar by English diplomats hopeful of gaining trading concessions. All of them were given some years after they were made.

If the tradition of more private dining spelled the end of "livery" plate, it did not mean that display silver ceased to be made, however. It was just that a lavish display of silver and gold was made for one's family and social equals rather than for all classes. Indeed the original function of many objects was subsumed in their magnificence, and their sole purpose was for display. Before the introduction of the fork in the seventeenth century, the ewer and basin had been used to rinse a guest's hands with perfumed water at intervals throughout the meal. It is unlikely, however, that the Earl of Kent's exquisite ewers and accompanying basin (figure 4) existed for any reason other than to form part of a buffet of plate, and to act as a support for elaborately engraved heraldry. The English love of heraldry was often decried by the French who, while just as obsessed with genealogy, never gave the engraving of coats of arms the same attention on their silverware. "The boast of heraldry, the pomp of power," as the poet Thomas Gray described it, saw expression in the art of engraving, brought to a height of skill at the end of the seventeenth century hitherto unmatched in England. Ironically, though, most of the prime exponents of this new silver were French rather than English craftsmen and engravers, many of them Protestant refugees from absolutist France, forced to flee when, in 1685, Louis XIV revoked the Edict of Nantes which had given them a certain degree of religious tolerance in their homeland. Yet not all of them sought refuge on religious grounds—some, like the engraver Blaise Gentot, were economic immigrants. Attracted by the opportunities offered by London, fast becoming the largest and most prosperous European capital, as well as by the relatively free atmosphere of trade, these ambitious craftsmen and artists were to revolutionize the decorative arts in England. Gentot was in fact a Catholic, who worked in England for a number of years until bankruptcy forced him to return to his native France. His great achievement was to bring a new dimension to heraldic engraving on silver, with his use of dramatic draperies and cherubs. The mythological dragons which support the coat of arms in the center of the dish sit firmly on a ledge against a backdrop of ermine—the depth of the composition and intricacy of the detail render the function of the silver dish itself quite superfluous.

Anthony Grey, 11th Earl of Kent, whose coat of arms is the subject of Gentot's engraving, had been one of the pallbearers at the funeral of Queen Mary in 1694; he bore the Sword of State at the coronation of Queen Anne in March 1702. His son, who succeeded him a few months later, was for a time Lord Chamberlain of the Household to Queen Anne and in 1710 was created Duke of Kent. But for all these honors, neither father nor son seems to have made much of a mark on the political or social scene of their day, and on the death of the duke in 1740 their estates passed to distant relatives and the new

4. Rosewater dish and pair of ewers, silver gilt, London, 1699/1700, maker's mark of Benjamin Pyne; engraving attributed to Blaise Gentot. The advent of the fork had made the practice of pouring rosewater over a diner's hands obsolete by the beginning of the eighteenth century, but lavish ewers and dishes such as these continued to be made as display pieces, the flat dish providing a surface for the elaborate engraving of decorative armorials. Cat. no. 5

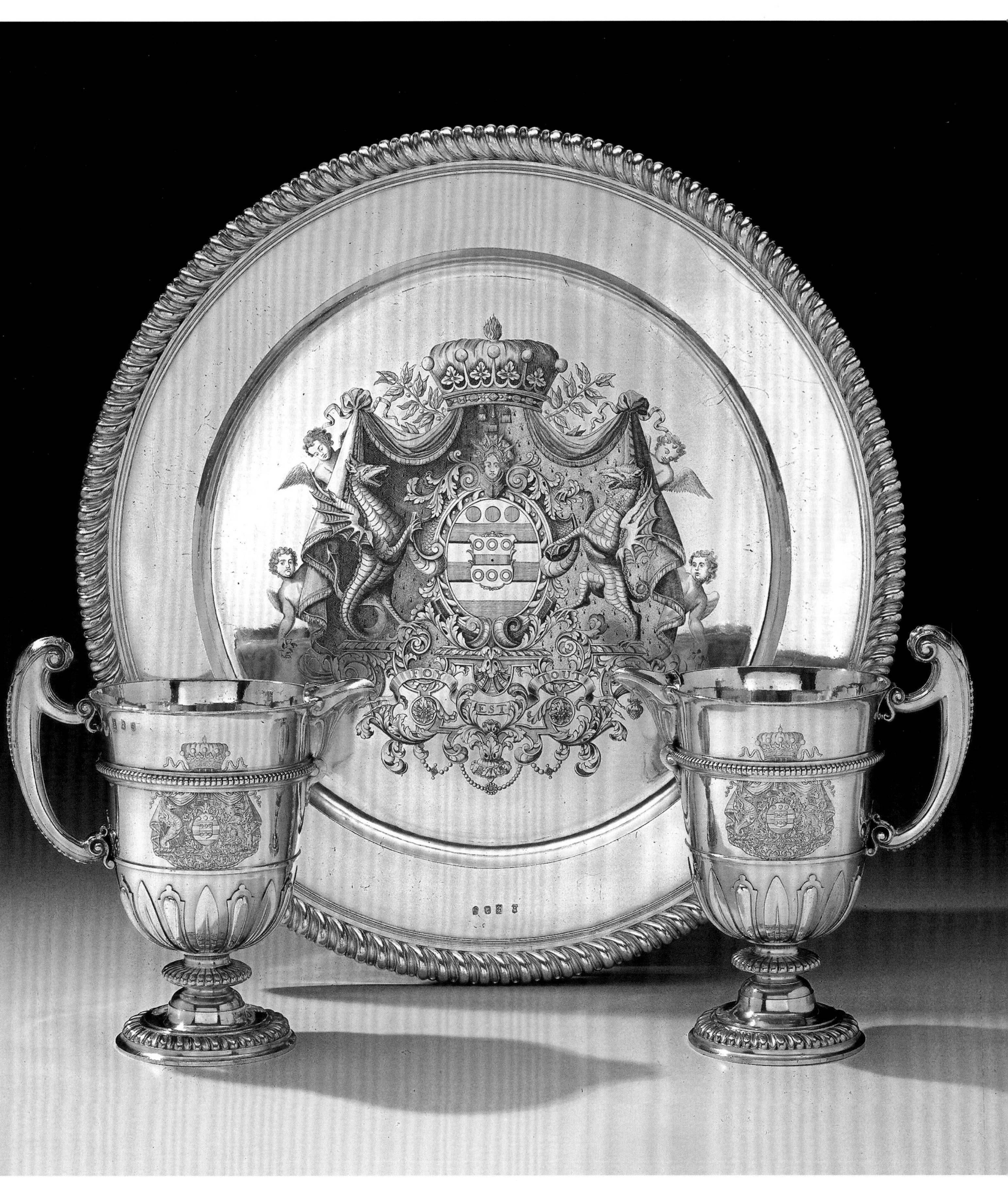
FOY
EST
TOUT

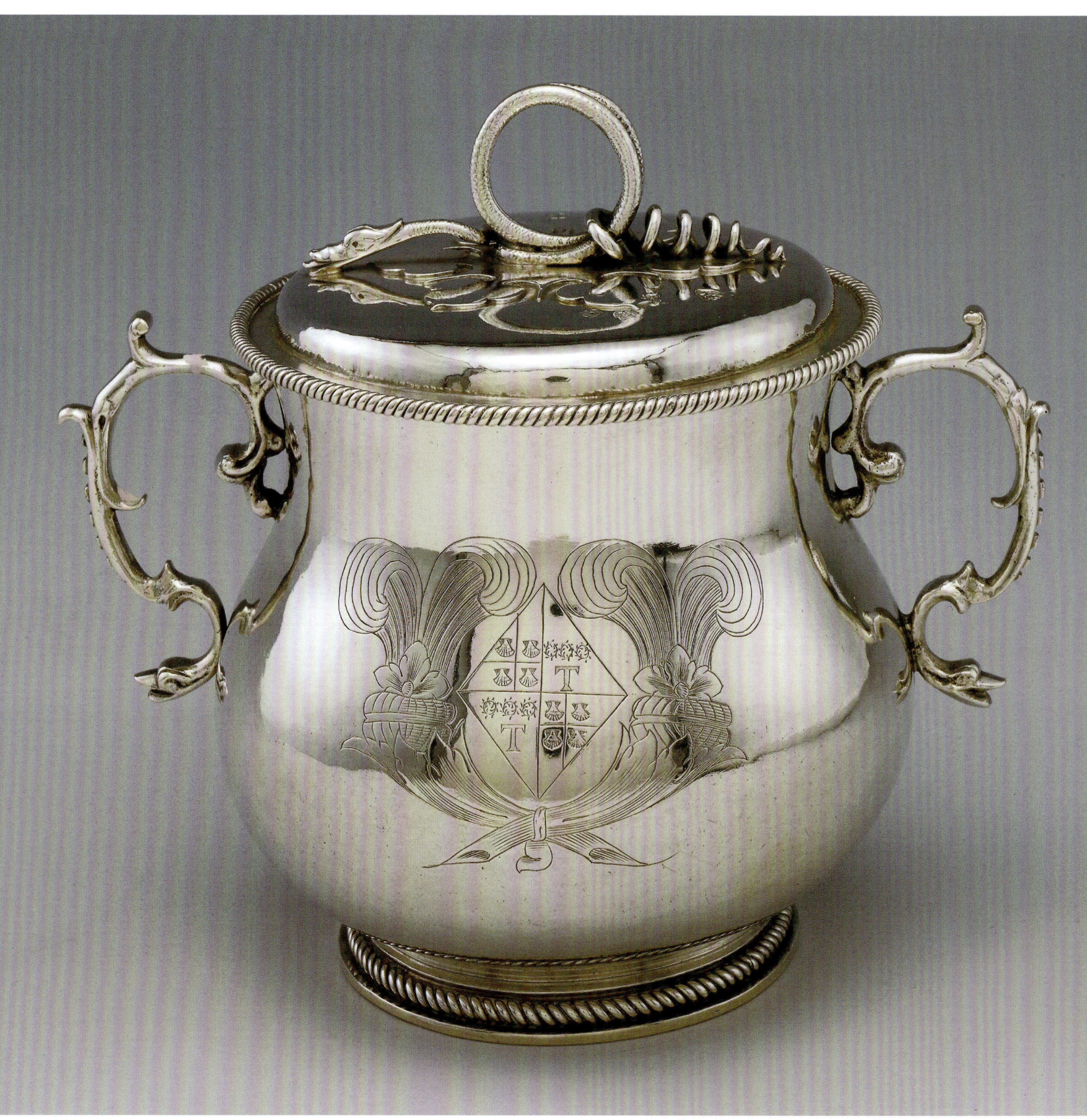

5. Two-handled cup and cover, silver, London, 1661/62, maker's mark of Robert Smythier. Variously known as "porringers" or "caudle cups," these multi-purpose vessels were used for drinking the hot, richly spiced alcoholic concoctions popular in the seventeenth century, as well as the meat stews recently introduced from France and the Iberian peninsula.
Cat. no. 3

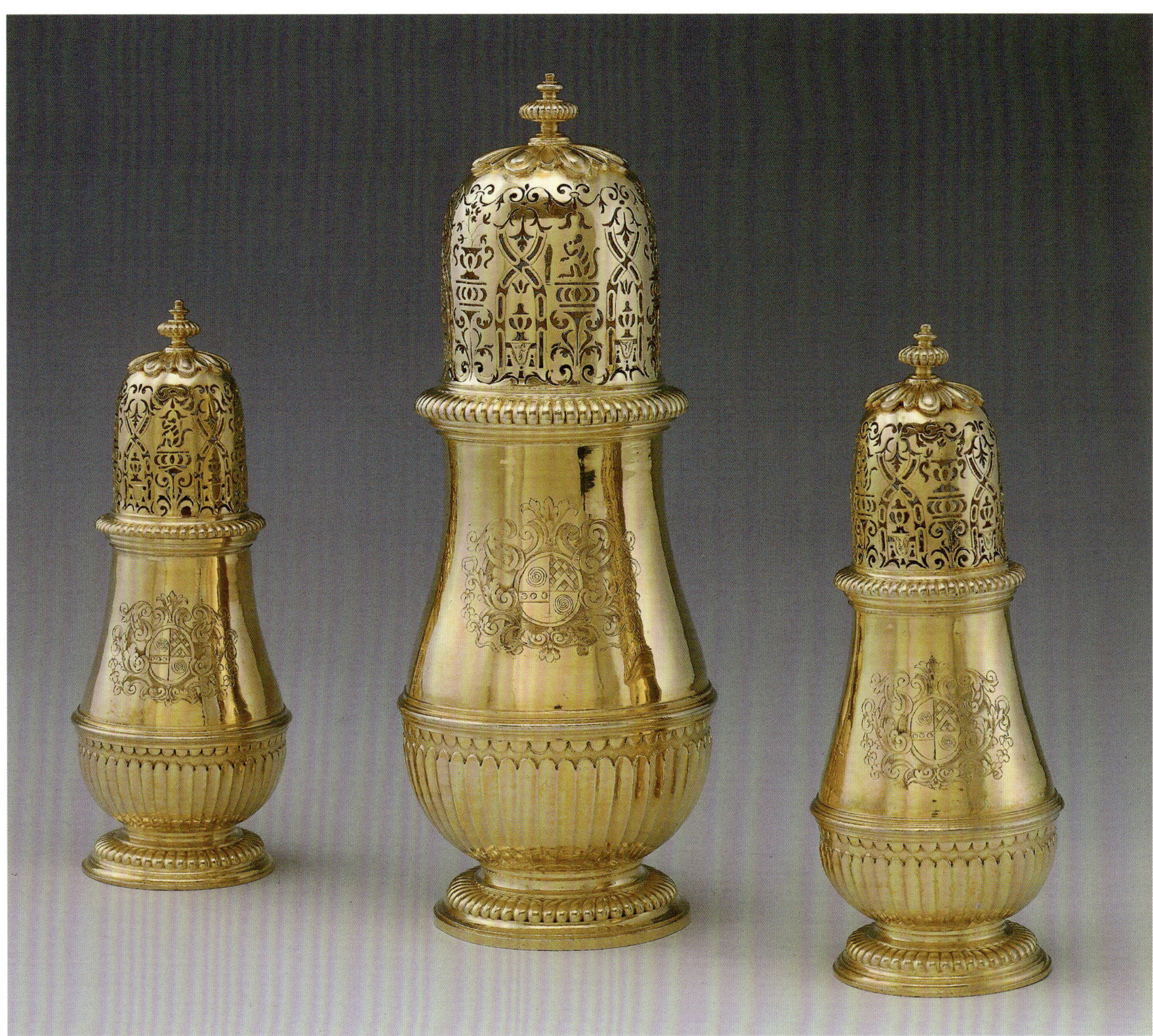

6. Set of three casters, silver gilt, London, 1704/5, maker's mark of David Willaume I. Formal dinners were concluded with a "banquet," or dessert, course using silver gilt. Sweet wines, exotic fruits, and sugary delicacies were consumed.
Cat. no. 6

dukedom became extinct. This may explain in part how the set has survived, and in such good condition, as no subsequent Duke of Kent sought to have the dish re-engraved with new ducal arms, or have the set melted down and replaced with something in the new rococo taste fashionable in the 1740s.

The two-handled cup and cover in figure 5 show the trend towards more private pleasures. Used as a drinking vessel for hot liquids such as posset, caudle, or spiced beer, the porringer is one of the most common silver vessels to survive from the seventeenth century. Posset was a rich alcohol-based broth usually taken in bed before retiring. On March 10, 1617, Lady Anne Clifford noted in her diary "I was not well at night, so I ate a posset and went to bed." Caudle was a warm drink of thick gruel blended with wine, ale, or spirits and sweetened and spiced. The "porringer" could also be used with a spoon for the more liquid stews becoming fashionable in the second half of the seventeenth century, such as French *ragoûts* and *olio* (sometimes spelled *oleo*), a rich Spanish stew of game and fowl, which came to England via Portugal in the wake of the wedding of Catherine of Braganza to King Charles II in 1662. Shortly before his death in 1685, Charles was served with a "porringer of spoon meat," which he consumed in the room of his mistress the Duchess of Portsmouth.

Porringers were multi-purpose vessels for both food and drink, while tiny versions were employed for drinking distilled spirits. Used by the aristocracy, the gentry, and the middle

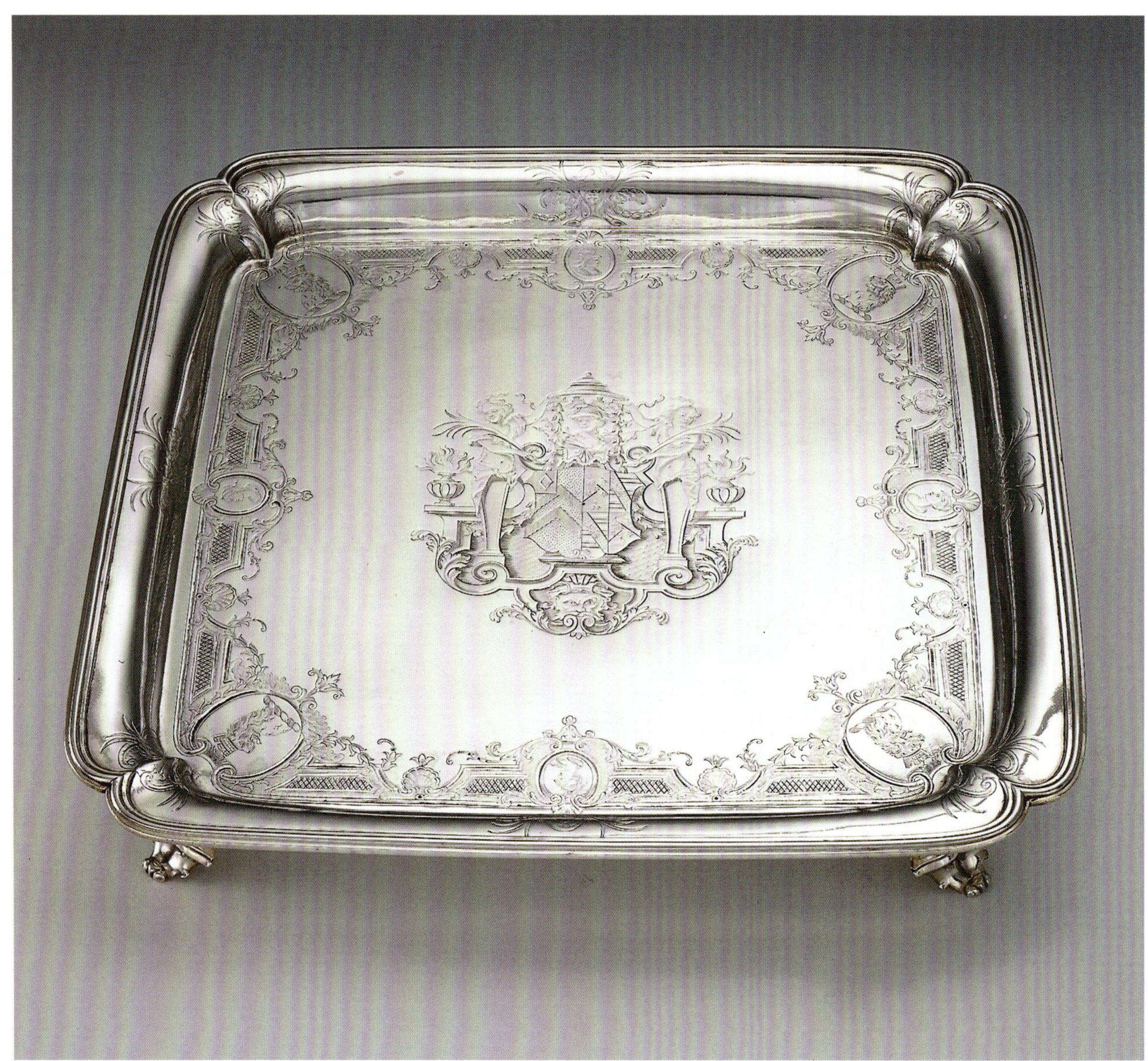

7. Salver, silver, London, 1727/28, maker's mark of Paul de Lamerie. Its form inspired by lacquer nesting trays imported from Asia, this tray was used for serving alcoholic drinks from the sideboard in the dining room, or for holding tea vessels in the withdrawing room.
Cat. no. 9

classes, silver examples were even to be found in taverns, where they were often engraved with the name of the proprietor. The example in the Gans Collection by Robert Smythier, made a year after the restoration of Charles II, is representative of the upper range in weight and quality. Smythier had the title of Subordinate Goldsmith to the King and, not unsurprisingly, this is borne out by the high quality of the object: the scroll handles and serpent-form finial are well modeled, in contrast to many contemporary examples which are coarsely molded and finished.

Since the Middle Ages, one aspect of aristocratic dining had always remained private. Besides meaning a formal feast, as it does today, the word "banquet" from the sixteenth century onwards could also denote the dessert or final course of a meal. It was often taken outdoors in the privacy of a banqueting pavilion in a formal garden or even, as at Longleat House in Wiltshire, in a summerhouse on the roof in order to enjoy the view. *Hippocras*, a spiced wine, would be served together with candied sweetmeats, exotic fruit, and other costly delicacies. By the end of the seventeenth century, the banquet had evolved into a formal component of the dinner itself, when the silver that had adorned the table for the first two courses would be removed, together with the tablecloth, and replaced with a new service of silver gilt. The set of three casters in figure 6 (p. 19) formed part of just such a banqueting service made for the Gorges family of Herefordshire on the Welsh border. The service also included footed salvers used to serve wine; these baluster-shaped casters were for sprinkling sugar and spices, such as nutmeg, onto the delicacies offered.

Contemporary travelers observed how in England it was not until this final course of a dinner that the drinking began in earnest. The English had a predilection for sweet wines such as sack, port, and Madeira, all of which were available when war with France—a constant feature of the political landscape for much of the time from the 1690s through the early 1800s—precluded the import of wines from Burgundy and Bordeaux. Sack was a rough white wine from Spain, while port was a strong red wine from the Douro valley in Portugal; both of these were found, in time, to benefit from the addition of brandy to preserve them in transit, sack becoming "sherry," an anglicization of Jerez, in southern Spain. At the beginning of the eighteenth century, port became the patriotic drink of the ruling Whigs, while the Tories and those among them who were Jacobites (secret supporters of the Stuart dynasty which had been deposed and exiled in 1688) drank red wine from the Bordeaux region, known in England as claret.

Drinking—and eating—habits changed radically, however, in the second half of the seventeenth century with the introduction of a new triumvirate of non-alcoholic drinks: coffee, tea, and chocolate. For us today, it is perhaps difficult to imagine a world without caffeine, but it was unknown to the Greeks and Romans, and to the medieval world. Liberal quantities of sugar, sprinkled onto meats and savories as well as desserts, had given the nervous system a gentle kick; but following the adoption of tea and coffee, food became markedly less sweet and more savory. As tea and coffee took hold, consumption of ale—which had hitherto been the drink of all classes throughout the day (in preference to the often unpleasant tasting water that came up from wells in London)—declined drastically.

Francis Bacon had first mentioned coffee in his *Sylva Sylvarum* at the beginning of the seventeenth century, and a coffeehouse had been opened in Oxford in the 1640s, but it was not until the years immediately following the restoration of King Charles II in 1660 that coffee and tea gained social acceptance. Tea was first thought of as a medicine and an effective cure for any ailment. On June 28, 1667, the diarist Samuel Pepys came home to find his wife "making of tea; a drink which Mr. Pelling, the Pitticary [apothecary], tells her is good for her cold and defluxions." Tea cost an astonishing £10 a pound, which was more than twice the annual wage Pepys paid his cook, so at first it was the drink of the very wealthy. Asian lacquer, porcelain, and metalwork provided the inspiration for the new vessels required to serve tea, coffee, and chocolate. For example, the square salver of 1738/39 (figure 7) copies the Japanese lacquer nesting trays imported into Europe during the period.

The salver is struck with the mark of one of England's most celebrated silversmiths, Paul de

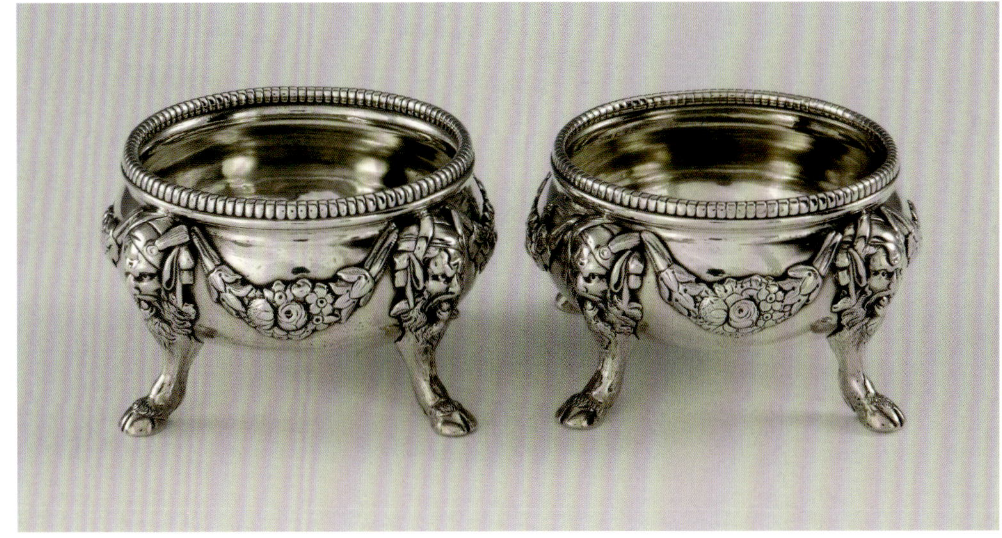

8. Pair of salts, silver, London, 1731/32, maker's mark of Paul de Lamerie. With delicate hoof feet inspired by French design prints, small salts like these were placed between diners around the table. Cat. no. 11

Lamerie (working from the end of his apprenticeship in 1710 to his death in 1751). De Lamerie's workshop dominated the London silver trade for much of the first half of the eighteenth century. Born of French immigrant parents, de Lamerie was one of the second generation of Huguenots who did so much to bring English decorative arts into the European mainstream through their contact with the latest French designs and their superior manufacturing techniques. The Gans Collection has nearly thirty objects from de Lamerie's workshop, more than from any other silversmith. It would nonetheless be a mistake to think of de Lamerie as an artistic virtuoso. Indeed, it is unlikely that he was involved in making silverware on a day-to-day basis. On the other hand, he directed a studio of designers and modelers, as well as a bustling workshop that was large by the standards of his day, and included hammermen, chasers (embossers), engravers, and casters. De Lamerie was also at the center of a web of "outworkers," who could be used to perform highly specialized skilled tasks. All this in no way lessens our appreciation for de Lamerie, for his vision and enterprise in coordinating this team resulted in the creation of some of the greatest silver ever produced in England.

Early works from de Lamerie's shop are plain, often with the French-inspired *Régence* ornament of pilasters and panels of criss-cross patterns known as diaperwork, a feature of silver produced by Huguenot silversmiths working in London. In the 1730s de Lamerie was among the first English silversmiths to adopt features of the rococo, the new style of restless movement, asymmetry, and naturalism that had taken France by storm. The pair of shells of 1734/35 (figure 9) takes naturalism to the extreme, for they were probably cast from real scallop shells and then finished painstakingly by hand. Their original function is something of a mystery. Shell dishes first appear at the end of the seventeenth century, usually in sets. In 1727 the Earl of Chesterfield received "sevon scallop shells" as part of the dinner service he took with him as ambassador to The Hague, while in 1740 John Trevor bought "5 scollops for oysters" from the silversmith George Wickes. Oyster sauce was a popular accompaniment to roast beef and it is possible that these shells were filled with sauce and set around the table. The fact, however, that their meticulously detailed outsides do not sit neatly on the tabletop (they tend to topple randomly) suggests that they may instead have been intended to be held in the hand, for eating oysters browned under heat. A 1723 recipe directs: "Lay a piece of Sweet Butter at the Bottom of your Silver Scallop Shell; then get a quantity of Large Oysters, and cut off the fins; put four in a shell, with some of their own liquor strain'd, grated Bread, a little Salt, Pepper, and a spoonful of white wine, and cover them with grated Bread, and set them over your stove to stew; and hold over them your Browning-Iron; half an hour will stew them."

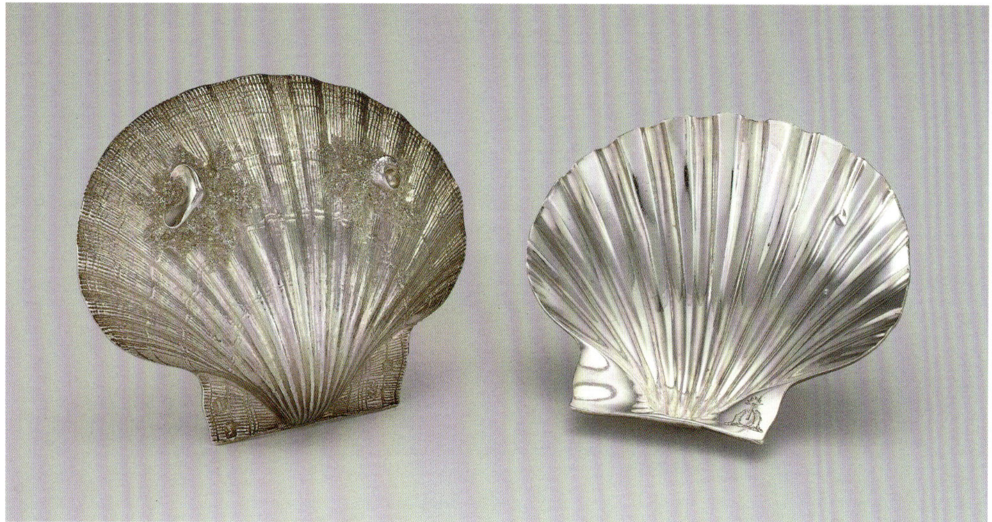

9. Pair of shells, silver, London, 1734/35, maker's mark of Paul de Lamerie. The original function of these dishes, apparently cast from natural scallop shells, is not clear. One possibility is that they were used for oysters *au gratin*. Alternatively, they could have been used to hold oyster sauce, into which diners would dip pieces of roast meat.
Cat. no. 13

Entremets I

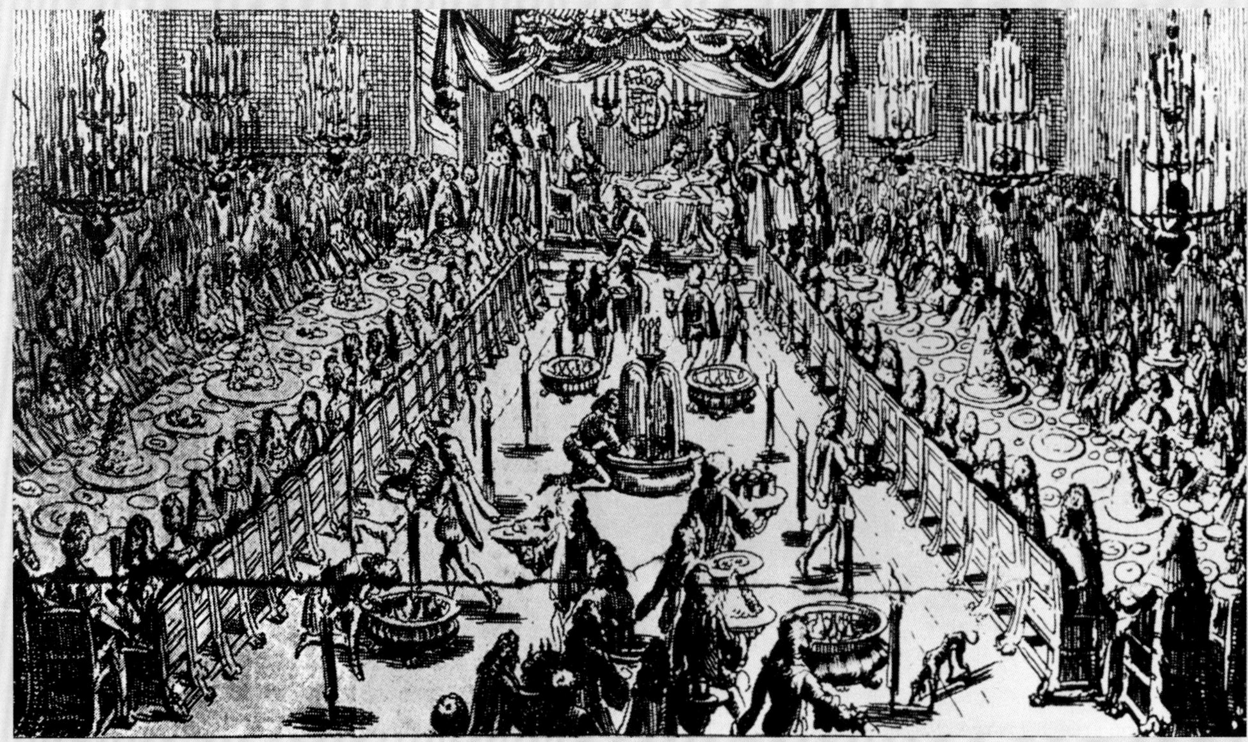

French Influences, 1660–1750

Philippa Glanville

In spite of all the Refinements which the English have undergone Eating and Drinking is still the Groundwork of whatever they call Pleasure …

The Champion, August 5, 1742

10. Anonymous engraving of the coronation banquet of William and Mary in Westminster Hall, 1689. In the late seventeenth century, food was still highly decorated and left little room on the table for decorative silverware. *Private Collection.*

When Charles II employed Jean Tattau to work as his "Pottagier" [soup maker] in the royal kitchens in December 1674, it marked the opening of fifty years of dramatic change in English eating practices. This extraordinary period saw the birth of the dinner service, the arrival of *haute cuisine*, and the triumph of the fork.

The Stuart king's new French employee specialized in *bisques*, *olios*, and *terrines*, which now opened the first course of formal dinners. "Proper for all Feasts and Entertainments," as the English writer Charles Carter described them in 1730, these prestigious dishes were not soups as we understand them, but densely seasoned, mingling different kinds of meat and vegetables, with little liquid and dressed with cockscombs, mushrooms, and artichoke bottoms. They took hours of cooking, required many costly ingredients, and were served in large, ornamented containers. Termed "terrines" or "olios" after their contents, these novel vessels were designed to be the focus of attention, raised up on feet and set on a stand, unlike the series of open serving platters familiar to the Stuart court. When diners sat down and the cover was lifted, the dish and its lavish garnish constituted a piece of theatre. Roasts or large fish then replaced the soups. François Massialot's influential *Cuisinier roial et bourgeois*, first published in Paris in 1691, and then in London in 1702, expressed the essence of court cookery. A generation later, thick meaty soups gave way to the *nouvelle cuisine* of the 1720s, which emphasized clarity of flavors and produced wetter mixtures. Although the final dishes appeared and tasted simpler, the two kinds of soup—the clear broths and the thick bisques—in fact required more preparation. The cook was now working from the basics of classic French cooking such as concentrated broths, *coulis*, or *essences* to produce a whole variety of dishes.

While a salmon or a pike might arrive hot from the kitchen as a *grosse entrée*, competing with the roast at the first course, more refined hot fish dishes such as those of sole, smelts, turbot, or crayfish appeared at the second course with their freshly made cream sauces. New implements, notably the silver fish slice (figure 17, p. 31), were invented so that these delicacies could be elegantly served.

The English were eating more fresh vegetables, herbs, and salads, as advocated by John Evelyn in his 1699 *Acetaria: A Discourse of Sallets*. Mixing salad dressing, based on oil and vinegar, at the table in a porcelain bowl was, like the art of carving, a skill taught to young women. Around 1710 new seasoning, ketchup from China based on anchovies and mushrooms, and soy sauce from Japan, supplemented the vegetable pickles already popular.

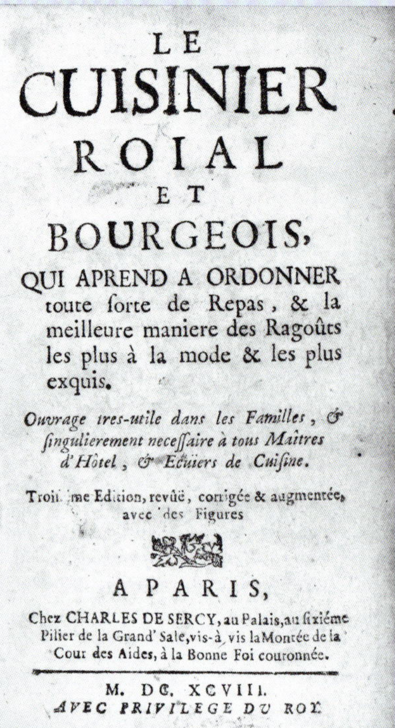
LE
CUISINIER
ROIAL
ET
BOURGEOIS,
QUI APREND A ORDONNER
toute ſorte de Repas, & la
meilleure maniere des Ragoûts
les plus à la mode & les plus
exquis.

Ouvrage tres-utile dans les Familles, & ſingulierement neceſſaire à tous Maîtres d'Hôtel, & Ecüiers de Cuiſine.

Troi[illegible]me Edition, revûë, corrigée & augmentée, avec des Figures

A PARIS,
Chez CHARLES DE SERCY, au Palais, au ſixiéme Pilier de la Grand' Sale, vis-à vis la Montée de la Cour des Aides, à la Bonne Foi couronnée.

M. DC. XCVIII.
AVEC PRIVILEGE DU ROY.

11. Title page from *Le Cuisinier roial et bourgeois*, Paris, 1698. François Massialot's great cookery book, which first appeared in 1691, exerted tremendous influence on European tables for the next fifty years. Massialot described himself as "a cook who dares to qualify himself royal, and it is not without cause, for the meals which he describes … have all been served at court or in the houses of princes, and of people of the first rank." A good deal of Vincent la Chapelle's book, published some forty years later, plagiarizes Massialot's. *The British Library.*

During the second course, *morilles* [morels], young peas, new potatoes, radishes, cucumbers, and celery formed the *hors d'œuvres*, which were set out on small dishes flanking the larger ones. Veal olives—parcels of forcemeat wrapped in flattened veal, a popular French recipe—had to be picked from their cooking liquor with a slotted "olive" spoon. Cream-based sauces such as *béchamel* demanded a more sophisticated serving vessel, unlike Queen Anne's favourite sauce of melted butter, whisked to an emulsion with water, flavored with lemon, and poured into an open boat. Porcelain dishes contained fish, eggs, liver, and other second-course delicacies, which would not be palatable if served or eaten from silver. Such dishes also brought color to the table, since fresh flowers were permitted only as a garnish for desserts.

For summer parties, a Soho *traiteur*, or caterer, could supply French wine and cheese, truffles, *cornichons* [gherkins] and Bayonne ham, and a *pâtissier*, or confectioner, the meringues, puff pastries, and ices then fashionable. Dessert kept its character as a lavish display of hothouse fruit, cheese, and sweet biscuits. Stilton cheese, which ripened in December, was satirized by the English writer Daniel Defoe in 1724 as "an English parmesan, brought to table with mites and maggots" and was the centerpiece of a winter dessert.

French chefs were to blame for the costly and competitive display of silver in aristocratic dining rooms of the 1720s and 1730s. The art of food was as much a display of connoisseurship as a prince's horsemanship, or a nobleman's ability to design a garden pavilion. Although the Duke of Richmond's *maître d'hôtel* [steward] might have in reality devised the table settings and the forty or sixty dishes making up a formal dinner menu, it was the host's taste that was being judged.

Innovations in cuisine demanded new vessel designs. Leading food historians such as Barbara Ketcham Wheaton and more recently Gilly Lehmann have largely overlooked serving vessels, while art historians discussing rococo tableware have credited inventive draftsmen, rather than clever chefs, as the artists who devised the new tableware. But food history gives us a fresh perspective; the *maître d'hôtel* was a key figure, delivering the integrated theatrical effects expected at a fashionable dinner.

In the hope of invoking a better understanding of a vanished world, dinners of three centuries ago were reconstructed at Versailles in the early 1990s and more recently in New York. But they cannot tell us how the food tasted or what the diners experienced. Were the new cream-based sauces tepid? Why did the sauceboat become deeper and acquire a cover? Is the lack of a silver bread basket in French dinner services a genuine difference from Anglo-Saxon eating habits, or did the French simply keep to the ancient idea of a woven straw basket for bread? Why in England was mustard still sprinkled dry from a caster fifty years after the French and Dutch served it as a paste, in pots?

Far more cookery books were published in England than in France. No new ones appeared in Paris between 1700 and 1740, when the *nouvelle cuisine* was directly driving new vessel forms. In London twice as many were published between 1730 and 1750 as in the first two decades of the century, an index of how keen English stewards and cooks were to master the new recipes and serving ways. Fortunately the Frenchman Vincent La Chapelle, chef to the Earl of Chesterfield and later to the Prince of Orange, created a vivid snapshot of Chesterfield's high style of eating in *The Modern Cook*, an illustrated book published in London in 1733. Re-published in London three years later and then in Paris and The Hague, its large engravings show the silverware he deployed to impress his patrons' guests, with their purpose explained.

Through fifty years of emulation—despite wars, tax barriers, political hostility and the mockery of satirists—French cooking inexorably insinuated itself onto English tables. The household book of Katherine Windham, mistress of Felbrigg Hall in Norfolk, England, shows how she composed a dinner in the 1720s. She opened the first course with soups, large pieces of beef or venison, boiled suet puddings (much mocked by French visitors), mince pies, and fish, stewed. This mingling of savoury and sweet dishes was typical of English, but no longer of French, cooking. For her second course Katherine listed poultry and small game birds, lamb, vegetables from asparagus to hop buds, from turnip stalks to parsnips, and shellfish, potted meat, pancakes, fritters, custards, tarts, cheese cakes, and fruit pies, all delicacies which needed to be served hot or might spoil if left standing.

Meal times were drifting later, so dinner moved from 2 P.M. around 1700 to 3 P.M. by the mid-century, and supper was developing its own character. Families enjoyed the absence of servants at supper, and exploited the private pleasures of dishes on heaters, or omelettes prepared at a chafing dish. Even the grandest families could dress the supper table with an epergne with a lamp underneath, as Lord Fitzwalter did in the 1730s, to keep the dish warm and dispense with servants. Candle branches slotted onto the base created an intimate pool of light.

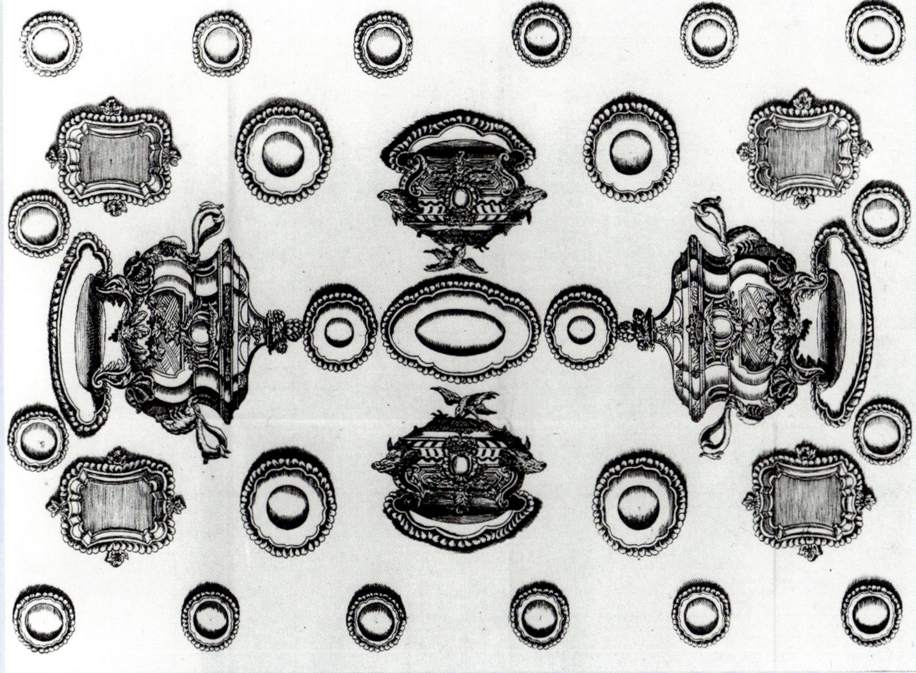

12. Table plan, engraving from Vincent La Chapelle's *The Modern Cook*, first published in 1733. Like most cookery books of the period, *The Modern Cook* was written by a professional cook and was intended for professionals. It includes not only recipes but also directions on how to set a table. *The Schlesinger Library, Radcliffe Institute for Advanced Study, Harvard University*.

Georgian Splendor

So much is the blind Folly of this Age that they would rather be imposed on by a French Booby, than give Encouragement to a good English *cook!*

Hannah Glasse, *The Art of Cookery, Made Plain and Easy; Which far exceeds any Thing of the kind ever yet published*, London, 1747

Although the end of the seventeenth century had finally seen the demise of much of the strict hierarchy of medieval dining and its almost religious atmosphere, certain elements of the old formality, such as the buffet of display plate in the dining room, survived into the eighteenth. Magnificent pieces like the Earl of Kent's ewers and rosewater dish (figure 4) were still the focus of the display; but things were changing. More and more decorative silver was finding its way onto the dining table itself, in the shape of centerpieces and tureens. Gradually, the ritualistic element of dining, with its battalions of servants, was yielding to a new intimacy in which dishes and their accompaniments were within easy reach of diners. Salt and pepper, mustard (served either as the paste we know today or sprinkled as a powder over roasts), as well as oil and vinegar for "sallets," could all be clustered together on a raised central platform, known as a *surtout*, often fitted with candle branches and a central tureen for soups or *oille*. Like all innovations in fashion, this new tableware came from France. On April 25, 1698, the 1st Earl of Portland described in a letter to King William III how he had been entertained by Monsieur (the French king's brother) at St. Cloud, where the table was decorated with a "milieu de table" in several tiers. Inevitably, there was a time lag of a few years before such revolutionary things were to be produced in England. In 1715, the 2nd Earl of Stair was issued with a "sourtoote finely enchased," presumably one of these newfangled ensembles, by the state Jewel House. Stair was going to France as ambassador and in order to entertain in the lavish style expected of the personal representative of the monarch, was supplied with a service of silver. It was only natural that he would want to show himself in Paris as a man of the latest fashion, equipped with the *dernier cri*. Six years before, the 1st Earl of Galway, ambassador to Portugal, had been issued with that equally innovative object: a "toureene." Pies, presented in their decorative pastry casings, were being replaced with runnier dishes that required silver receptacles to serve them. Little by little, table decoration was shifting from an ephemeral splendor of colored pastries and sugar sculptures to the enduring magnificence of richly decorated silver vessels.

Among the earliest surviving English silver tureens is a pair issued to Philip Dormer Stanhope, 4th Earl of Chesterfield, by the Jewel House in 1727 (now in the Hartman Collection, Museum of Fine Arts, Boston). Like all the components of this dinner service, given to Chesterfield to take with him as ambassador to The Hague, these tureens are copies of contemporary French silverware. Chesterfield, who was fastidiously Francophile, exhorted his son to "imitate the French" in all things. The next logical step was to engage a French cook and, while at The Hague, Chesterfield asked his friend the Duke of Richmond, then in Paris, if he could help him find a "maître cuisinier." Shortly afterwards, Chesterfield engaged Vincent La Chapelle as his cook. La Chapelle in time felt that there was a market in England among the cooks and stewards of noblemen for a guide that not only gave recipes for French dishes but also showed how to dress a table in the French manner. His book *The Modern Cook*, published in 1733, includes engravings of table plans (figure 12, p. 25), of a "Sourtout, to

13. *Pot à oille*, or soup tureen, silver, London, 1736/37, maker's mark of Paul de Lamerie. With its baroque dynamic surfaces and vertical emphasis, its panels of delicate chasing, and naturalistically cast handles and finial, this tureen is probably an exact copy of a French example. A pair of the same form appears as illustrations to Vincent la Chapelle's 1733 cookery book *The Modern Cook*, and may depict actual pieces owned by his employer, the Francophile Earl of Chesterfield.
Cat. no. 15

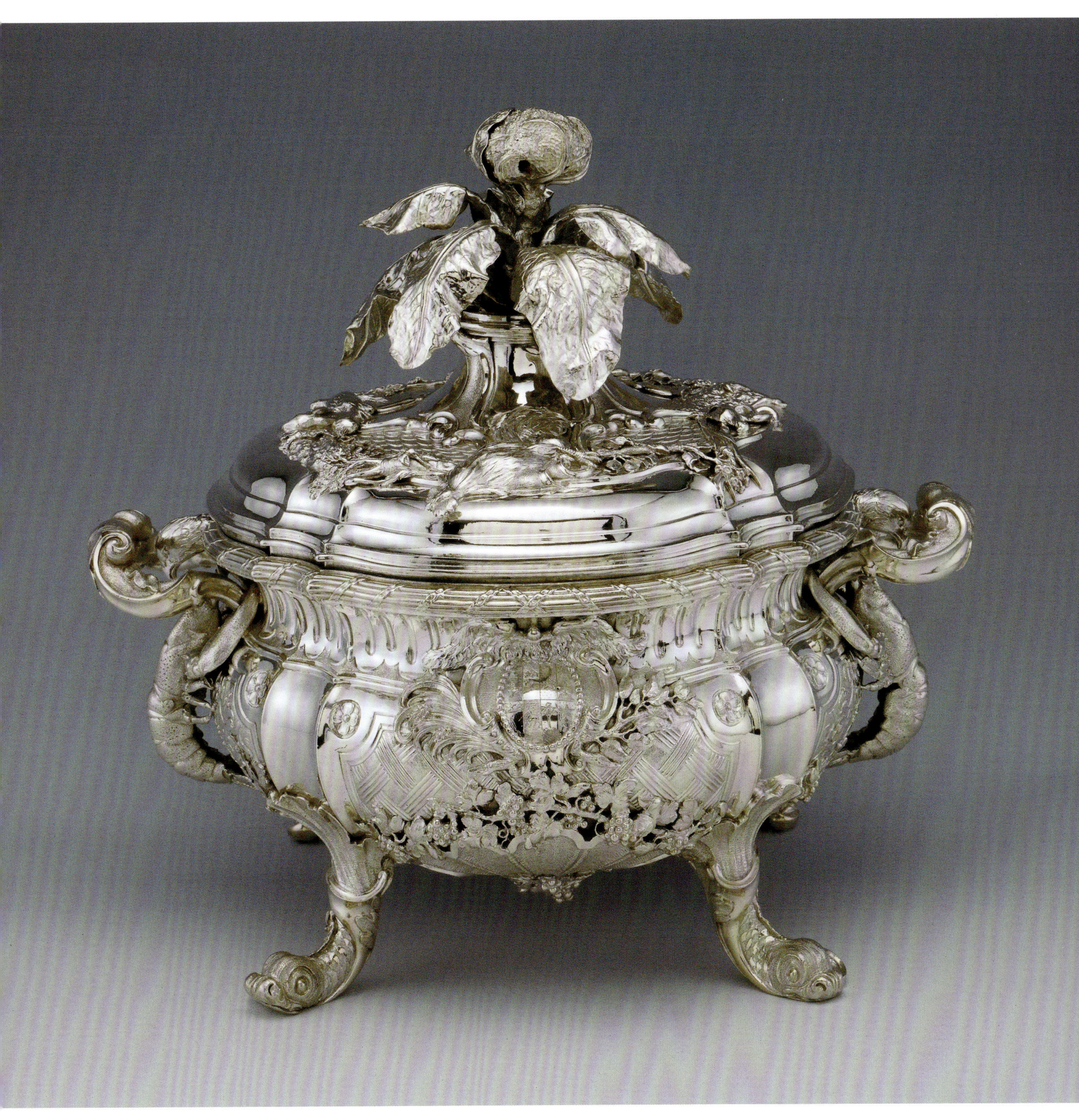

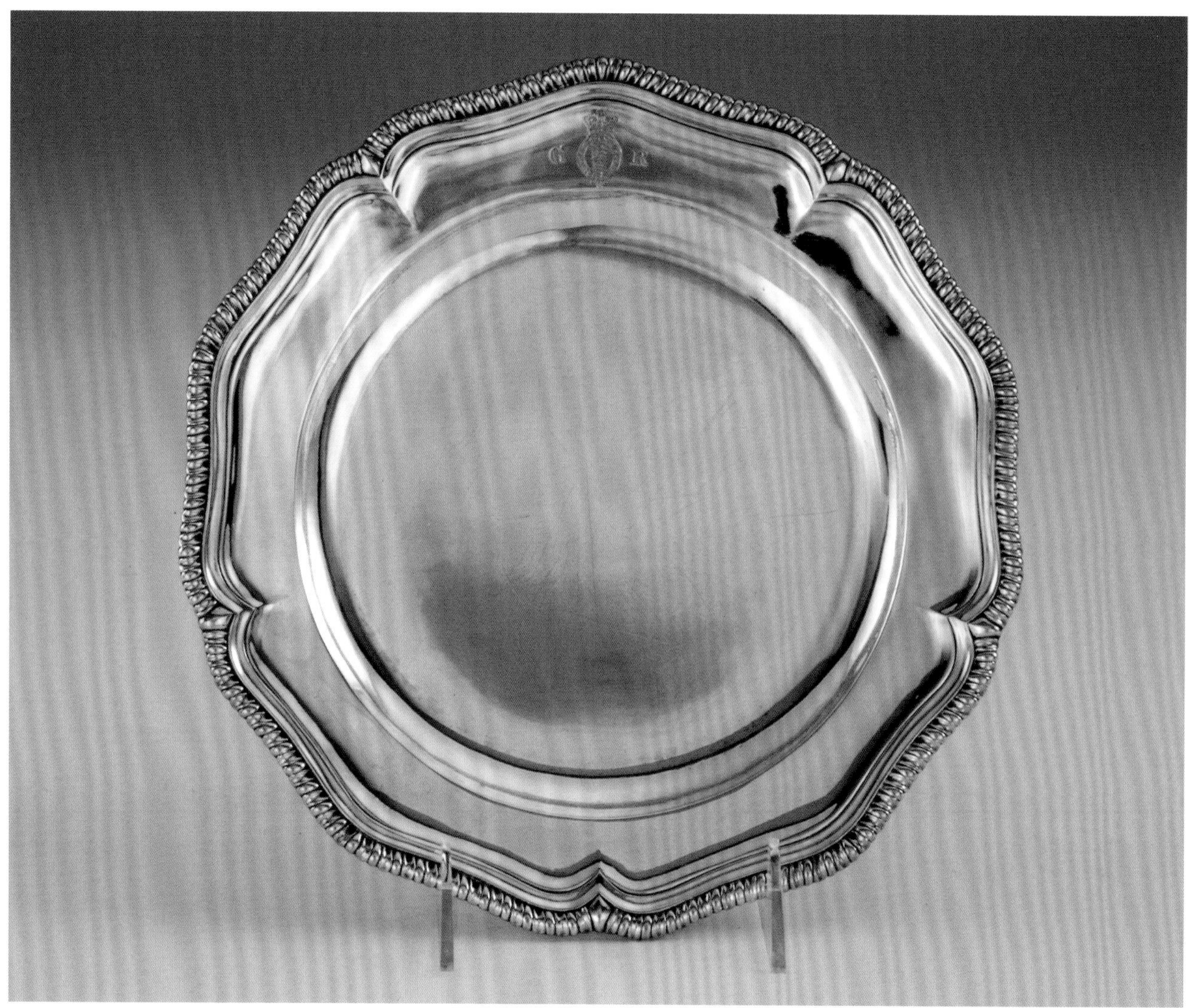

14. Set of twelve dinner plates, silver, London, 1741/42, maker's mark of Paul de Lamerie. Engraved with the royal badge of a lion and the initials of King George II, these plates were doubtless issued by the Jewel House to an ambassador or officer of the Royal Household.
Cat. no. 21

be left upon the Table till the Dessert is serv'd," and of two pairs of soup tureens. One pair of tureens is virtually identical to the example of 1736/37 from de Lamerie's workshop in the Gans Collection (figure 13, p. 27). The tureens in La Chapelle's engraving of a table plan are so meticulously delineated that they are most likely to be real pieces of silverware belonging to his employer, Lord Chesterfield.

Interestingly, while Chesterfield's tureens of 1727 in Boston are entirely baroque in style, the Gans tureen is replete with elements of the new rococo style that had taken France by storm in the early 1730s. Indeed, it is possible that the tureen depicted in La Chapelle's book was in fact French, and that de Lamerie's 1736/37 example is a copy made in London a few years later. Like the French-model wine coolers which Chesterfield received in 1727 as part of his dinner service for The Hague, the Gans tureen is a product of collaboration between Paul de Lamerie and his fellow Huguenot, Paul Crespin, whose mark appears on the liner.

The Gans tureen was originally one of a pair—the other, in the Metropolitan Museum of Art, New York, had its vegetable finial replaced in the early nineteenth century with the English royal badge of a lion. The armorials engraved on the two tureens are also different. Those on the Metropolitan Museum tureen were borne by the Reverend John Dymoke (1764–1828). Dymoke was hereditary King's Champion, and in that capacity his son had appeared on a white charger at the coronation banquet of George IV in 1821. It was the job of the King's Champion to throw down the gauntlet, daring all present to challenge the right of the new king to succeed to the throne. It is possible that the Dymoke family received its

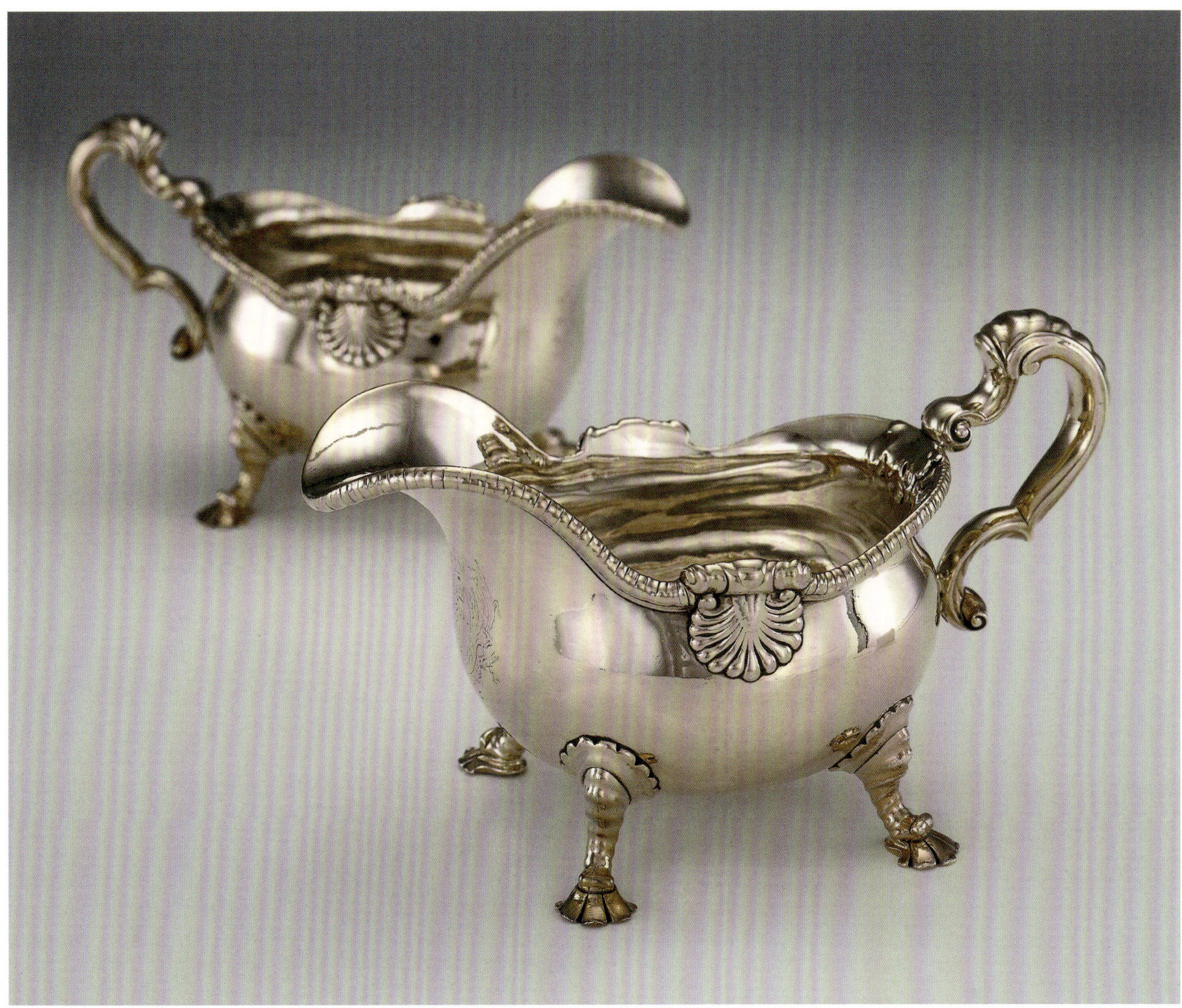

15. Pair of sauceboats, silver, London, 1742/43, maker's mark of Paul de Lamerie. The fashion for rich sauces poured over food was a French one, and the prototypes for the first English silver sauceboats were French. But the English habit of pouring melted clarified butter over roast meats persisted, and items like these are usually referred to in contemporary bills as "butter boats."
Cat. no. 23

tureen from the Jewel House as a perquisite, or gift of silver, for performing that ancient ceremonial function, and the Jewel House replaced the naturalistic finial with the royal badge. The arms on the Gans tureen are those borne by William Drury-Lowe (d. 1827). Since the history of both tureens can only be traced back to the 1790s, it seems likely that they appeared as secondhand on the market around that time and were then separated.

Circular tureens like the Gans example were intended for *oille* (the French word for olio), while elliptical ones were for soups. The French custom, copied in England, was to set a table for the first course with a pair of each type, as shown in La Chapelle's plan. Platters holding meat and fowl dishes were arranged around the center of the table, with smaller dishes of hors d'œuvres, or side dishes, placed in the spaces in between. For the second course, the tureens would be removed and new dishes of roast meats with sauces, fish, pies, and savouries would follow. Diners' plates would be changed with each course. Silver dinner plates had been known since the early sixteenth century, when the medieval trencher plate made of stale bread had begun to disappear from fashionable dining. By the eighteenth century, a dinner service required several dozen dinner plates, as well as one or two dozen soup plates.

English sauces of the seventeenth century had been highly flavored reductions into which diners dipped pieces of roast meat. On the other hand, the French sauces—with their base of cream, flour and butter— became popular in the early eighteenth century. They were as eagerly favored by some as they were despised as being un-English by others. As one Frenchman quipped, the French had innumerable sauces but only one religion,

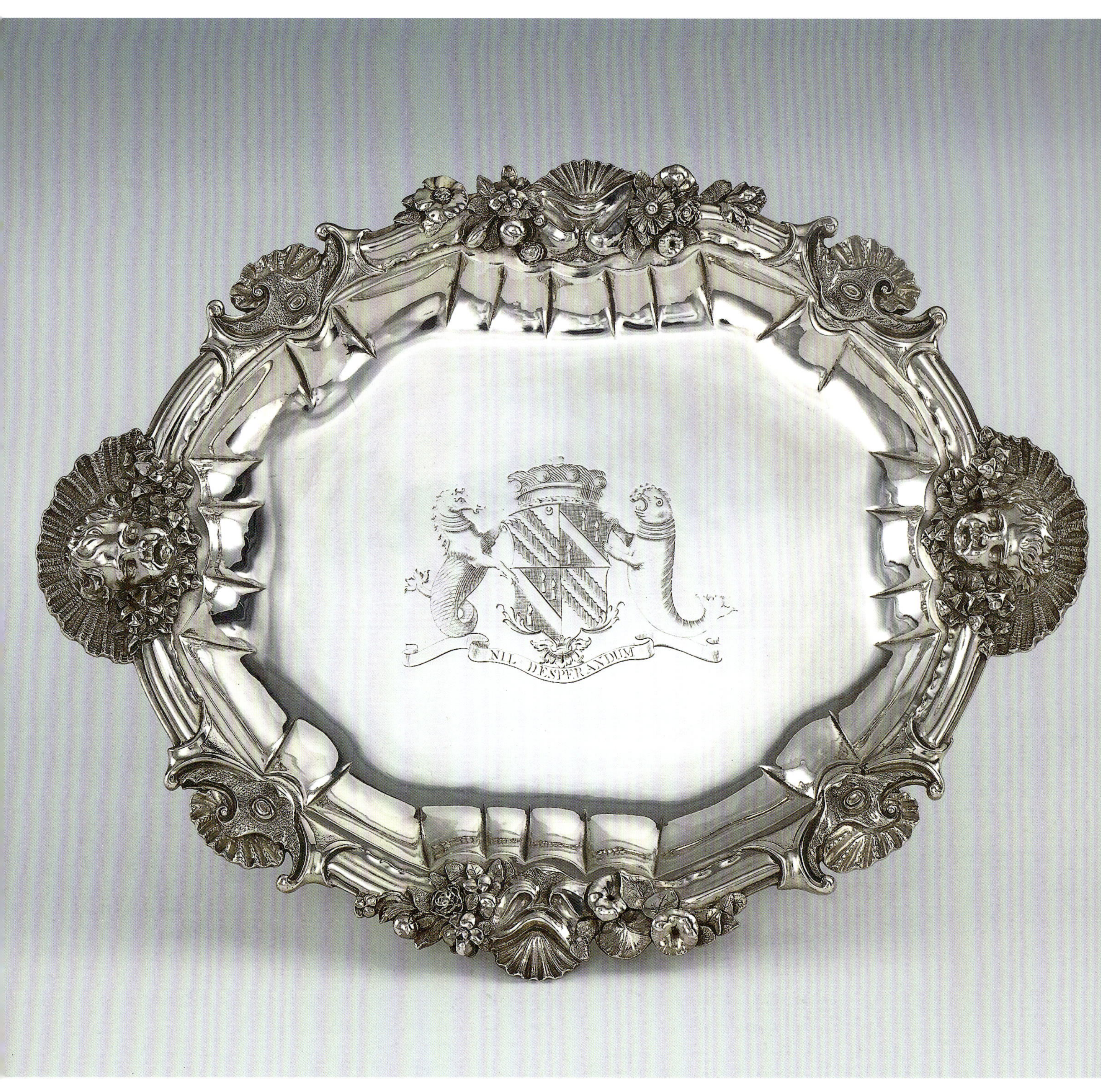
NIL DESPERANDUM

while the English had countless religions but only one sauce. The French form of sauceboat—with either one or two lips for pouring the sauce over the food—was copied in England, but paradoxically this new form of tableware was usually described by London silversmiths as a "butter boat," because most people, especially the "middling sort," continued to favor the English custom of pouring hot clarified butter over roast meats. Dr. Samuel Johnson had been known to pour it over his plum pudding.

There was, moreover, a proportion of the English who continued to resist French cuisine for nationalistic reasons. The anonymous writer of a 1747 pamphlet inveighing against naturalizing immigrants declared, "In these our modern days, we see a set of men of taste (as they are pleased to call themselves) who despise Englishmen, English food, and English liberty, for no other reason, that they are the product of the places of their nativity; whilst they furnish themselves from a foreign climate with every vice, and every species of luxury."

For the cosmopolitan English elite, however, who could travel abroad, who spoke French among themselves, and who patronized the leading silver suppliers such as Paul de Lamerie, France was the wellspring of taste and fashion. But when it came to silver, not all French fashions were adopted with the same alacrity. Stands, or undertrays, for tureens and sauceboats, designed to protect the tablecloth, were a French feature that was seldom adopted in English silver. Interestingly, the four sauceboats acquired from de Lamerie secondhand by Lord Anson in the 1740s had stands accompanying them (figure 16), elaborately decorated with rococo foliage. Anson, a naval captain who had made a fortune for himself, his crew, and the British government by seizing a Spanish treasure galleon, the *Nuestra Señora de Covadonga*, in the Pacific, had on his return been made a peer and married the Lord Chancellor's daughter. His father-in-law, Lord Hardwicke, was already a big patron of Paul de Lamerie. Besides his own extensive purchases from de Lamerie, he had given his friend Bishop Secker a complete dinner service, and it may have been Hardwicke who gave Anson the extravagant silver dinner service engraved with Anson's coat of arms held up by two fish (a privilege recently granted to the naval hero). The service was in the most advanced rococo style: even a modest component, such as the fish serving slice (figure 17),

16. One of a set of four sauceboat stands, silver, London, 1739/40, maker's mark of Paul de Lamerie. Engraved with the armorials of Admiral George Anson, 1st Baron Anson (1697–1762). Unlike the French custom, soup tureens and sauceboats were seldom given stands in England; instead, the tablecloth was changed frequently. Cat. no. 20

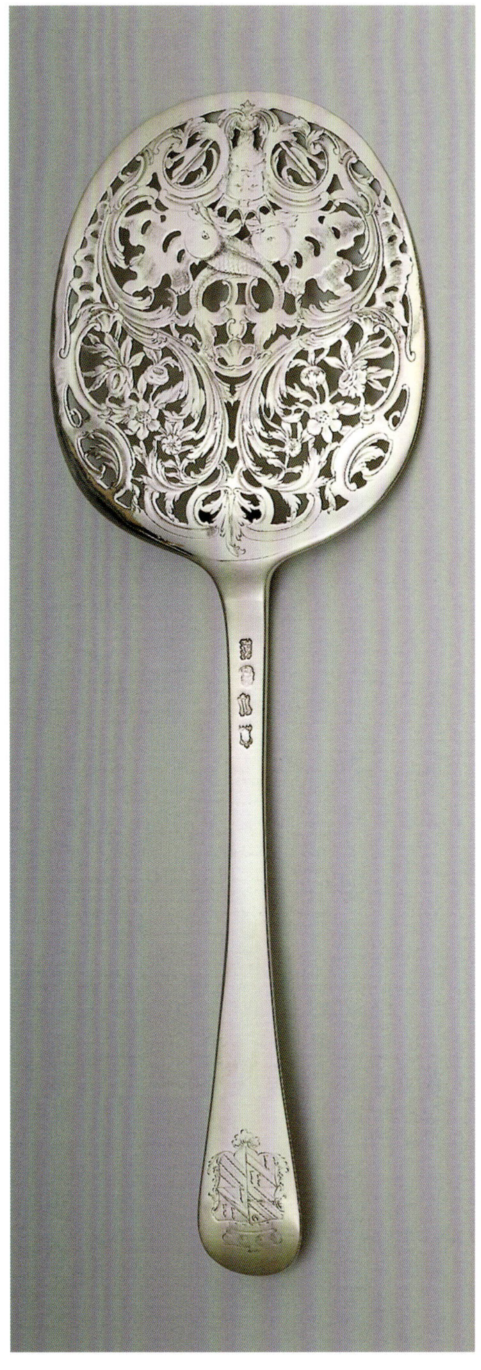

17. Fish serving slice, silver, London, 1746/47, maker's mark of Paul de Lamerie. Engraved with the armorials of Admiral George Anson, 1st Baron Anson (1697–1762). Cat. no. 29

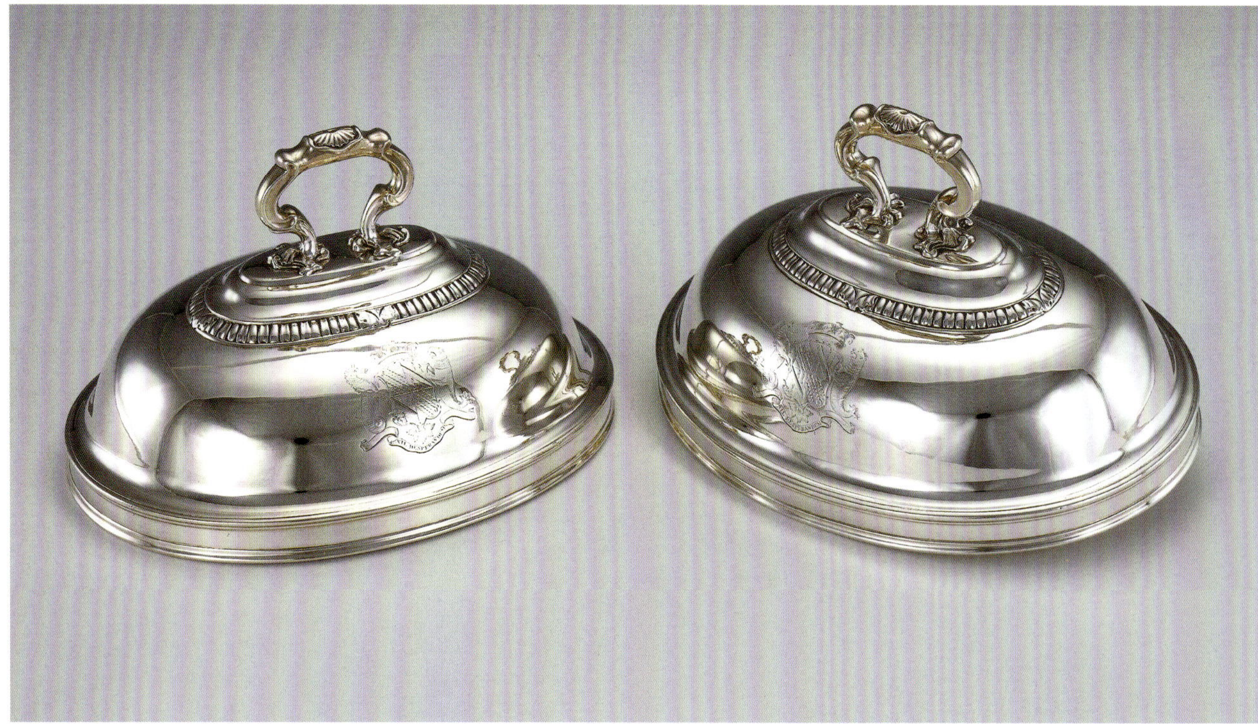

18. Pair of dish covers, silver, London, 1749/50, maker's mark of Paul de Lamerie. These small-size covers are rare survivals of the fashion for serving food *à la française*, where all the dishes of a particular course were placed on the table and, after the covers had been lifted, the diners helped themselves. This custom was replaced in the early nineteenth century by service *à la russe*, where each component of a course was brought around to diners by the servants. Engraved with the armorials of Admiral George Anson, 1st Baron Anson (1697–1762).
Cat. no. 36

is meticulously decorated with a depiction of Neptune and attendant fish.

The Anson service, most of it dispersed at auction in London in 1893, is interesting in that it epitomizes the transition between the hegemony of the baroque sideboard of display plate and the rise to widespread use of the soup tureen, the sauceboat, and other items of decorative silver for the dining table itself. The magnificent ewer and basin (now in the Fowler Museum of Cultural History, UCLA, Los Angeles), completed in 1739/40, are among the very last examples of a tradition of display pieces stretching back to the Middle Ages. By Anson's day, however, lavish display in silver was more likely to be found on the dining table, not the sideboard. Anson himself owned two pairs of tureens, one large and one small, as well as many variously sized dishes and plates for the table. The pair of oval domed dish covers of 1749/50 (figure 18) is a rare survival, for most heavy dish covers were melted down when service *à la française* went out of fashion at the beginning of the nineteenth century.

Yet even if what was spent on buffet plate dwindled next to what was spent on the table silver, the sideboard nevertheless retained its importance for serving drink. Foreign visitors remarked on how the English retained what was seen as a medieval custom of toasting each other at dinner, something which required new glasses of wine to be brought by a servant and afterwards returned to the sideboard to be rinsed. At the beginning of the nineteenth century, the German visitor Christian Goede observed: "Each lady must be solicited to drink wine by a gentleman, who first drinks to her, then to the hostess and the master of the house, and so on, until he has gone through the whole company." He added that it would be indecorous "to touch a glass with your lips previous to such challenges." The most convivial of drinks was punch which, unlike port or French wines, came with no political baggage. Indeed, it was considered patriotic to drink punch.

With such ornate dinner services, all eyes would be drawn not to the sideboard but to the dining table. Here the silverware conveyed quite a different message. Instead of the monumentality of sideboard plate, with its elaborate heraldry intended to advertise the status of the host, the silver on the table was now in all likelihood replete with classical imagery. For all its emphasis on status and show, silver was in truth among the most personal of accoutrements: while an aristocrat's clothes or the decoration of the state rooms of a noble household were seen by every supplicant at his levée, his table silver was only for the eyes of his chosen dinner guests. It was also perhaps the most scrutinized aspect of

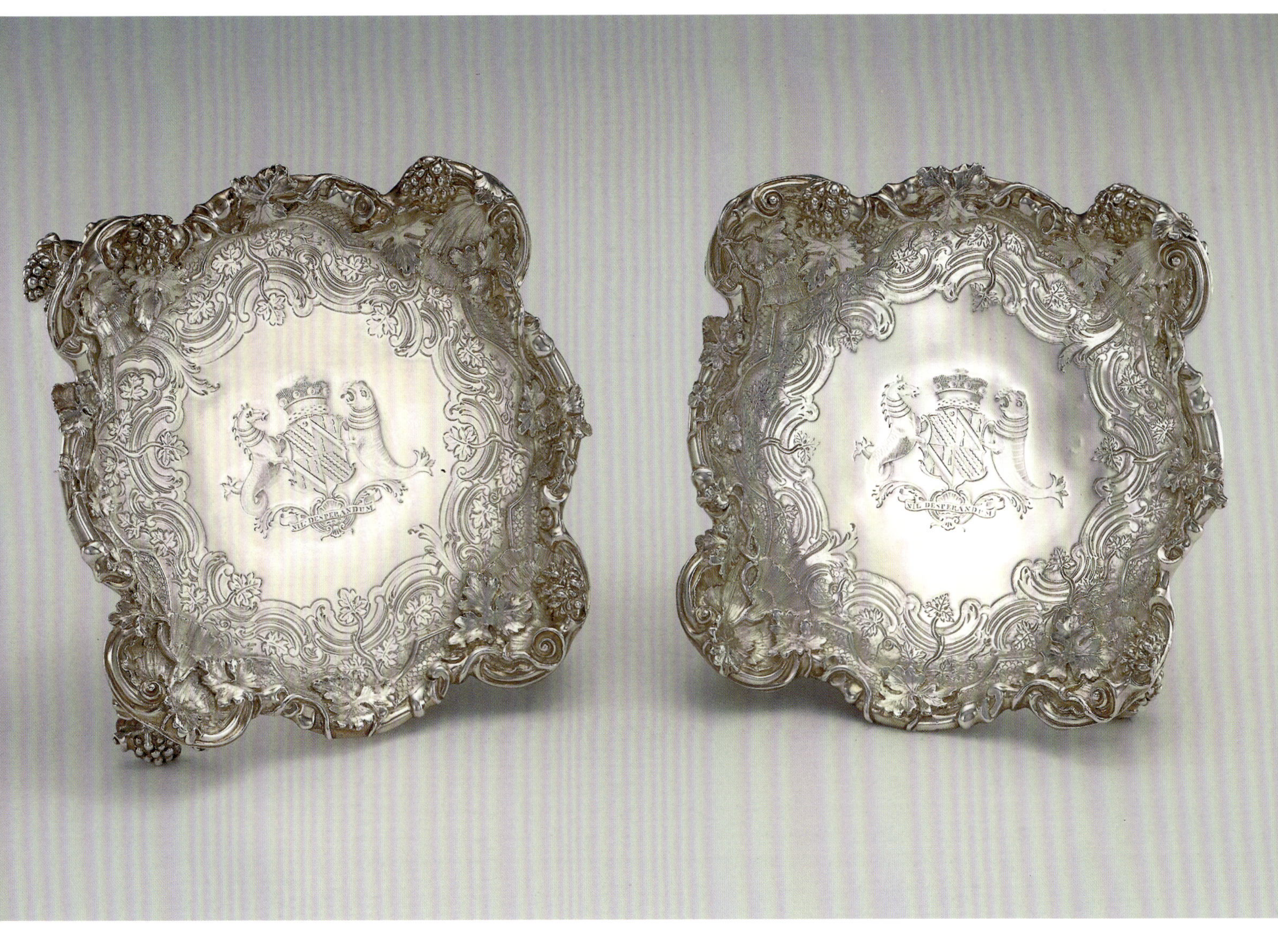

19. Pair of waiters, silver, London, 1747/48, maker's mark of Paul de Lamerie. Small salvers, known to collectors today as "waiters," were used to bring wine in small glasses from the sideboard to the table. In 1788 the Reverend John Trusler, author of *The Honours of the Table, or, Rules for Behaviour during Meals,* directed readers to "give nothing but on a waiter." These two are engraved with the armorials of Admiral George Anson, 1st Baron Anson (1697–1762). The shield is supported by a sea horse and a seal. Anson was granted the privilege of bearing these supporters in his armorials in 1757.
Cat. no. 30

an aristocrat's wealth, for it was seen, and some of it even handled, by guests at close quarters during a long Georgian dinner of many courses. So, in Alexander Pope's words, it was appropriate that the decoration of the silverware should "point a moral and adorn a tale."

The most popular iconographic themes for the dining-room silver were depictions of Bacchus, the god of wine, and Ceres, the goddess of the harvest, often accompanied with a quotation from the classical poet Terence's play *The Eunuch:* "Sine Cerere et Libero friget Venus"—without food and wine, love withers. The ability to "read" an object and understand the meaning of its classical allusions was a highly prized attainment in the eighteenth century, as befitting the Age of Enlightenment. Even when dining with a bluff sea dog like Admiral Anson, guests expected

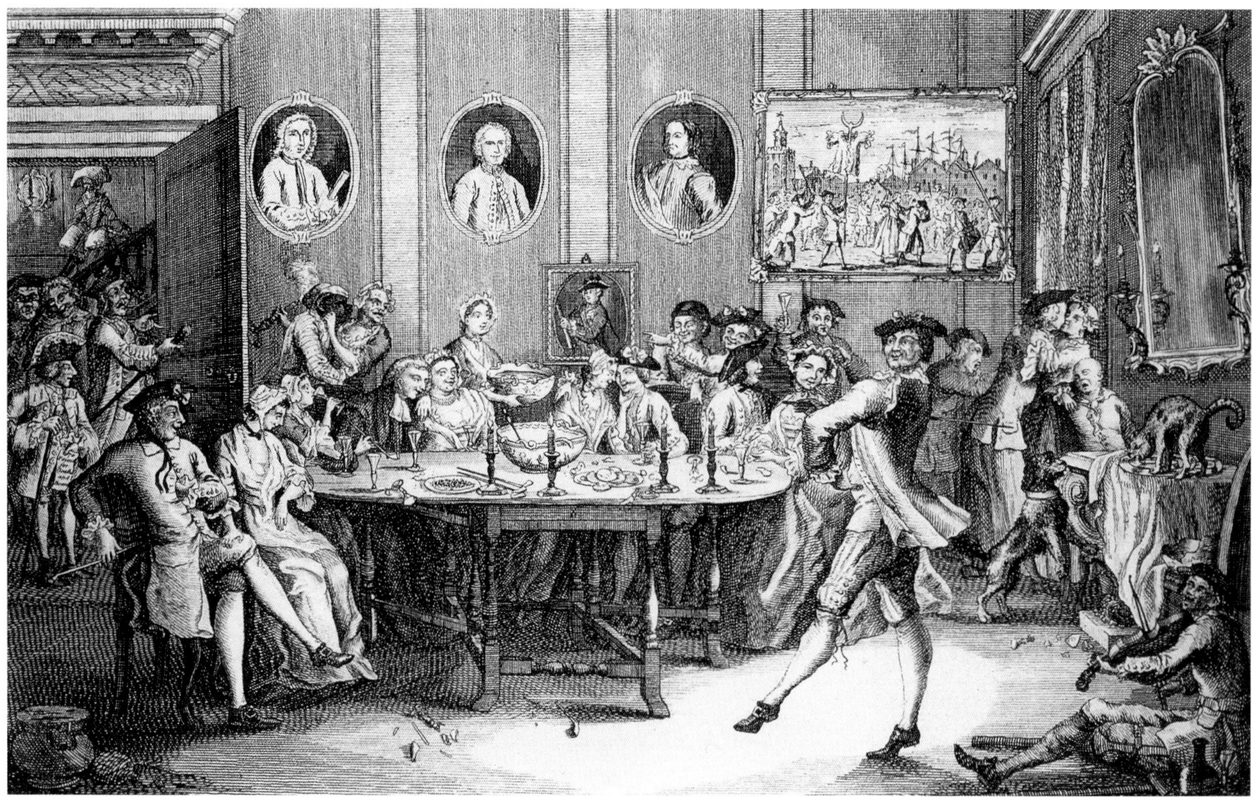

to enter into a classical world of fauns, satyrs, and goddesses.

The bread basket of 1739/40 from de Lamerie's workshop (figure 22, p. 36) illustrates this concept very well. The heads of Ceres mingle with symbols of Bacchus, while the basket's feet, formed of compressed lions' faces, show that the might of the lion is subdued by the power of love. This complex iconography is contained in a swirl of foliate scrolls and baroque and rococo motifs. It was a peculiarly English style that de Lamerie and a few of his contemporaries made their own, with a curious commingling of motifs taken not only from French rococo, but also from the baroque, even at times the sinuous, molten style known as auricular that was popular in Germany and the Low Countries in the early seventeenth century.

The cup and cover of 1742/43 (figure 23, p. 37), one of the masterworks of English decorative arts, is a cornucopia of detail that is as much sculpture as it is silver. Indeed, in this example, the modeler and chaser (who may or may not have been the same person) turned the medium of silver into a molten mixture from which putti and lions' faces emerge amid a controlled confusion of foliage, scrolls, and the distinctive rockwork, known as *rocaille*, that was a recurring feature of the rococo. Contrasting with this are expanses of plain silver, making the intense activity look as if it is bursting out of the confines of the cup. The form of the cup itself, a sinuous vase shape with two grapevine handles, is based on baroque designs of the previous century. The delight in ostentatious display had not waned in spite of the new interest in practical silverware for the table. Like the Duke of Kent's two ewers and dish (figure 4, p. 17), this cup is not a functional object but exists merely for display and to imbue the dining room with its complex message of food, wine, and love. The Gans cup was decorated by an anonymous master who has been dubbed "the Maynard Master" after his most celebrated creation, the Maynard Dish (produced in de Lamerie's workshop in 1739/40 and now in the Cahn Collection, St. Louis). Most of the Maynard Master's very idiosyncratic work—in which meticulously rendered animal and human heads and naturalistic foliage contrast with patches of plain silver enlivened with changes in texture—is struck with Paul de Lamerie's mark. There is evidence that he also worked for other silversmiths, such as James Shruder.

20. ***A Convivial Company*****, engraving, mid-eighteenth century. Punch remained popular through the eighteenth century and was thought to be patriotic (in other words, non-French) compared to French wines.** ***Private Collection.***

21. Salver, silver, London, 1743/44, maker's mark of Paul de Lamerie. This large salver, some 22 inches across, is of a type often described as a "table" in contemporary bills. Cat. no. 25

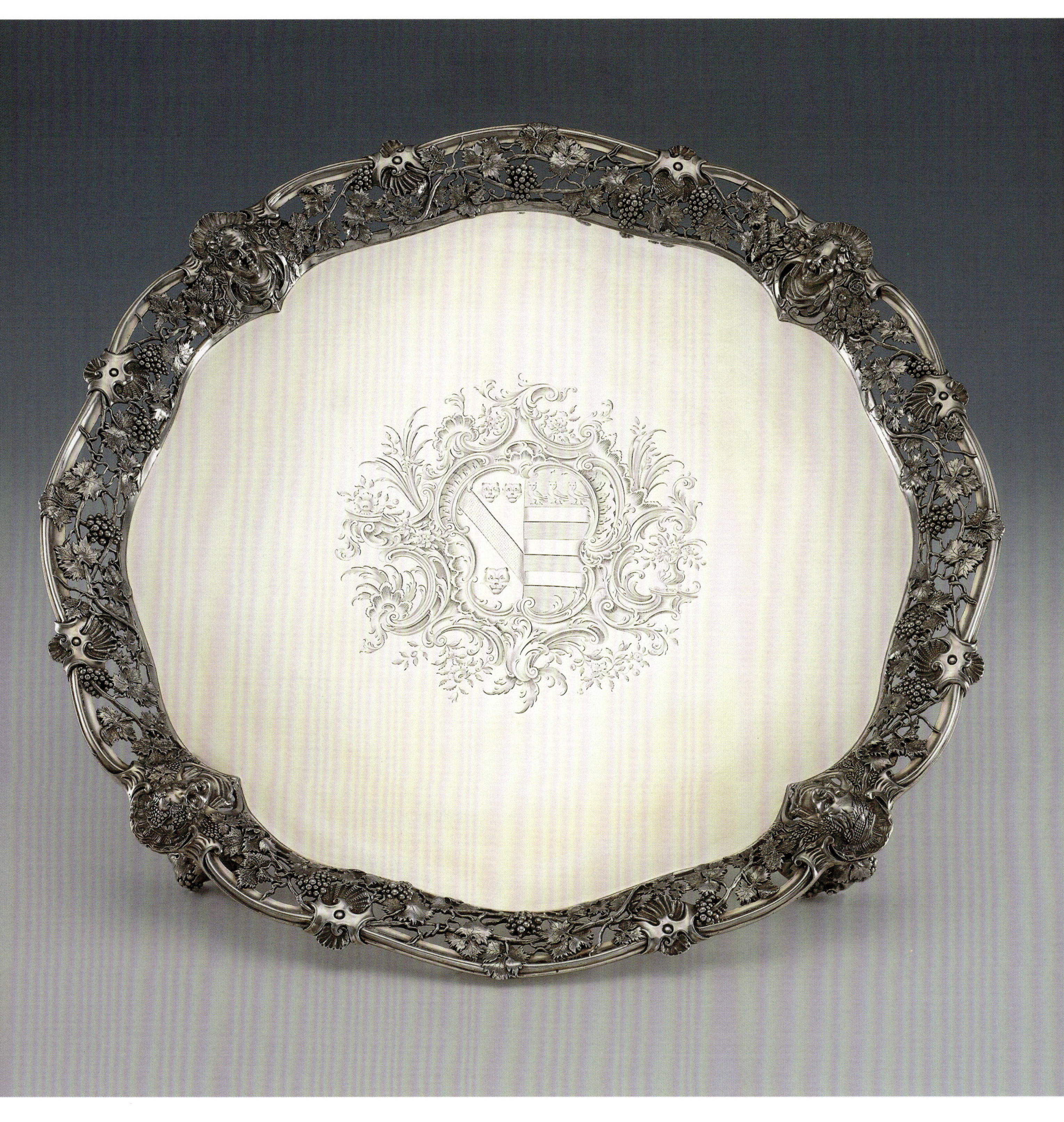

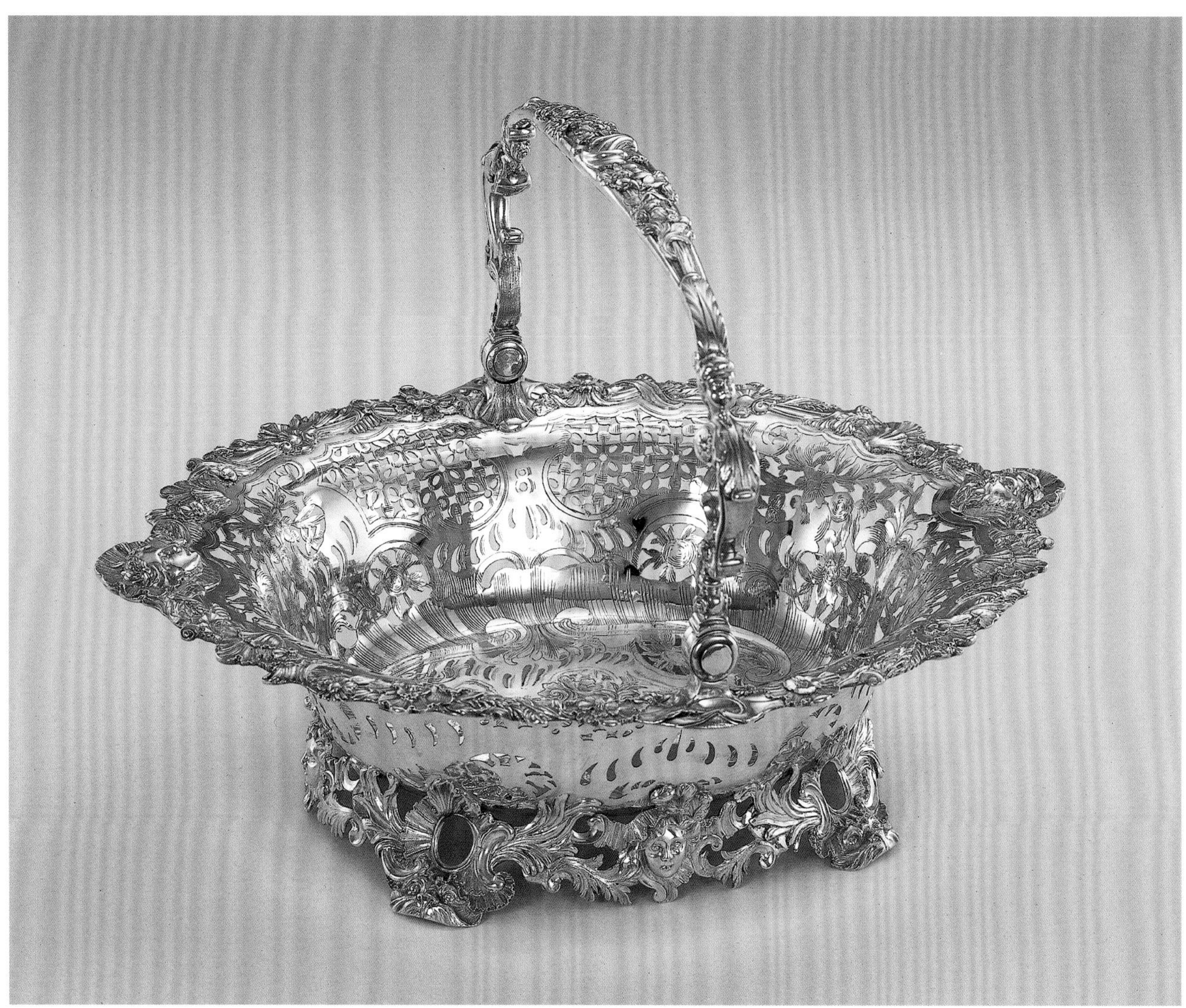

22. Basket, silver, London, 1739/40, maker's mark of Paul de Lamerie. Decorated with symbols of Bacchus, the ancient Roman god of wine, and Ceres, goddess of the harvest, this basket illustrates the oft-quoted line from the Roman poet Terence, "Sine Cerere et Libero friget Venus,"—without food and wine, love withers.
Cat. no. 18

Classical allusion was not confined to the dining room, but the gods and goddesses, bacchic fauns and satyrs adorning wares for tea and coffee are often more decorative than symbolic. French visitors were amazed at the English habit of ladies retiring at the end of the dessert course, leaving the men to drink and "talk broad." Coffee and tea would be served in the withdrawing room. The growth in popularity of these caffeine drinks, as well as chocolate, meant that a host of new silver vessels was required—not only coffee pots and teapots, but also small jugs for milk and cream, sugar bowls, tongs for sugar lumps, and teaspoons. For coffee pots, a bulbous ginger-jar shape, based on Chinese ceramics, enjoyed a brief vogue in the 1680s but was soon replaced by the tapering cylinder still popular today. Early examples of this kind of pot were made of sheet silver, wrapped into a tapering tube and soldered along the join. With the growing demand for more elaborate decoration in the early eighteenth century, however, the more advanced workshops, like that of Paul de Lamerie, raised up (in other words, hammered into shape) deep pots from single disks of silver and added foliate embossing and cast components. One characteristic of coffee pots struck with de Lamerie's mark is their recessed bases, only visible when the pot is turned over (figure 25, p. 39). To make a pot like this involved much more work than the simpler pots produced by de Lamerie's contemporaries, but it resulted in greater capacity and de Lamerie probably regarded it as his "trade mark." Coffee pots and teapots did indeed become bigger as the eighteenth century progressed, for the price of coffee and tea became less prohibitive with burgeoning

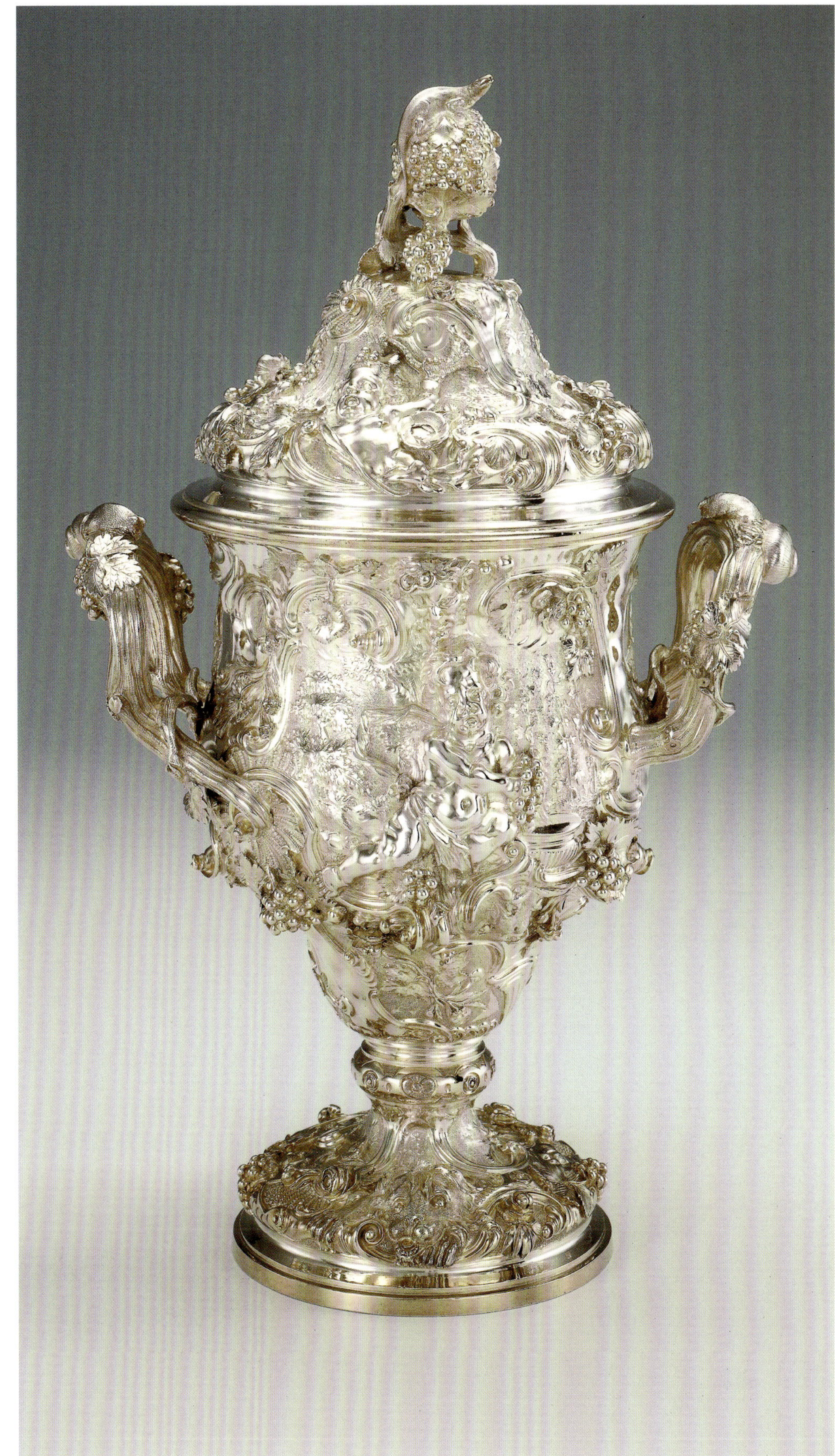

23. Cup and cover, silver, London, 1742/43, maker's mark of Paul de Lamerie. A *tour de force* of the modeler's and chaser's skills, this cup and cover are as much sculpture as silverware. The decoration appears to burst forth out of the constraints of the form—a vase—and the medium—silver. Cat. no. 22

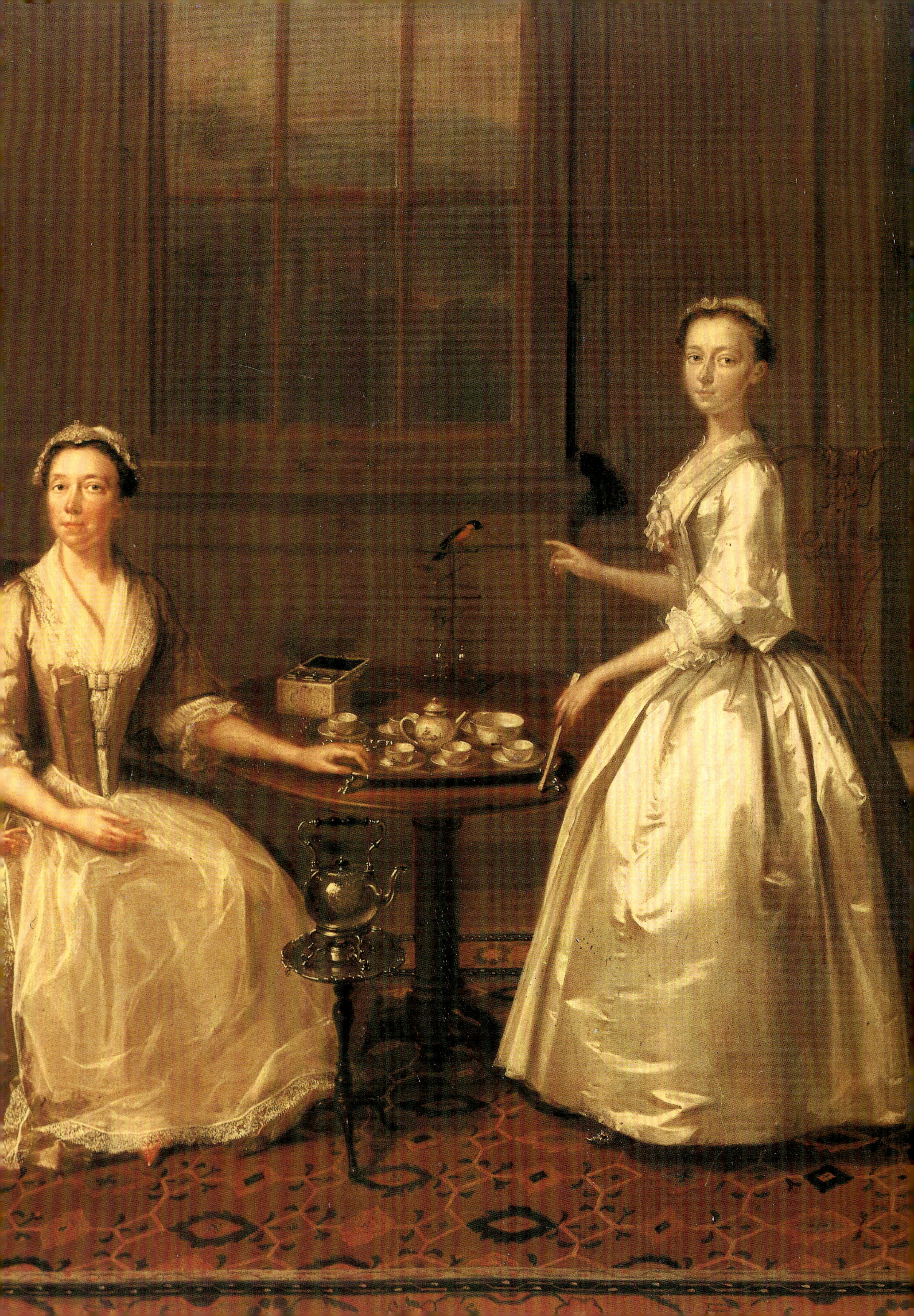

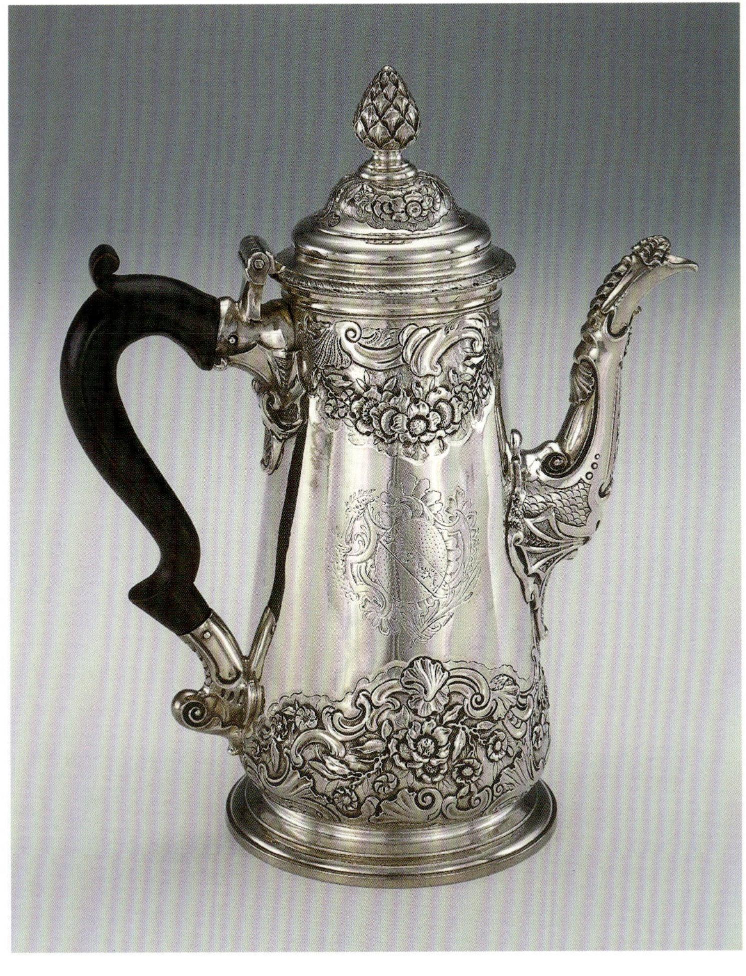

trade with Asia and Africa. Nevertheless coffee remained too dear for all but the upper classes in the eighteenth century, while tea became progressively cheaper as the century advanced and was thus available to a wider spectrum of society. Not everyone was happy about this. In his *Essay on Tea* published in 1757, Jonas Hanway, a colorful controversialist, lamented in particular the rise in popularity of tea at the expense of ale: "I am not YOUNG, but methinks there is not quite so much beauty in this land as there was. Your very chamber maids have lost their bloom by SIPPING tea."

The tea ceremony, which the English took from the Japanese and made into a particularly English institution, was now the height of fashion and led to a surge in demand for special silverware. Yet the commodity of tea itself was still costly enough to be kept under lock and key, often in an elegant wooden chest containing two tea boxes (or caddies, from the Malay word "kati," a unit of measure) and a sugar container (figure 26).

While Paul de Lamerie's tea caddy set of 1738/39 has panels of restrained rococo decoration, the two tea caddies of 1751/52 (figure 27, p. 40), in contrast, which date from the very end of his career, are exuberantly adorned with decoration enclosing panels depicting Chinese

25. Coffee pot, silver and fruitwood, London, 1738/39, maker's mark of Paul de Lamerie. As tea became progressively cheaper during the eighteenth century, its consumption spread to all social classes, but coffee always remained a drink of the aristocracy. Cat. no. 16

24. Detail from William Verelst (d. after 1756), *The Gough Family*, 1741, oil on canvas. In this conversation piece, a square salver or "table" similar to the one shown in figure 21 (p. 35) is on the table. A kettle is on a three-legged stand. *Private Collection.*

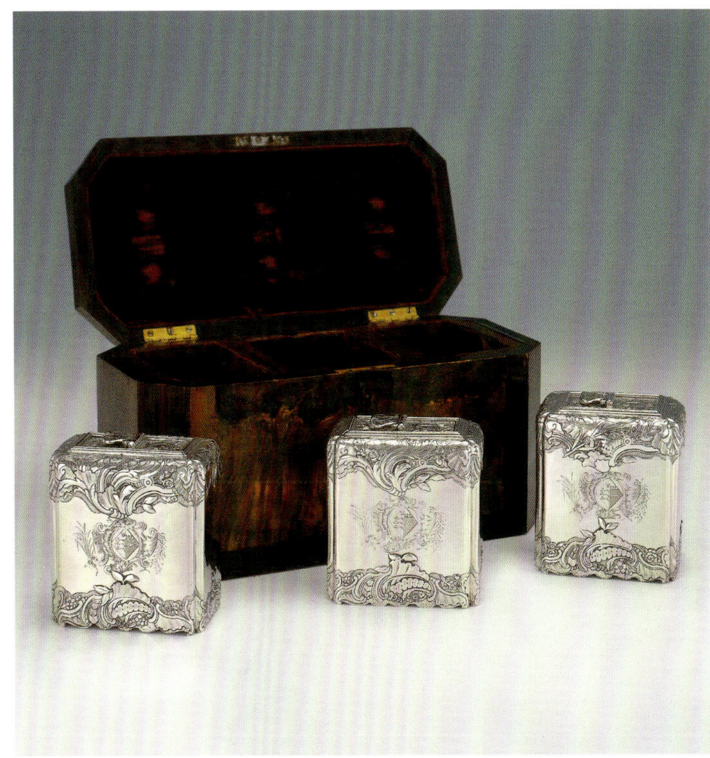

26. Pair of tea caddies and a sugar box, silver, London, 1738/39, maker's mark of Paul de Lamerie. The restless movement of the rococo foliage and waves chased on these boxes is only put to rest when they are returned to their wooden box. They were engraved some thirty years after they were made with the arms borne by Catherine Maria, widow of Sir Henry Moore, 1st Baronet and Governor of New York from 1765 to 1769. Cat. no. 17

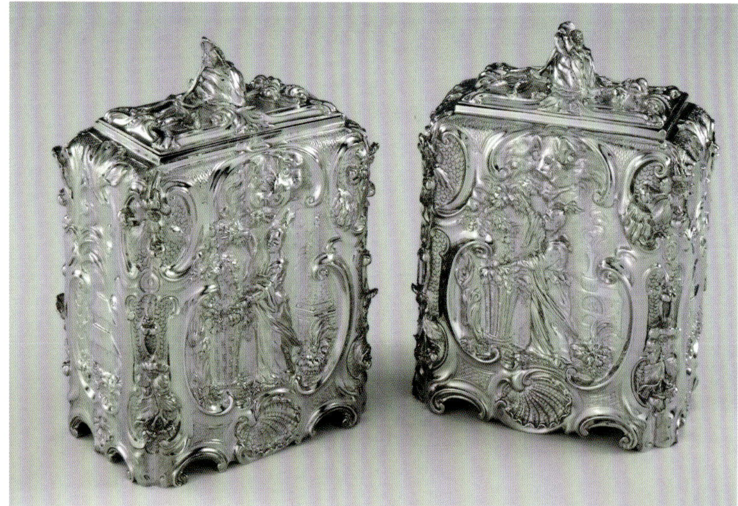

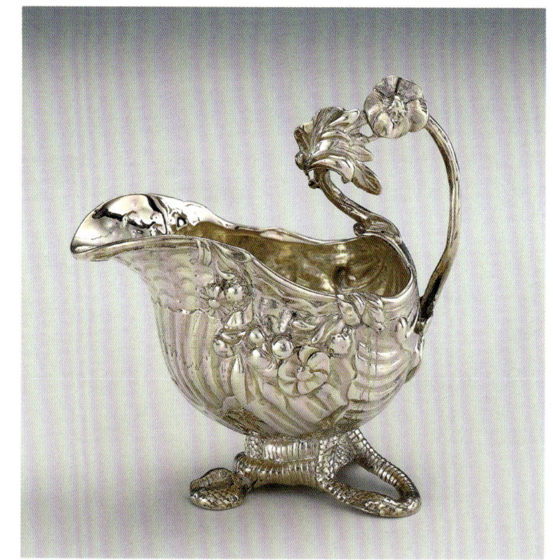

27. Pair of tea caddies, silver, London, 1751/52, maker's mark of Paul de Lamerie. The rococo of the caddies and sugar box of 1738/39 (figure 26) is restrained compared to the riot of rich decoration on these examples. Picturesque scenes of tea pickers are enclosed by molten scrolls, foliage, and lions' heads.
Cat. no. 40

28. Cream jug, silver, London, 1744/45, maker's mark of Paul de Lamerie. At first, tea was drunk in England in the same way as in Asia, but the habit of adding milk or cream, either hot or cold, gained favor in the early eighteenth century. Great imagination was lavished on these small decorative jugs, which were intended to cause a stir when presented at the tea table.
Cat. no. 26

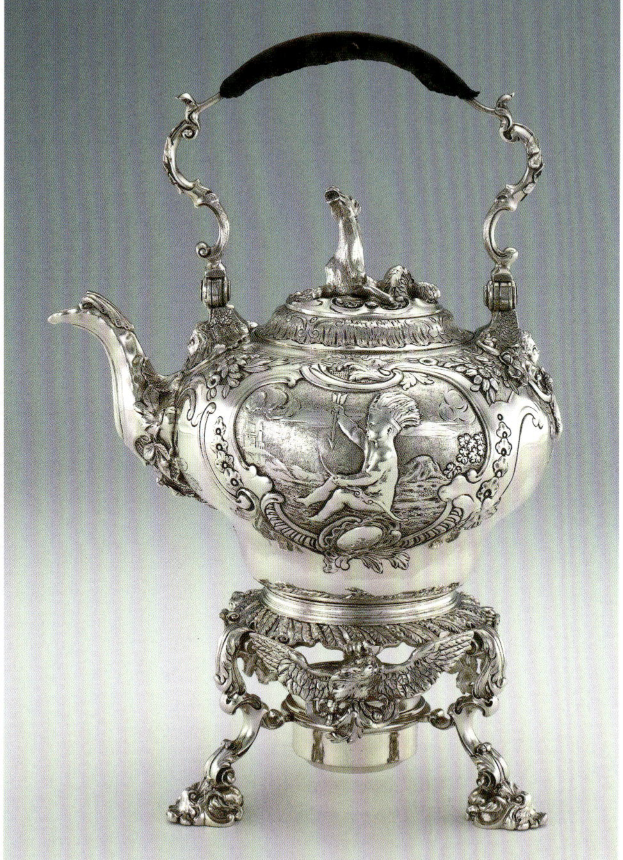

29. Tea kettle and lamp stand, silver and leather, London, 1745/46, maker's mark of Paul de Lamerie. As tea continued to be an expensive commodity, the precious leaves in a small teapot were continually refreshed with boiling water from a large kettle, hinged at the front so that it could be tipped off the stand.
Cat. no. 28

tea pickers. Chinoiserie was a whimsical style that evoked the East and enjoyed a brief vogue as flat-chased decoration on silver during the 1680s; it was revived in the mid-eighteenth century as embossed decoration on tea caddies, coffee pots, and cream jugs. Loosely based on engravings published in travel books, these exotic figures perhaps tell us more about an eighteenth-century Londoner's perception of Asia than anything about China itself.

The chasing on these chinoiserie caddies lacks the brilliance of the "Maynard Master" and identical caddies struck with other makers' marks during the same period suggest that they were produced speculatively rather than as special commissions like the basket (figure 22, p. 36) or

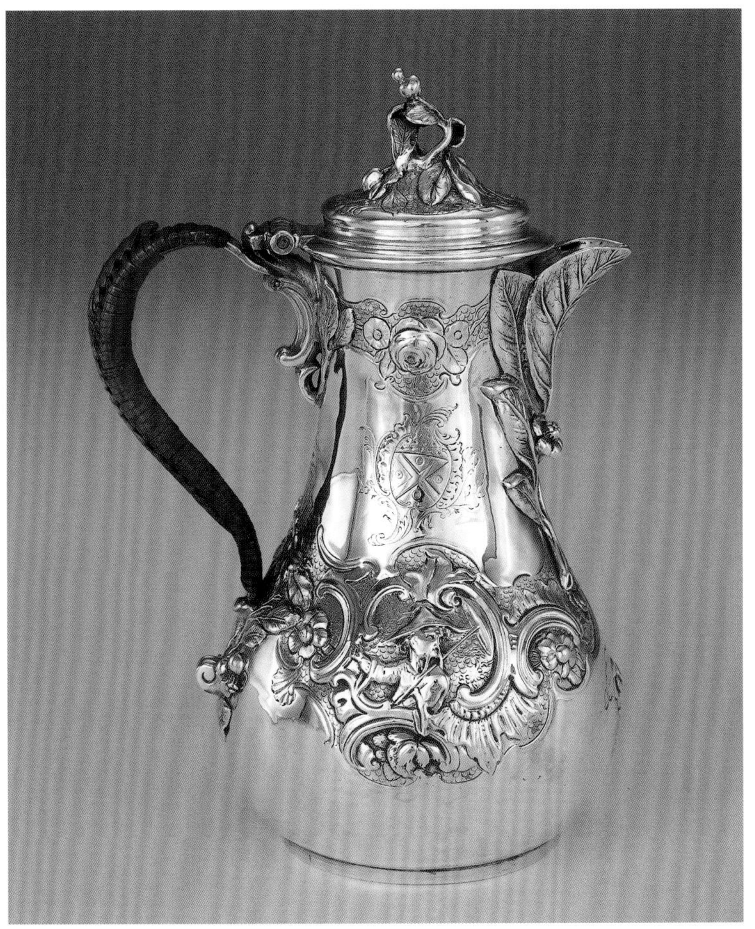

30. Coffee pot, silver, London, 1749/50, maker's mark of Paul de Lamerie. There was a brief vogue for Turkish coffee in the middle years of the eighteenth century. The ledgers of the silversmith Edward Wakelin contain references to "Turky" coffee pots, which were probably small pots like these with lip spouts.
Cat. no. 35

the cup and cover (figure 23, p. 37). A kindred awkwardness is found in the embossing on the large kettle on a lamp stand of 1745/46 (figure 29). There, the cherub who has donned a feather headdress to represent the New World also contrasts with the refinement of the work of the "Maynard Master."

Whether alluding directly to the origins of tea itself or employed simply for visual excitement, exoticism at the tea table was the order of the day. Presided over by the lady of the house, the silverware of the tea ceremony was also expected to delight and surprise with novelty and whimsy, even femininity, but its decoration was not constrained to follow a programme of classical iconography as the silver in the more masculine setting of the dining room so often did. The delightful cream jug formed of leaves, with a snake for a base (figure 28), is redolent of the love of naturalism that appears from the mid-1740s. Several versions of this jug are known, all bearing the mark of de Lamerie, but with minor variations in execution. An example in the Fogg Art Museum at Harvard University is more proficiently chased, and a watered-down version is in the Clark Art Institute at Williamstown, Massachusetts. All three jugs were evidently finished by different hands, for the tooling is quite different on each, and it becomes clear that a number of skilled craftsmen worked for de Lamerie in his heyday.

An obituarist writing following the death of Paul de Lamerie in 1751 observed that he "was particularly famous in making fine ornamental Plate, and has been very instrumental in bringing that Branch of Trade to the Perfection it is now in." Work marked by de Lamerie, however, does not tell the whole story of silver produced in London during this golden age, for the trade was an intricate and widely scattered network of individuals and small workshops supplying large shops. Ironically enough, the system of hallmarking often clouds the picture of what really went on. The law stipulated that before submitting a piece of silver for assaying (testing the composition of the alloy) and marking (to show that its alloy was of the legal standard, required before a piece could be offered for sale in a shop), it had to be stamped with the personal punch of the guild member submitting it for assay. Although traditionally referred to as a "maker's mark," this mark did not necessarily belong to the person who made the piece. Indeed there is enough evidence to show that the process of making silverware in the eighteenth century was already an industrial one involving many different specialists. We do not know the identity of the person or persons who chased the greatest creations bearing de Lamerie's mark, such as the cup and cover in figure 23 (p. 37), but it is very unlikely to have been de Lamerie himself. Much of the talent that de Lamerie relied on belonged to fellow Huguenots, many of them working in poverty in basements and garrets not far from his workshop in Gerrard Street, Soho. But although the Huguenots were by far the largest group of foreign talent working in London, they do not constitute the whole picture. As we have seen, the engraver Blaise Gentot, who worked in London at the end of the seventeenth century, had immigrated on economic rather than religious grounds. During the reign of George II, other craftsmen came to London because of the business opportunities it afforded. Among them were Charles Kandler from Saxony, Nicolas Sprimont from Liège, and James Shruder, who appears to have come from Germany and arrived in London sometime before 1737.

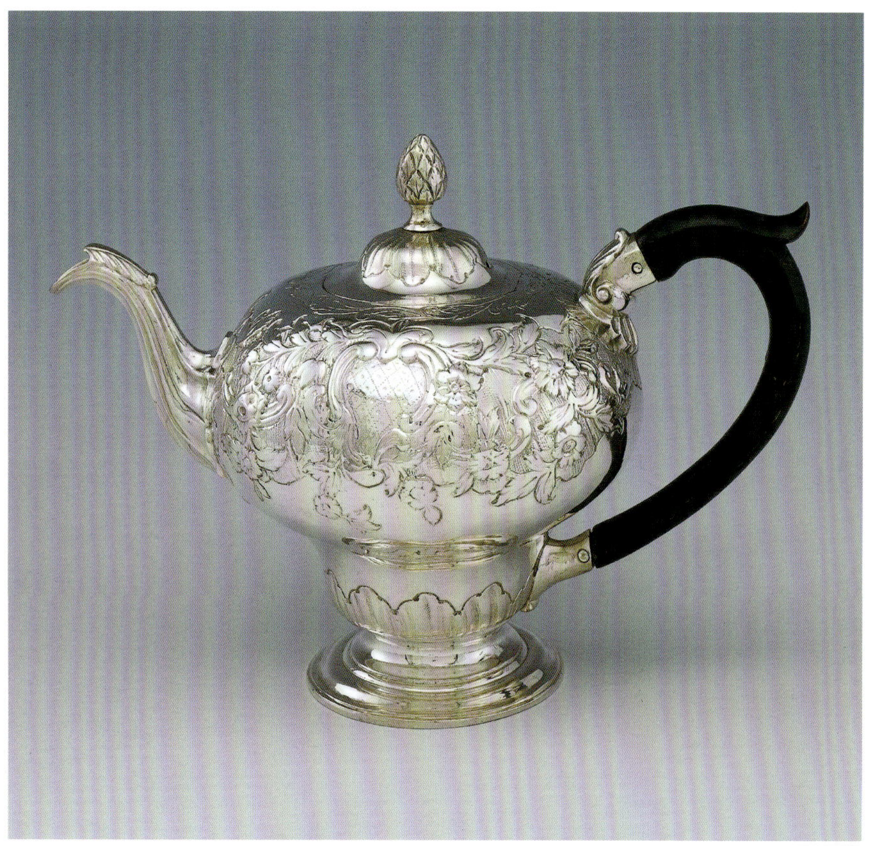

31. Teapot, silver and fruitwood, New York, c. 1765, maker's mark of Myer Myers. Like the English, the American colonists were avid tea drinkers, but in the 1770s tea became a political pawn in the growing revolt in America. When the British government lowered the rate of duty on tea to three pence a pound in America and made the tea trade a monopoly of the British East India Company, the "Sons of Liberty," as members of the radical American opposition called themselves, pre-empted what they saw as a potential sell-out to London in their fight against taxes imposed by the British government. As an act of political demonstration they organized "the Boston Tea Party," in which patriots disguised as Mohawk Indians threw hundreds of crates of tea bricks into Boston harbor. Supporters of independence made coffee into America's most popular beverage and tea never recovered its popularity in America.
Cat. no. 102

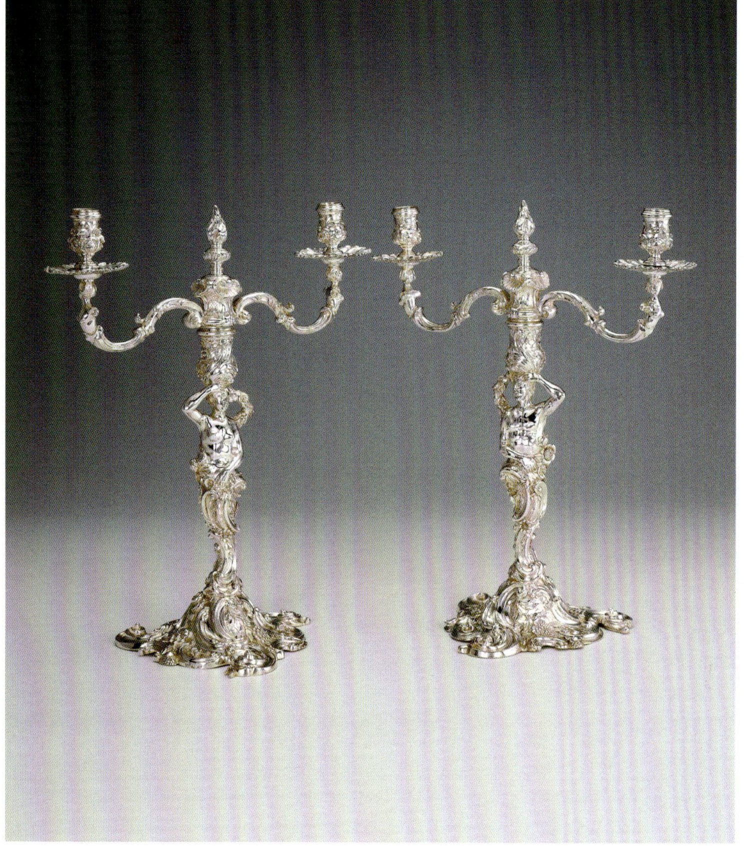

32. Pair of two-light candelabra, silver, London, 1748/49, maker's mark of Paul de Lamerie. As the fashionable hour for dinner became later, illumination was needed on the dining table. Candlesticks became more slender and branches higher and lighter.
Cat. no. 31

33. Tea kettle on lamp stand, silver and ivory, London, 1749/50, maker's mark of James Shruder. This extravagant creation of superbly modeled marine motifs marks the high point of English rococo naturalism.
Cat. no. 38

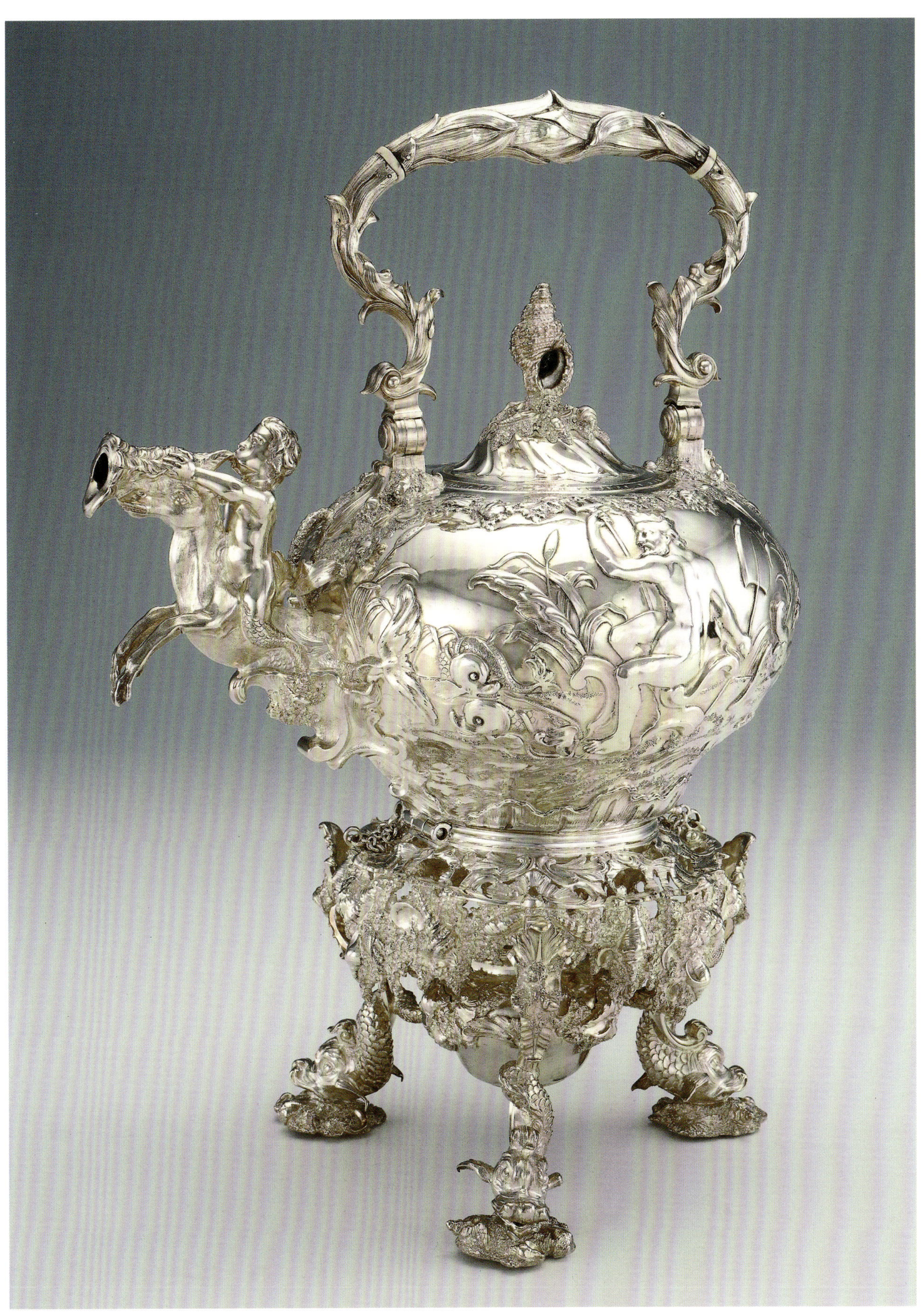

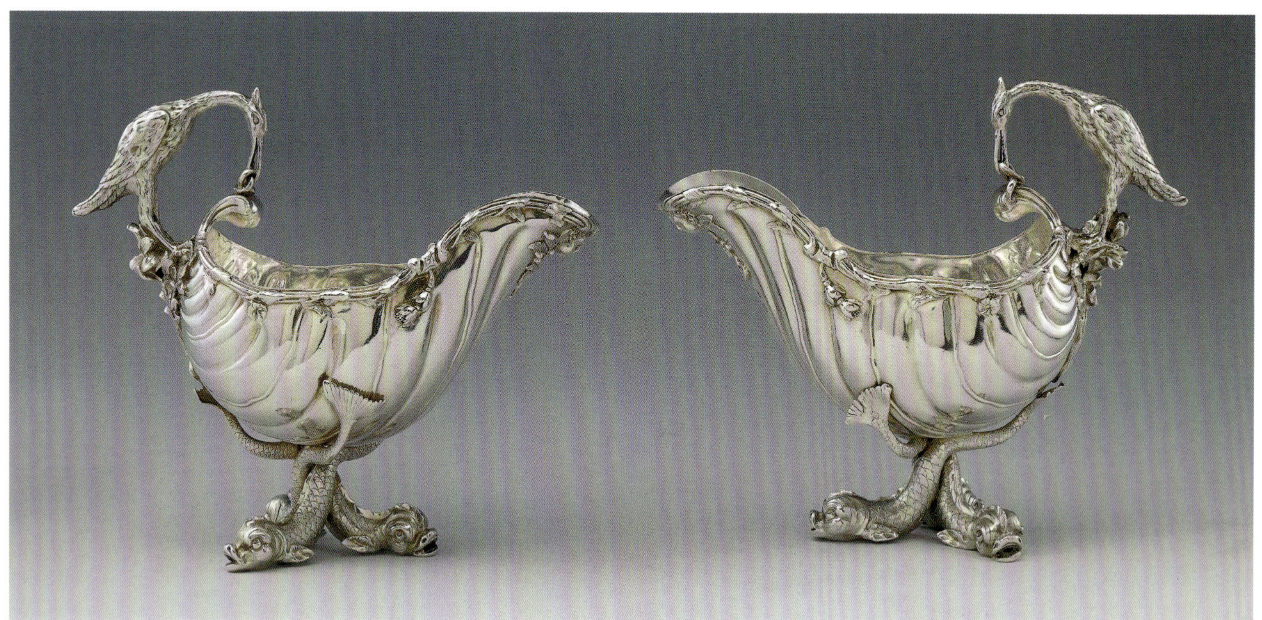

Work bearing Shruder's mark is uncommon, but what does survive shows superb modeling and chasing as on the magnificent tea kettle on lamp stand (figure 33, p. 43) of 1749/50, with many elements similar to those found on silver marked by de Lamerie in the 1740s. It is likely that Shruder worked as a modeler for de Lamerie during this period; he was a witness to de Lamerie's will in 1751. With its ocean spray, coral work, and Neptune rising from the ocean, the kettle is a *tour de force* of imagination that has never been surpassed. Its strength lies in the way that everything operates strictly within the confines of form and material (a metal vessel). Unlike the anonymous "Maynard Master," Shruder never makes function subservient to the decoration. It is not surprising that such an extravagant creation, and its matching coffee pot (now in the Victoria & Albert Museum, London), were made for Leake Okeover (1701–1765), a Staffordshire landowner whose love of marine themes is evident in the expensive service of Chinese export armorial porcelain he ordered in 1738.

The Okeover kettle must have caused a stir

34. Pair of sauceboats, silver, London, 1749/50, maker's mark of William Cripps. These whimsical creations in the picturesque style are purely decorative, lacking the complex classical allusions on the basket (figure 22, p. 36) or the cup and cover (figure 23, p. 37). Cat. no. 34

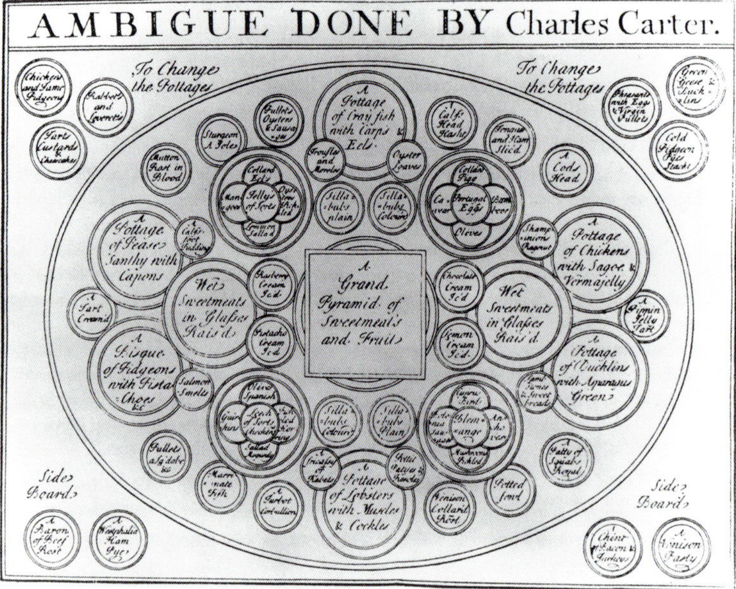

35. *Ambigue done by Charles Carter*, plate from the 1730 edition of Carter's book *The Complete Practical Cook*. Carter inveighs against "French customs and French cookery," yet he plagiarizes French recipes. For instance, his "ambigue" is in fact a French invention from the end of the previous century: a collation of cold dishes, both sweet and savory, served together and known in French as an *ambigu*. *The British Library*.

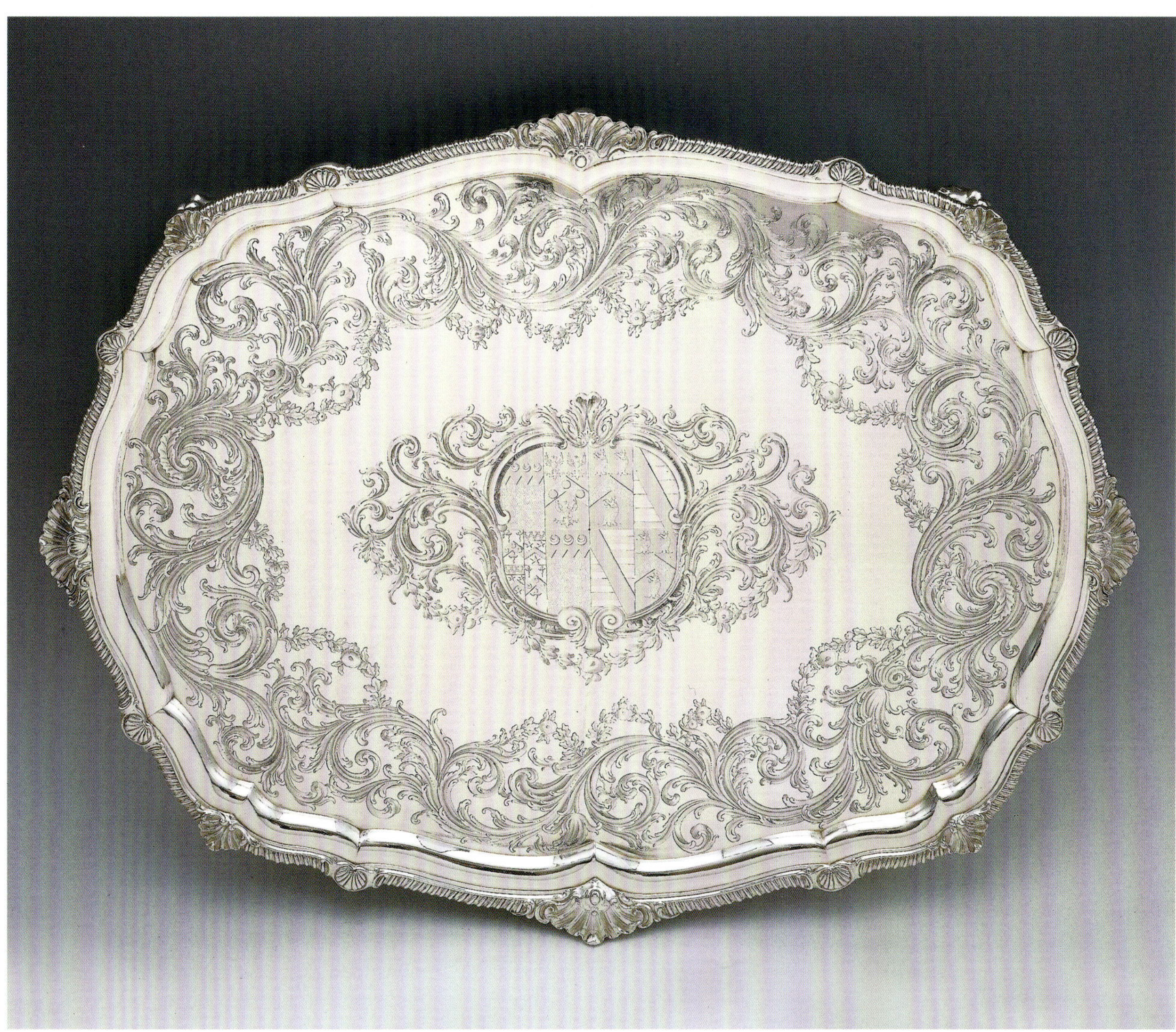

36. Salver or "table," silver, London, 1749/50, maker's mark of Edward Wakelin. Intended either as a stand for an epergne, or as a large tray for tea and coffee wares, this salver is exceptional for the high quality of its engraved border and the complex armorials in the center.
Cat. no. 39

when it first appeared on the tea table. Its decoration contains no allusion to love or the other concerns of the classical gods; its only "message" is a nautical allusion to the kettle's contents. Its generous proportions were suitable for large-scale entertaining, not only after dinner—when the men at last joined the ladies in the withdrawing room after several hours spent in hard drinking—but also in the new custom of serving tea in mid-afternoon during the widening gap that had appeared between breakfast and dinner, as the latter had gotten later and later during the eighteenth century.

In the sixteenth century, dinner had been served at midday; in the seventeenth, fashionable Londoners like Samuel Pepys sat down to dinner in mid-afternoon. By the end of the eighteenth century, the Prince of Wales and others of polite society would be dining in the early evening. All this was to have an impact on the demand for different types of silverware. Candlesticks and candelabra, not needed on the dining table in the previous century, started to make their appearance in the dining room as dinner more and more often took place after sundown. As a result, the scale of candlesticks changed. They became taller, so that the view was not restricted across the tabletop, and branches for candelabra became lighter and higher. The caryatid, or figural, stem for a candlestick had appeared in the 1680s; by the 1740s mythological nymphs and satyrs held candles aloft, often from sockets enriched with sunflowers, the symbol of Apollo, god of the sun. The pair of two-light candelabra of 1748/49 (figure 32, p. 42), with their garlanded female caryatid stems, conjures up visions of an

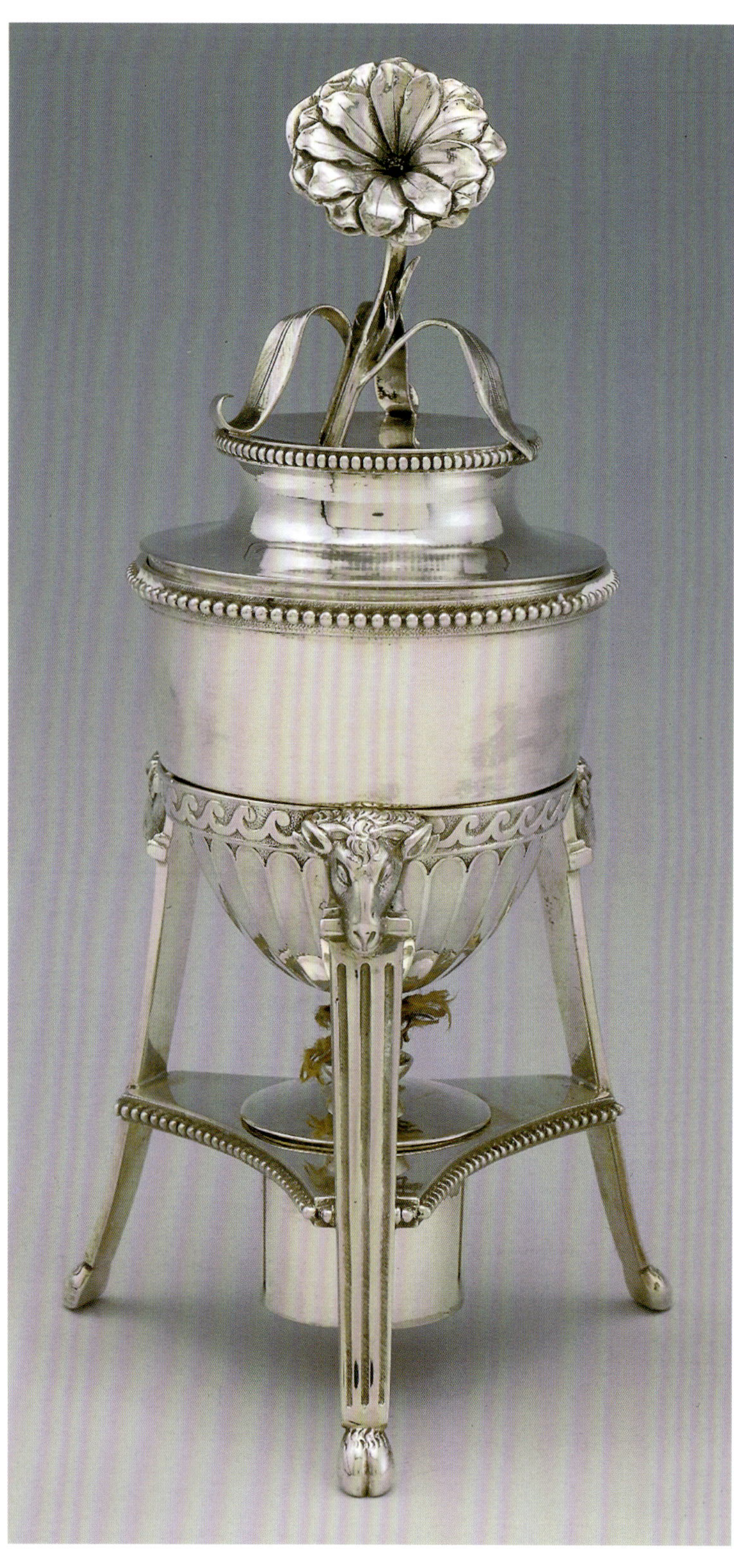

37. Perfume burner, silver, London, 1785/86, maker's mark of Andrew Fogelberg and Stephen Gilbert. The simple elegance of classicism, with its emphasis on line rather than ornament, had all but replaced the rococo by the 1780s and is well illustrated by this burner, which would have been used to perfume a dining room. Cat. no. 41

Arcadian landscape inhabited by nymphs, satyrs, and deities.

The sauceboats of 1749/50 (figure 34) take this picturesque style even further. Naturalism, shown by the birds that form the handles and the foliage around the rims, is grafted on to shells to form the bodies of the boats. With their shells they are reminiscent of Venus, but the allusion is slight; the powerful classical images of a few years earlier have become mere decorative motifs. How much of this change was due to a widening consumer base and to increasing numbers of customers who had no interest in being able to read a mythological message on their silverware, is difficult to assess.

The sauceboats are struck with the mark of William Cripps, a native Englishman who appears to have supplied Philips Garden and other retailers with finished silver. One of the most fashionable retailers at that time was Edward Wakelin, who in the late 1740s ran the business started by George Wickes some years before. By a happy chance, most of the business ledgers of this firm survive in the Victoria & Albert Museum and provide us with a tantalizing glimpse of the silver trade in mid-eighteenth century London. They also provide valuable information about the names given to specific items of silverware. The large tray or "Nurl'd Table," as it was described in Wakelin's *Gentleman's Ledger* (figure 36, p. 45), was made for Stephen Skynner in 1750 to present to his daughter Emma and her new husband, William Harvey. The tray itself cost £106 10s., and the additional outlay for engraving his new son-in-law's arms as well as a decorative border of foliate scrolls was a staggering £10, nearly a tenth of the price of the tray itself. A red leather case for it cost a mere eight shillings.

A tray of this scale, some thirty inches wide, could be placed under an epergne or centerpiece on the dining table. With candles ranged round it, the shiny surface of the metal would reflect the light. On the other hand, it could also be fitted into a wooden stand and used as a tray for tea wares. The English love of heraldry is still apparent in the skillful delineation of the many shields that both Harvey and his new father-in-law were entitled to bear, but there seem to have been no qualms about standing a coffee pot on top of them. What a great shift had taken place, away from the pride embodied in the baroque splendor of the Duke of Kent's heraldic ewers and dish to the decoratively functional.

Entremets II

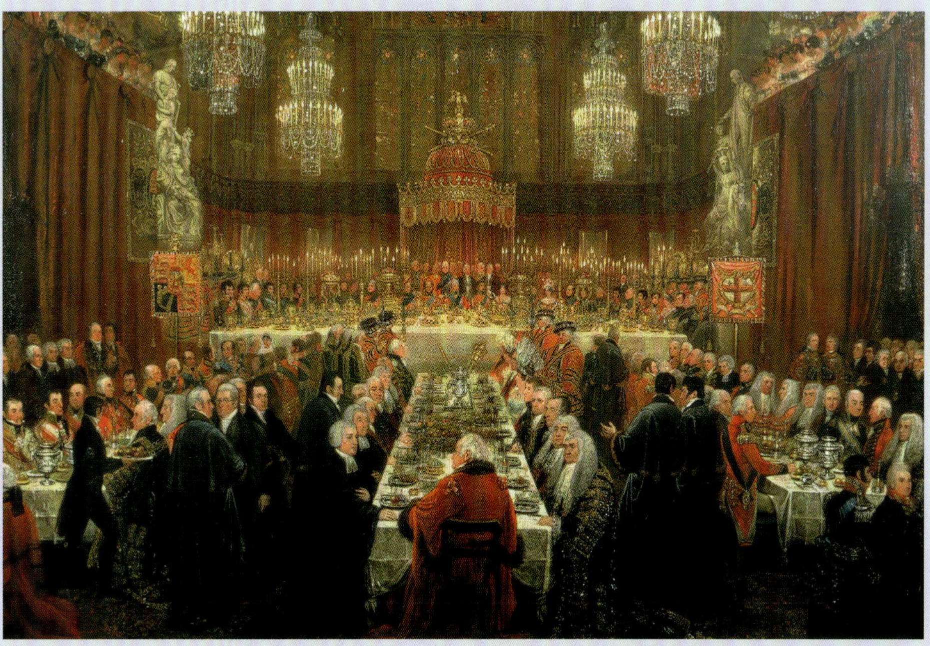

38. *The Banquet given by the Corporation of London for the Prince Regent, the Emperor of Russia and the King of Prussia on 18 June 1814*, oil on canvas. Luke Clennell's painting shows the profusion of both silver and silver gilt on crowded tables. "There never perhaps was an occasion when more plate was brought together in one place," remarked one observer. The wine coasters and coolers are a new feature on the tabletop. *Guildhall Art Gallery, Corporation of London/Bridgeman Art Library*.

Regency Delights, 1800–1830

Philippa Glanville

The tablecloth is then removed: under it, at the best tables, is a finer, upon which the dessert is set. At inferior ones, it is placed on the bare polished table. It consists of all sorts of hot-house fruits, which are here of the finest quality, Indian and native preserves, stomachic ginger, confitures, and the like. Clean glasses are set before every guest, and, with the dessert plates and knives and forks, small fringed napkins are laid. Three decanters are usually placed before the master of the house, generally containing claret, port, and sherry, or madeira. The host pushes these in stands, or in a little silver waggon on wheels, to his neighbour on the left. Every man pours out his own wine, and if a lady sits next him, also helps her; and so on till the circuit is made, when the same process begins again.

A German visitor, Prince Hermann von Pückler-Muskau, in a letter to his wife, 1826

Table culture in the Regency period, associated with conspicuous consumption, glittering plateaux, compotes for fruit and elaborate *pièces montées* (tiered desserts), presents a paradox. Although Britain was at war with France during the 1790s and from 1803 until 1815, fashionable English dining remained nevertheless acutely responsive to French fashions. Indeed, from Vienna to St. Petersburg, the top echelon in society, constantly meeting at dinner for diplomatic purposes, commented on new recipes, poached top chefs and shared connoisseurship of novel ideas in presentation. The Parisian *pâtissier* Marie-Antonin Carême found a keen audience in London for his inventions of *vol-au-vent* (puff pastry with a savory filling), large meringues, and fish cooked in champagne.

Warfare had a direct effect on the English table. Bread, pastry, and raised pies—all traditional dinner fare—fell from favor and the humble potato, virtually ignored in cookery books of the eighteenth century, became the patriotic carbohydrate, because of the high price of wheat during the Napoleonic Wars. A fourfold increase in the price of flour stimulated the adoption of substitutes for pastry, from potato toppings to ceramic pie dishes.

International hostilities dictated changes in drinking habits too. Napoleon's blockade of the West Indies stifled the supply of rum for after-dinner punch. Brandy, champagne, and French wines, already highly taxed, became almost unobtainable and even those English staples, port and Madeira, were scarce. The strong old English ales admired by Prince von Pückler-Muskau, a German visitor, appeared on smart London tables in the early nineteenth century as a gesture of patriotism.

Diplomacy drove the most significant shift in English dining practices, even though it took a generation to seep down through society. At the Congress of Vienna in 1814/15, when hundreds of diplomats gathered to decide the shape of post-Napoleonic Europe, Tsar Alexander I of Russia introduced the Anglo-Saxon world to a novel way of dining, termed *à la russe*. In this form of service, familiar today, dishes are served in sequence and from the sideboard, rather than laid out on the table in a mass to welcome the arriving diners in the well-established formula *à la française*. This new practice called for more serving staff, but created a different rhythm in the kitchen, as dishes could be served just as they were brought to perfection.

Dinners struck foreign visitors as a typically Anglo-Saxon device; Richard Rush, American ambassador from 1817 to 1825, noted that "the English are very remarkable for dinners." They were written up in newspapers, 10,000 references in *The Times* of London in one year, citing both guests and bill of fare. They were arranged to raise money for good causes, to acknowledge public service, and as annual celebrations. The Royal Academy dinner on May 3, 1818 at Somerset House, presided over by the American artist Benjamin West, began at 6 P.M., now the fashionable hour, with sun pouring through the skylights. As the meal went on, shaded lamps hanging above brought a rich glow to the scene, and the shining damask admired by Rush set off the glittering silver.

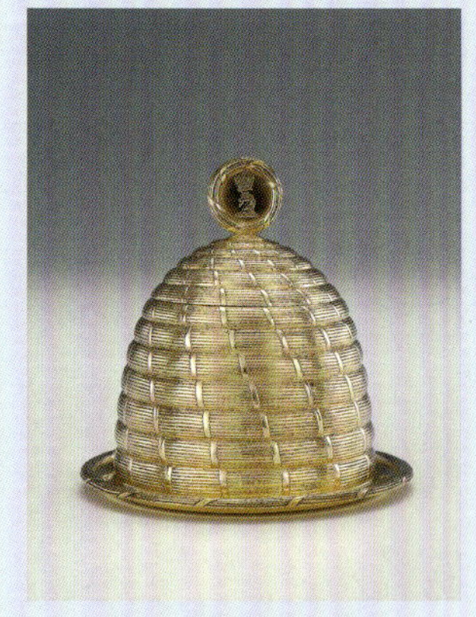

39. Honey pot and stand, silver gilt, London, 1798/99, the stand 1797/98, maker's mark of Paul Storr. Realistically formed as a woven bee skep, this pot is typical of the more elaborate items made for the breakfast table from the end of the eighteenth century onwards, reflecting the rise of the country-house party.
Cat. no. 42

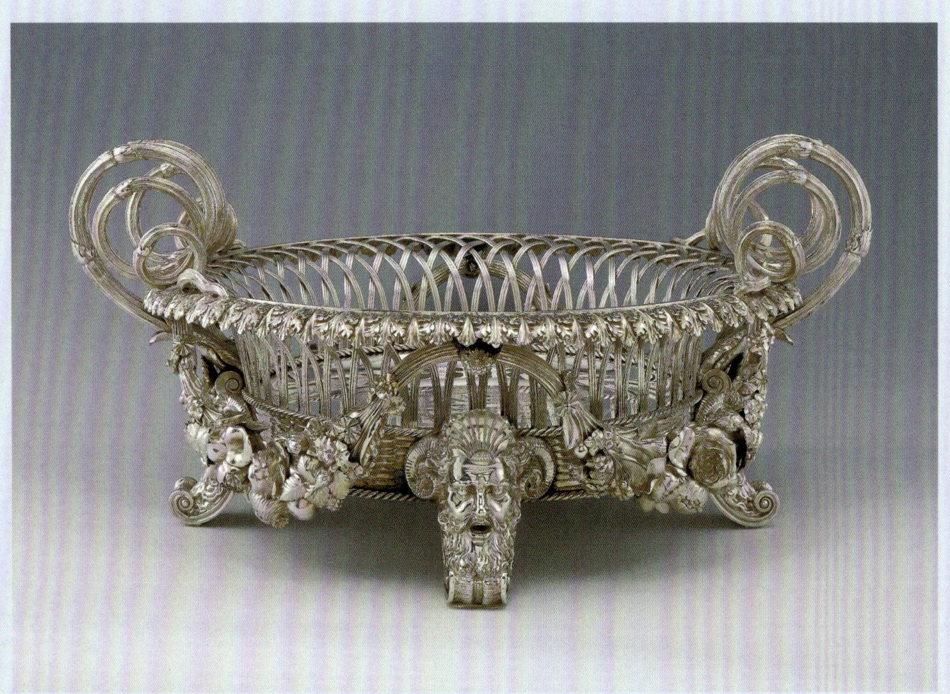

40. Basket, silver, London, 1813/14, maker's mark of Paul Storr. This monumental basket, originally one of a pair, is unlikely to have been used for serving bread, but was probably intended for display. It belonged to an extensive service purchased over a seven-year period by George Wyndham, 3rd Earl of Egremont, from Rundell's for use at Petworth, his house in Sussex. Artists such as J.M.W. Turner were welcomed at Petworth where, in the words of Benjamin Robert Haydon, another artist patronized by the earl, everything was "solid, liberal, rich and English."
Cat. no. 52

Most large dinners were supplied by caterers. They had a certain showy predictability and relied for effect on large sculptural *pièces montées*, hired out night after night and intended to please the eye rather than the stomach, although their decoration of crystallized fruit, small meringues, and other delicacies could be consumed. An exceptionally grand Anglo-German dinner at Windsor Castle in February 1805, during the Napoleonic wars, shows how strongly topical the message of the layout could be:

> The confectionery ornaments were designed with great taste, consisting of the emblems of traditional greatness, naval and military ornaments, temples, triumphal arches crowned with figures of Fame and Victory, lions and eagles, pavilions supported by columns enwreathed with laurel, and hung with festoons of silver gauze, fringed with gold, and with medallions of the Union Escutcheon, and portraits and ciphers of the KING and QUEEN …
>
> *The Times*, February 26, 1805

Wedgwood figures, set among the silver candelabra, brought both colour and a proud native product, although the original inspiration had been the sugar figures at Renaissance tables.

More revealing are the glimpses of daily meals for George III and Queen Charlotte found in the Lord Steward's accounts held in the English National Archives. Although the many dishes offered may surprise a modern menu planner, they ate simply. On February 4, 1802, for example, the king and queen were offered Flemish "Watersoutie," a comforting winter fish soup, a joint of beef from Hanover, lamb fried with spinach, and "Gallimaufre of Mutton" (a kind of stew), minced chicken (a favourite of the Queen's) and a smoked tongue. For the second course, stewed eels, pigs' feet and ears in a sauce, Spanish onions, and venison contrasted with more delicate fare: anchovy salad, eggs *remoulade*, and skewered sweetbreads. Dessert was fruit tarts and cream. Supper, a lighter meal, brought larks, guinea fowl, oysters, and mushrooms.

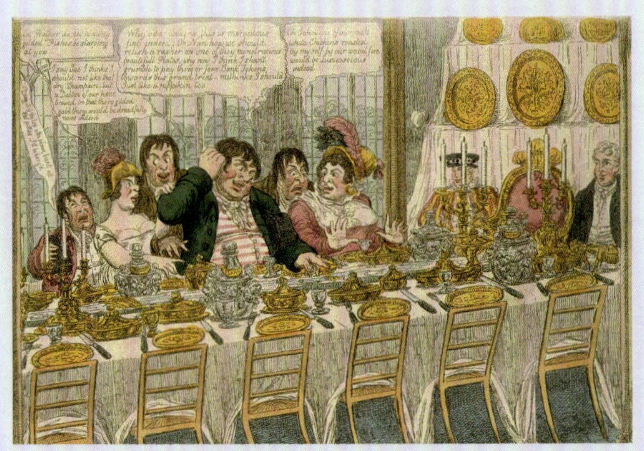

41. *John Bull in the Conservatory*, aquatint, 1811. This cartoon satirizes the fête held at Carlton House on June 19, 1811, by the Prince of Wales to mark the birthday of his father, King George III. A country bumpkin laments the absence of homely English fare amid the profusion of silver gilt crowding the table and the buffet. Instead of a newly fashionable plateau, the table had a stream running down the center of it, complete with live fish. *Private Collection*.

These relatively homely dishes contrast with the lavish, strongly French menus of their son, the Prince of Wales. At the Royal Pavilion, Brighton, he set up strong Argand oil lights in the ceiling. He also installed the latest catering equipment and a vast straw-insulated ice house, and set up lead-lined ice bins by the confectionery rooms. He acquired a thirteen-foot oval steam table to keep dozens of dishes hot for simultaneous serving—the essential theatrical ingredient of large dinners. Here the royal chef Carême produced the complex, rich, and delicious dishes such as *quenelles* (a kind of dumpling), soufflés, and puff pastry. Large *entrées* were ornamented with a frieze of silver attelets skewering oysters, kidneys, and *morilles*, intended for consumption at the second course.

Roasts still predominated; as Captain Rees Gronow commented in his *Reminiscences*, "the French or side dishes consisted of very mild but very abortive attempts at Continental cooking, and I have always observed that they met with the neglect and contempt that they merited."

As yet, drinks before dinner were offered only in Russia and there was little attempt to match particular wines with specific dishes, a practice that developed in England later in the century. After 1815, sherry became popular, drunk with the soup, and port (dry and strong, not the sweet after-dinner drink associated with club land and crusty dons) was available throughout the meal, but many people preferred to refresh themselves with home-brewed beer. The Prince of Wales, a leader of fashion in food and drink, could down three bottles of wine at dinner, punctuated with imported mineral waters that cost far more than the "fine Highland whisky," illegally distilled, which he sampled in Edinburgh in 1822. A year later, the huge duty on whisky dropped dramatically and whisky became a popular drink south of the Scottish border too.

Victorian Formality

This exit is the result of too many entrées.

Regency nobleman on his deathbed

The beginning of the nineteenth century ushered in a new golden age. For silverware it was literally golden, for silver gilt began to dominate the dining table and the sideboard. In earlier times, parts of objects, like the interior of a goblet, had often been gilded to prevent pitting caused by the acid in wine. Sometimes entire objects intended primarily for display, such as the livery pots (figure 3, p. 15) and the ewers and dish (figure 4, p. 17), had been gilded, at great expense. But the notion of gilding all the items in a dinner service had been completely unknown. The impetus for this, like so many trends in eating and drinking, came from France. Napoleon sought to surround his Consulate with an aura of gold; later, after he had become Emperor, gold dominated the interiors of Paris and the empire's satellite courts around Europe. Somewhat surprisingly, in England, the Prince Regent, who became King George IV in 1820, emulated his enemy assiduously. In fact, the prince became obsessed with Napoleon. He avidly collected Napoleonic memorabilia, and hired the imperial chef, Marie-Antonin Carême, to work at his exotic Pavilion at Brighton. It was the era of the great French chefs in England—Louis Eustache Ude (who worked for the prince's brother, the Duke of York), Auguste Escoffier, Charles Elmé Francatelli, and Alexis Soyer.

Dining assumed a new formality. Gone was the intimacy of the fashionable supper party, with a minimum of servants in attendance and everything within reach of the diners. Dining tables became laden with tureens, entrée dishes, and candelabra, all in a new classical, sculptural style. Richard Rush, the newly arrived United States ambassador, observed in June 1818 that everyone was "struck with this profusion of solid and sumptuous plate upon English tables, as unknown in any other capital to an extent at all approaching to comparison." The Duke of Wellington's official plate, issued to him by the Jewel House in 1814 when he became ambassador to France, included four tureens, four candelabra, twelve dozen plates, and a large centerpiece.

With the surge in the price of grain brought about by wars with the French, British landowners found themselves with a glut of cash, much of which they enthusiastically lavished on silver for their tables. The 12th Duke of Norfolk spent over £12,000 on two massive silver dinner services between 1815 and 1820, at a time when his cook was earning £50 a year. Naval and military heroes of the wars returned with new wealth, which they used to buy extravagant silverware, or else they received elaborate testimonial pieces from groups of grateful subscribers. Fulfilling this new demand were several large-scale manufacturers, but the firm of Rundell, Bridge and Rundell, who were appointed goldsmiths to the king in 1804, outshone the others.

If Paul de Lamerie dominated the silver trade in the second quarter of the eighteenth century, Rundell's, as the royal goldsmiths were known, did so in the first quarter of the nineteenth. But there the comparison ends. Although de Lamerie evidently used specialist outworkers as modelers and makers, his business always retained a personal stamp, and closed down when he died. Rundell's, on the other hand, was a partnership

42. Pair of entrée dishes and covers, silver, London, 1817/18, maker's mark of Paul Storr. Through Rundell's, Storr had supplied a dinner service embellished with panels of foliate scrolls and diaperwork to Bernard Edward Howard, 12th Duke of Norfolk. The decoration was copied from platters of the 1730s in the Norfolk collection. Rundell's used the same pattern for other services, including these examples made for the Davidson family. These high-domed covered dishes represent a transitional phase in table setting during the Regency period—the table continued to be set with a multitude of dishes for diners to help themselves, but some dishes were being handed round by servants, in the new service *à la russe*.
Cat. no. 64

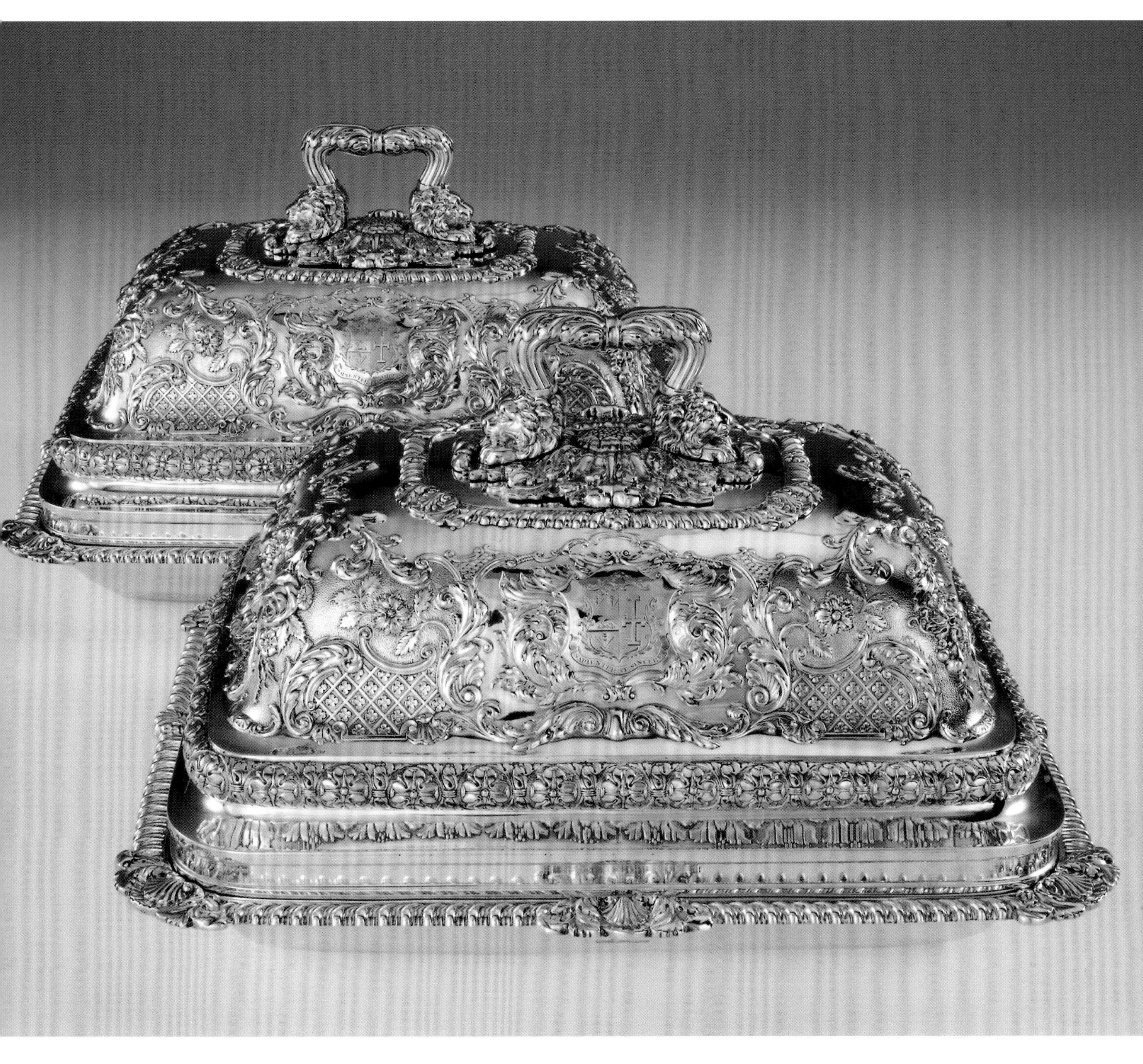

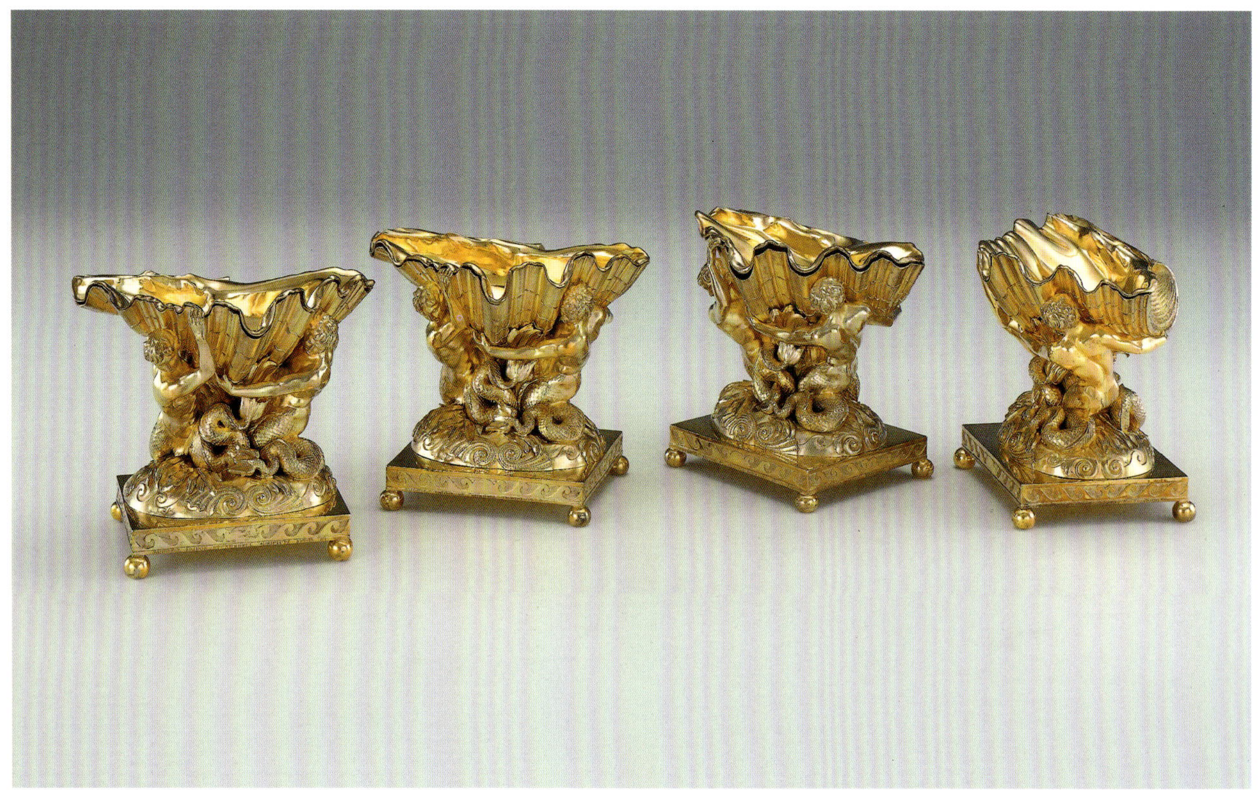

43. Set of four salts, silver gilt, London, 1813/14, maker's mark of Paul Storr. These salts were probably designed and modeled by the sculptor William Theed, head of Rundell's design studio, and made in their Soho workshops under the direction of Paul Storr. The maritime motifs allude to the most common source of salt at the time, the sea.
Cat. no. 53

from the outset and, by dint of building up unprecedented reserves, the firm could afford to have ambitious pieces of sculptural silver made speculatively for prospective clients rather than to order. Instead of being subjected to the whim of the client, who then might not pay for his order, Rundell's were able to drive the market for silverware and at the same time determine its artistic direction. Early on, Rundell's hired a stable of top sculptors and draftsmen who were employed in designing exclusively for the firm. Their two manufactories, the first directed by Benjamin Smith and Digby Scott and the second by Paul Storr, concentrated their manpower efficiently at two workshops where their designs and techniques were safe from their competitors.

It was the first time in the history of English silver that the customer was no longer the driving force in the adoption of new types of silverware and new styles. Even Rundell's greatest client, the Prince of Wales, or Prince Regent as he became in 1811, who spent more than £100,000 on silver alone during a ten-year period, purchased Rundell's creations ready-made, often after the same model had been made and sold to other, less illustrious, clients. One

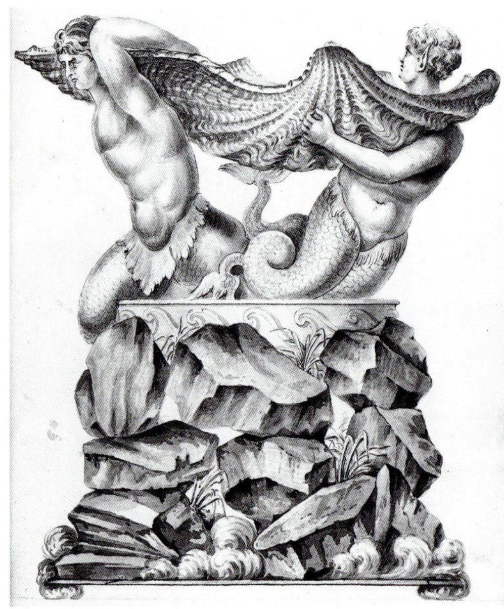

44. Design for a salt, pencil heightened with watercolor. From an album of fifty-five designs attributed to the sculptor Edward Hodges Baily, who was responsible for translating William Theed's designs for Rundell's into practical pieces of silverware. *Victoria & Albert Museum, London.*

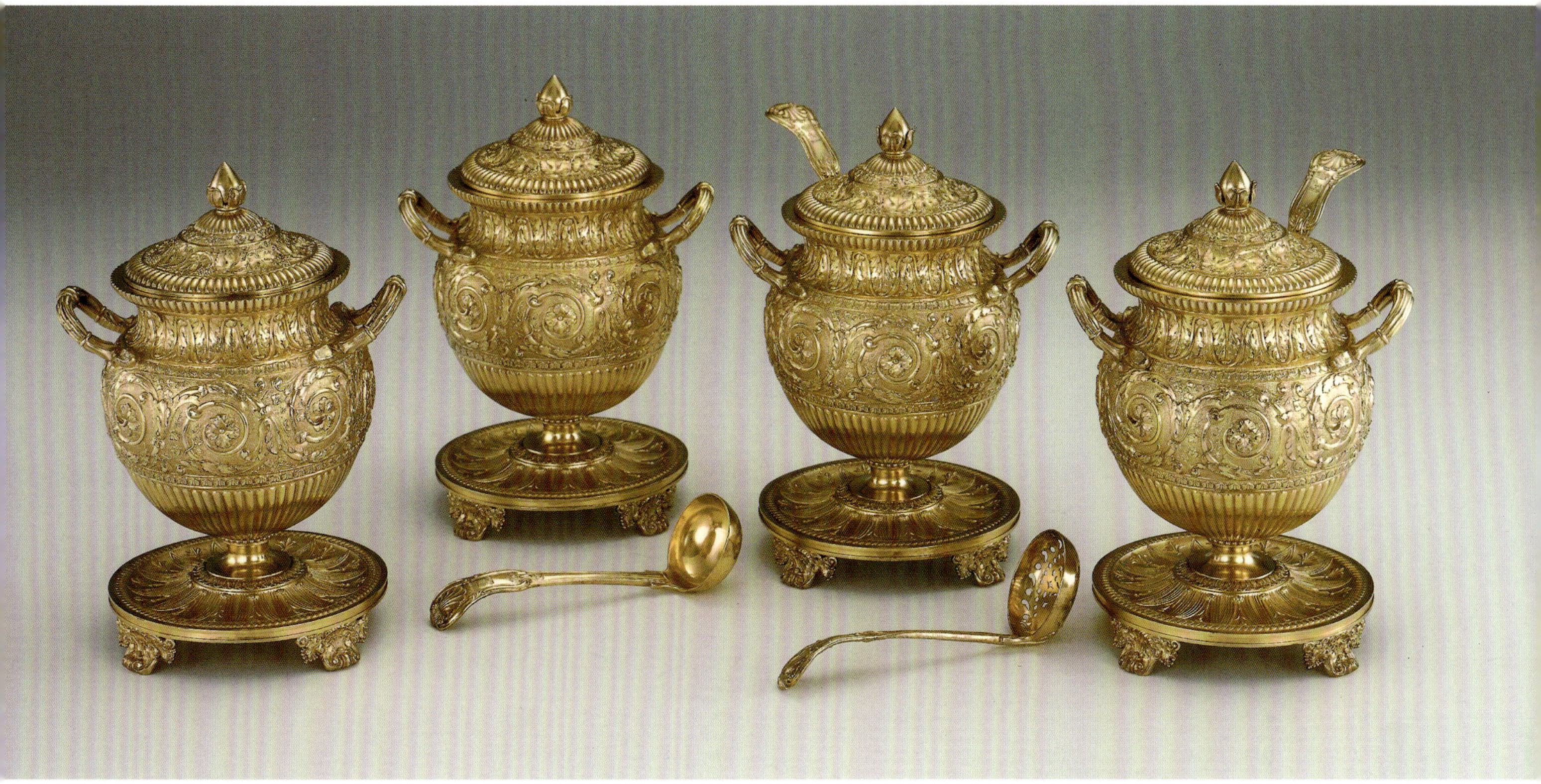

45. Four sugar or cream vases and ladles, silver gilt, London, 1816/17, maker's mark of Paul Storr. These are part of a set of eight "very richly chas'd Vases & Covers for Sugar & Cream for the Dessert" purchased from Rundell's by the 12th Duke of Norfolk in March 1816. The eight vases cost £241 4s. 1d. with a further £112 for "Gilding … all over in the very best manner 2 colors dead & red." "Dead" gilding was a bright gold color, while a redder hue could be obtained by increasing the amount of copper in the alloy.
Cat. no. 63

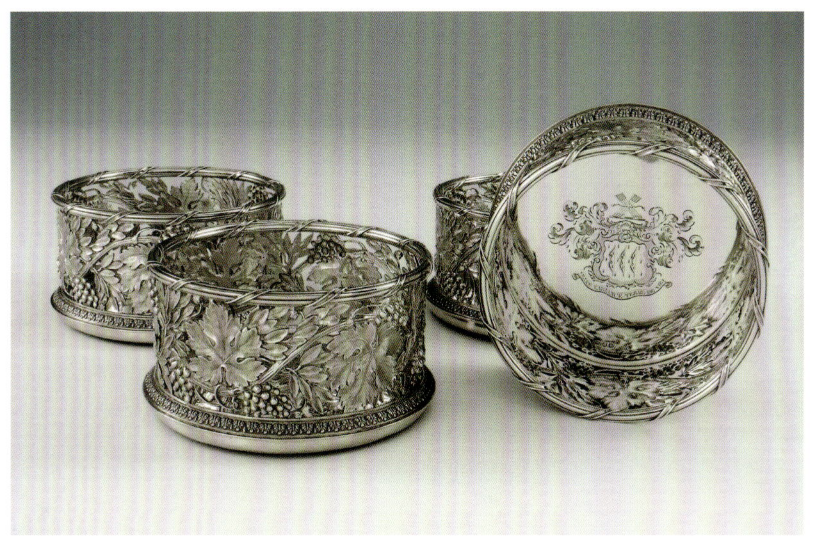

46. Set of four wine coasters, silver, wood, and baize, London, 1815/16, maker's mark of Paul Storr. At the beginning of the nineteenth century, the custom of serving wine from the sideboard yielded to placing wine glasses and decanters on the table itself so that diners might help themselves. Coasters with baize-covered bottoms enabled the wine to be pushed across the polished tabletop after the cloth had been removed at the end of the meal, when the port and other dessert wines began to flow in earnest.
Cat. no. 61

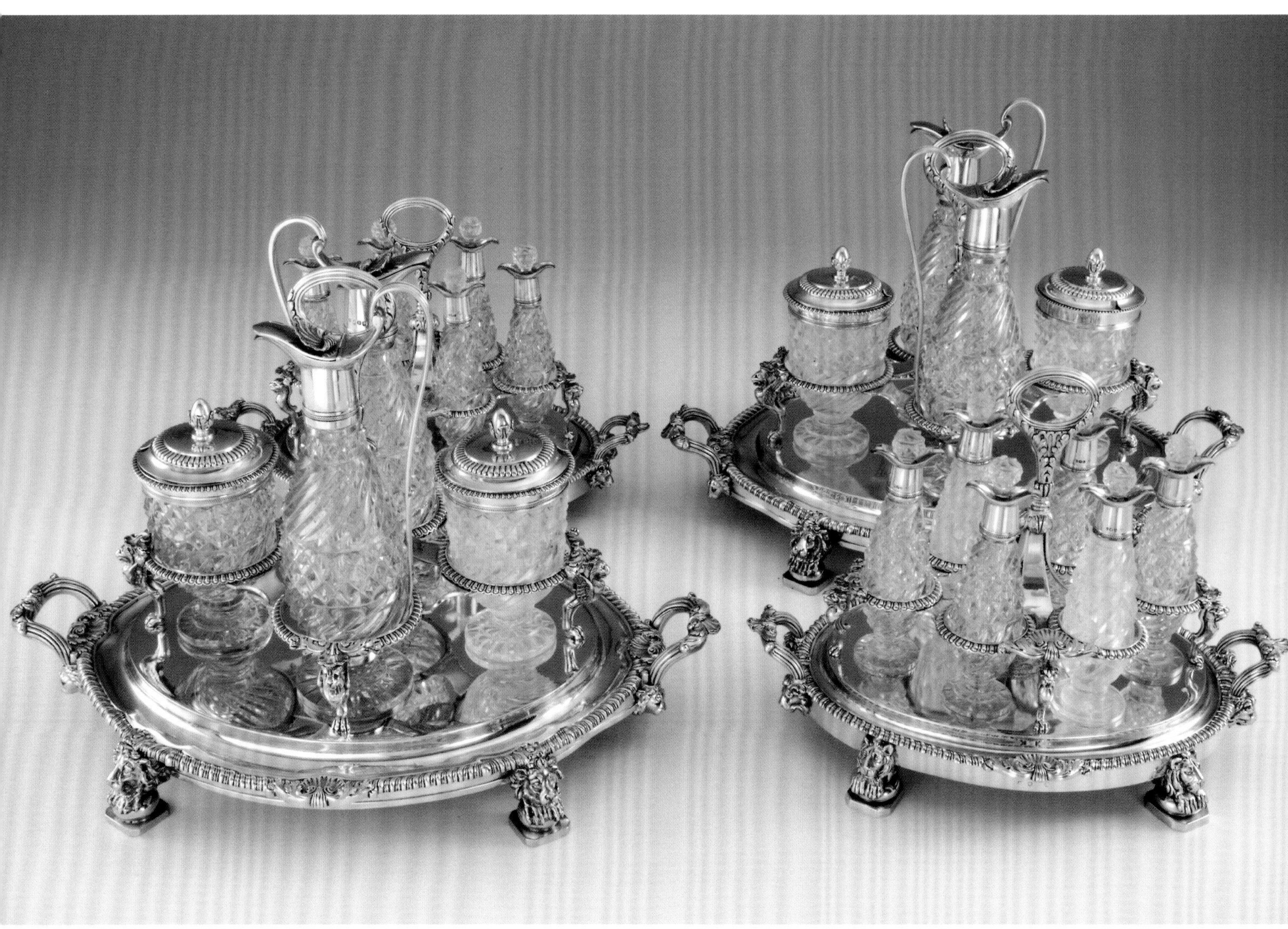

47. Four cruet stands, silver, partially gilt, cut glass, London, 1806/7, maker's mark of Paul Storr. Designed in the new Imperial style that Rundell's promoted in the first years of the nineteenth century, these stands formed part of a vast dinner service of some 278 pieces issued by the Jewel House to Douglas Alexander Hamilton, 10th Duke of Hamilton, on his appointment as British ambassador to the court of St. Petersburg. Cat. no. 43

key result was a greater homogeneity in design. Rundell's promoted a new imperial style in silver, which was only in part based on French prototypes. The whole realm of classical art was ransacked for models and motifs. It seemed only fitting that Roman marble funerary urns were the inspiration for silver-gilt sugar vases for the dessert table (figure 45, p. 53).

A great deal of the credit for this new silverware must go to Paul Storr, whose name became an icon among silver collectors, especially in America, during the twentieth century. The Gans Collection has nearly forty pieces struck with his mark. Like de Lamerie, Storr was probably not a practicing silversmith, but he was a gifted man of foresight and enterprise. In its heyday the workshop he set up in 1807 for Rundell's in Soho employed over 500 workmen. The capital provided by the firm enabled him to invest in the latest technology. This can be seen in the large-scale casting and stamping out of decorative motifs, which are often repeated on different items. A good example of this is the set of wine coasters of 1815/16 (figure 46, p. 53) which have borders of continuous grapevine stamped out with a highly finished steel die. It was a difficult and expensive process to cut a steel die of this size but, once done, it could be used over and over again.

The essential elements of a silver dinner service at this time remained soup and sauce tureens, platters, and plates. Candlesticks and candelabra were needed, as the hour of dinner had become progressively later. The entrée dish (figure 42, p. 51), a circular or rectangular deep dish with a domed cover, had appeared at the end

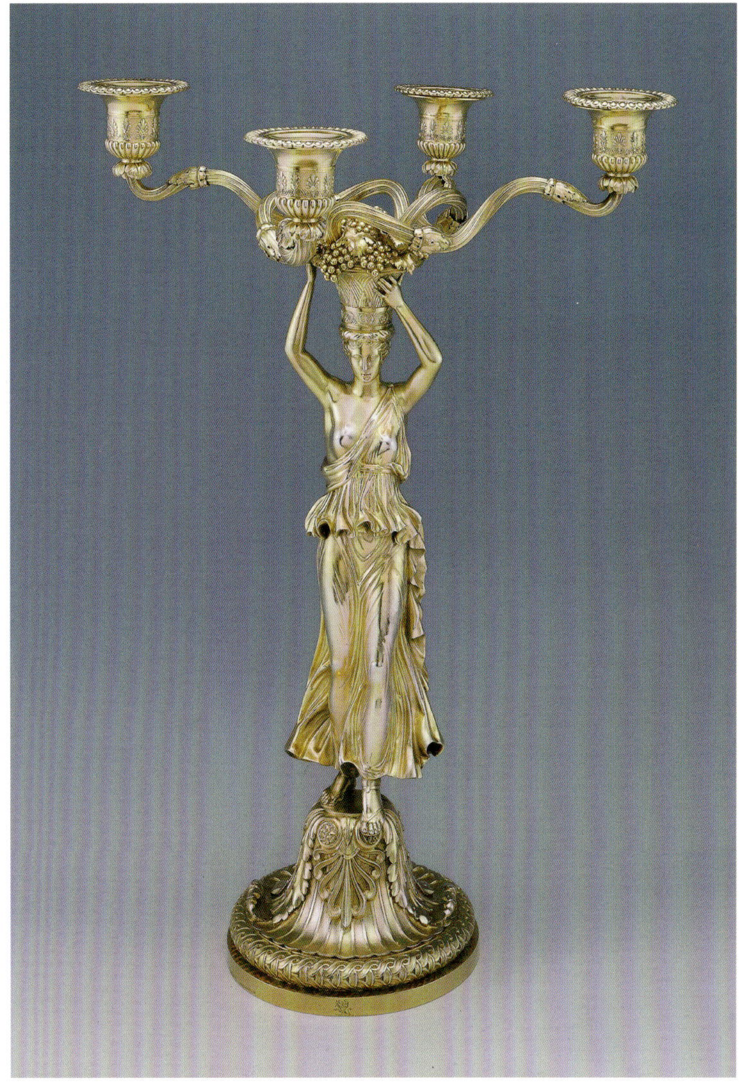

48. Candelabrum, silver gilt, London, 1815/16, maker's mark of Paul Storr. The female caryatid candlestick first gained popularity in English silver in the 1680s; it remained popular into the nineteenth century when, with the later hour of dining, it became a feature on the dining table, and was given branches high enough to allow an unhindered view across the table. Cat. no. 58

of the eighteenth century. Other traditional receptacles such as oil and vinegar frames (figure 47), salts, and mustard pots, acquired almost lofty proportions. Complete sets of flatware became the norm, and as fresh forks, knives, and spoons were required for each course, the sets became much larger. An innovation was the plateau, a platform running the full length of the table, with a mirror plate that formed the surface on which could be placed compotes, candlesticks, and arrangements of fruit or flowers. One of the largest of these platforms, the one designed by the Duchess of Northumberland, is still at Alnwick Castle in Northumberland.

Ironically, the Congress of Vienna, which convened in 1814, confirmed the status of France, the vanquished nation, as the cultural arbiter of Europe. It was there, though, that a new way of serving food first gained acceptance. Service *à la russe*, which did away with placing all the components of a course on the table at once, meant that fewer serving dishes appeared on the tabletop. But their place was quickly taken up by ever increasing numbers of candelabra, sculptural figures, and wine coolers. The idea of placing decanters of wine on the table—in coasters with baize bottoms or fitted with small ivory casters so they could be wheeled around the tabletop, or in ice-filled coolers—was revolutionary.

The dominance of the sideboard for serving wine was finally over—diners were given a selection of glasses at their place setting and were expected to help themselves, or be helped by a gallant neighbor. The lavish silver-gilt wine coolers of 1814/15 (figure 50, p. 57) are copies of the Buckingham Vase, a Roman marble urn

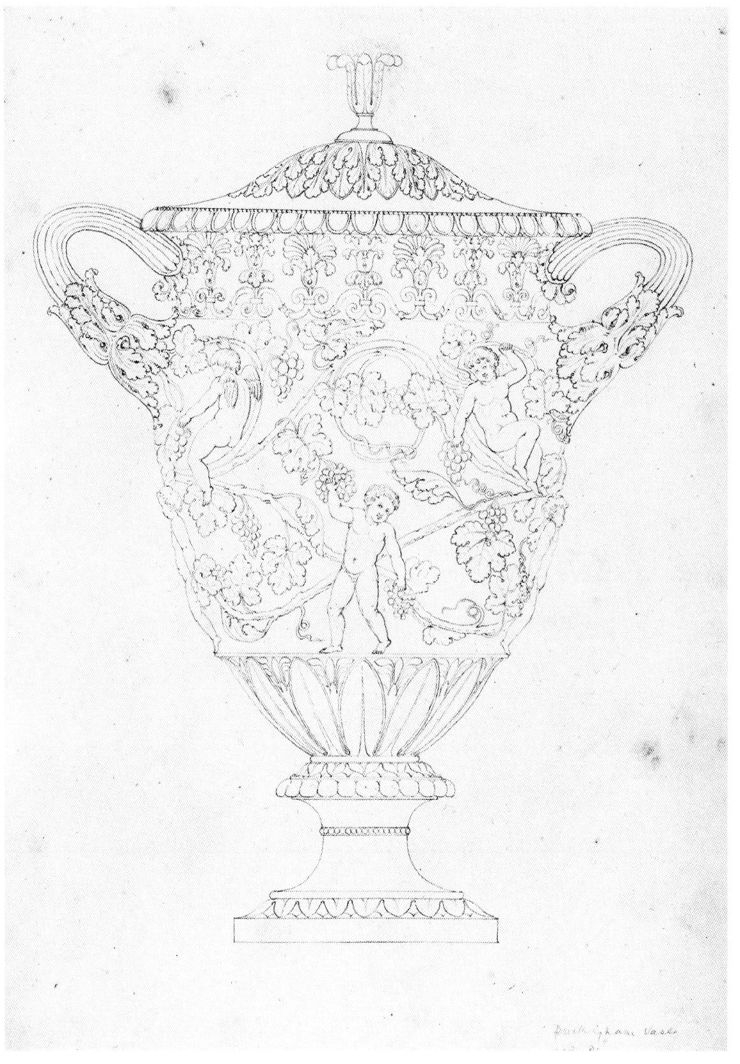

49. Design for an urn based on the Buckingham Vase, pencil. From an album of designs attributed to Edward Hodges Baily for Rundell's. The two great retailers of the Regency period, Jeffreys, Jones and Gilbert, and their great rivals Rundell's made versions of the Buckingham Vase for use as wine coolers and as racing trophies. This drawing is based on the engraving by Piranesi of 1778. ***Victoria & Albert Museum, London.***

which was discovered at the site of Hadrian's Villa outside Rome in 1769. It was acquired by the 1st Marquess of Buckingham in 1774 and prints of it were published by the Italian artist Piranesi a few years later. Such a famous work of art in a British collection was an obvious model for imposing silver wine coolers and Piranesi's engravings provided the blueprints for the silversmiths. Several examples in silver are known but the Gans set is the earliest. The marble urn itself is now in the Los Angeles County Museum of Art.

Once the main part of the meal was over and the chilled white wines had been replaced by decanters of sweet dessert wines placed in coasters, bowls of fruit could be chilled on top of the wine coolers. Their bodies are fitted with removable cylindrical liners and collars, allowing iced water to circulate around the decanter without making it wet. In the days before refrigeration it was the height of luxury to be able to produce ice during the summer months. Kept insulated with straw in ice houses built partly underground, ice had been a feature of aristocratic tables since the sixteenth century, but in the nineteenth century, commercial firms began to import ice in bulk from North America. As a result, wine coolers proliferated on the tabletop.

Hot drinks retained their popularity, too. Punch had been a mainstay of after-dinner drinking since the beginning of the eighteenth century. With a brandy base, it was a concoction of sugar, spices, lemons, and oranges; in the Regency period the brandy was sometimes replaced with gin, or in Scotland even with whisky. The punch set (figure 51, p. 58) of 1820/21 shows how even a stand for punch cups could be given a gilded monumentality. The cups are wreathed in meticulously delineated grape leaves and fit into a stand with applied borders of stylized honeysuckle and rosettes, motifs borrowed from classical architectural friezes.

By the time this punch set was produced in Rundell's Soho workshops, Paul Storr had already left the firm to set up his own business. Since Cato Sharp, his successor as manager, for some unknown reason never registered his own mark with the Goldsmiths' Company, the set was struck with the mark of Philip Rundell, the senior partner of the firm. Rundell's continued to operate their own workshops until the mid-1830s. Meanwhile, Paul Storr, at the helm of his own enterprise, was producing substantial quantities of silverware in competition to Rundell's. The stag-head cup of 1834/35 (figure 52, p. 58), marked by him, is typical of the bold modeling found on silver of this period and admirably suited to amusing objects such as stirrup cups, which could not be put down and had to be drained while the drinker remained in the saddle.

Storr had managed to entice Edward Hodges Baily, one of the leading members of Rundell's stable of modelers, to join him in his new venture. The monumental figure of Hebe (figure 54, p. 59) was produced in Storr's workshop in 1829/30 and probably modeled by Baily. Some twenty years earlier, Storr had produced another version on a square pedestal base, which Rundell's sold to Sir Francis Burdett, and it is evident that Storr had retained the designs and models from the earlier version. Standing

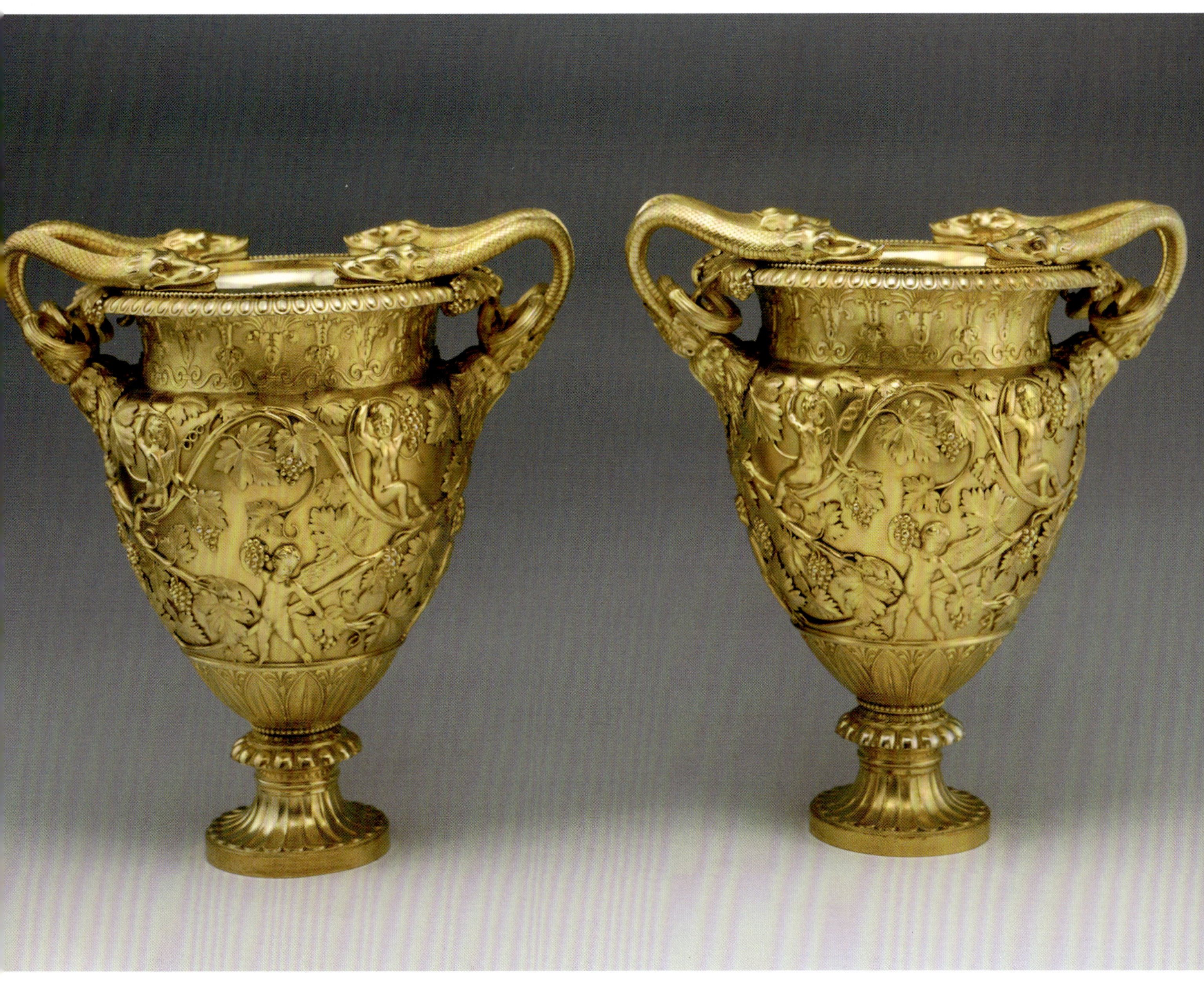

50. Pair of wine coolers, silver gilt, London, 1814/15, maker's mark of Benjamin Smith II. The whole of classical art was ransacked for models and motifs to be used for silver on the dining table during the Regency period. These coolers are replicas of the famous Buckingham Vase, an antique Roman urn in the collection of the Marquesses (later Dukes) of Buckingham at Stowe. Both the marble urn and these silver-gilt wine coolers were sold in the famous auction of the contents of Stowe in 1848 that lasted forty days.
Cat. no. 57

some three feet high, the figure of Hebe may have been intended as a table ornament, or merely as a freestanding sculpture. Based on Canova's celebrated marble sculpture, a version of which exists at Chatsworth (the Derbyshire estate of the Dukes of Devonshire), the figure illustrates the way in which silver was increasingly regarded as a sculptural medium. Hebe, as the goddess of youth who possessed powers of rejuvenation, was perhaps not the most suitable of figures to gaze down upon the many rich courses of a fashionable dinner.

This new monumentality was not confined to silver for the dining room, nor was it confined

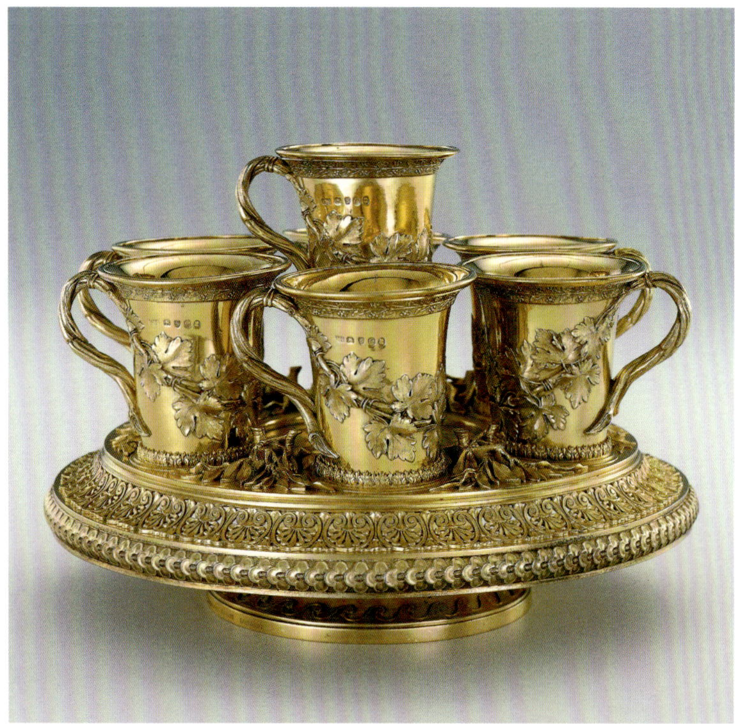

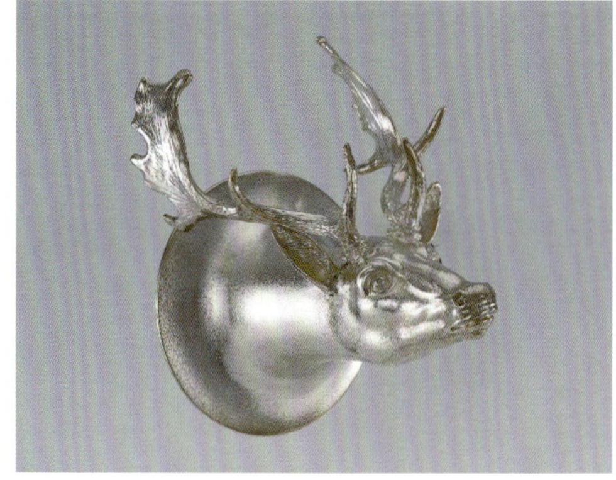

52. Stirrup cup, silver, London, 1834/35, maker's mark of Paul Storr. Cups in the form of fox heads and, less commonly, hound or stag heads, were popular from the mid-eighteenth century onwards and were often given as sporting prizes. Their lack of a foot made it necessary for drinkers, while still on horseback, to drain them in one draught.
Cat. no. 87

51. Punch set, silver gilt, London, 1820/21, maker's mark of Philip Rundell. What makes these individual punch cups look so imposing is the addition of an impressive stand that is embellished with grapevines as well as bands of decoration borrowed from Greek and Roman architecture.
Cat. no. 70

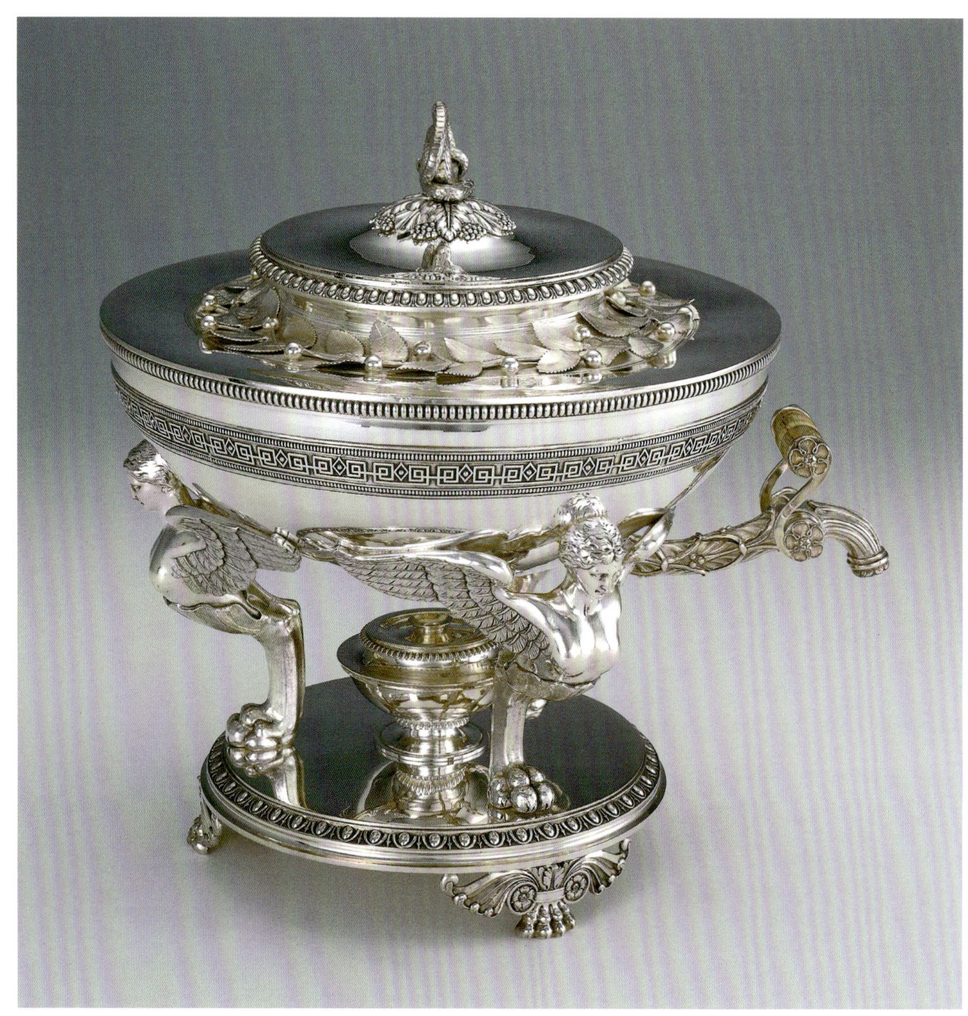

53. Tea urn, silver and ivory, London, 1814/15, maker's mark of Paul Storr. As the fashionable hour of dinner grew later, the widening gap between breakfast and dinner was filled with luncheon, eaten at midday, and tea, taken in mid-afternoon, which developed into a full meal during the nineteenth century. As a result, tea equipage became successively bigger and more imposing.
Cat. no. 56

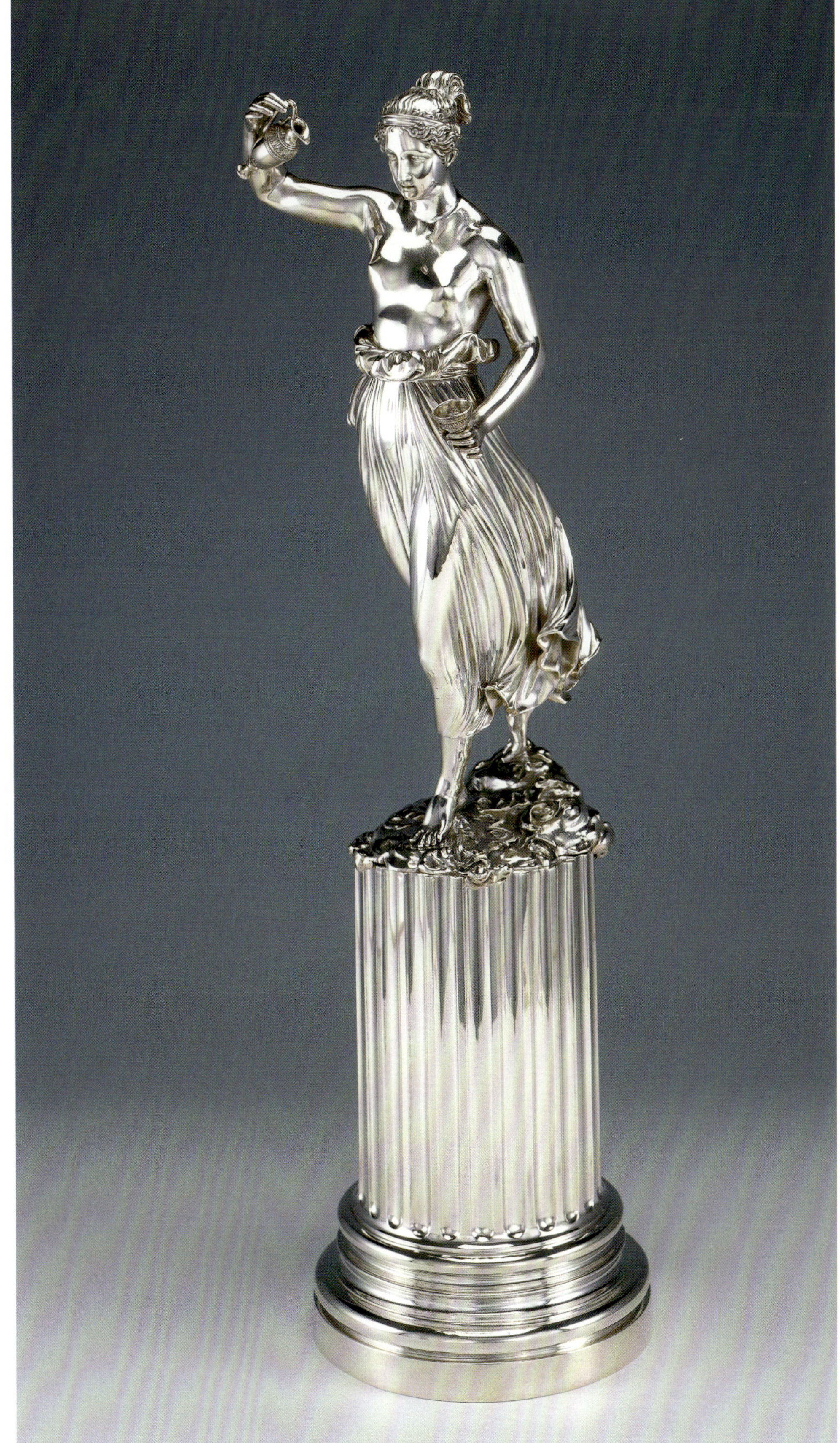

54. Statue of Hebe, silver, London, 1829/30, maker's mark of Paul Storr. Antonio Canova's statue of Hebe, the Greek goddess of youth who was believed to possess powers of rejuvenation, exists in several versions, including one at Chatsworth in Derbyshire. However, it was probably one of the many engravings published of the work that inspired the design for Storr's silver versions.
Cat. no. 82

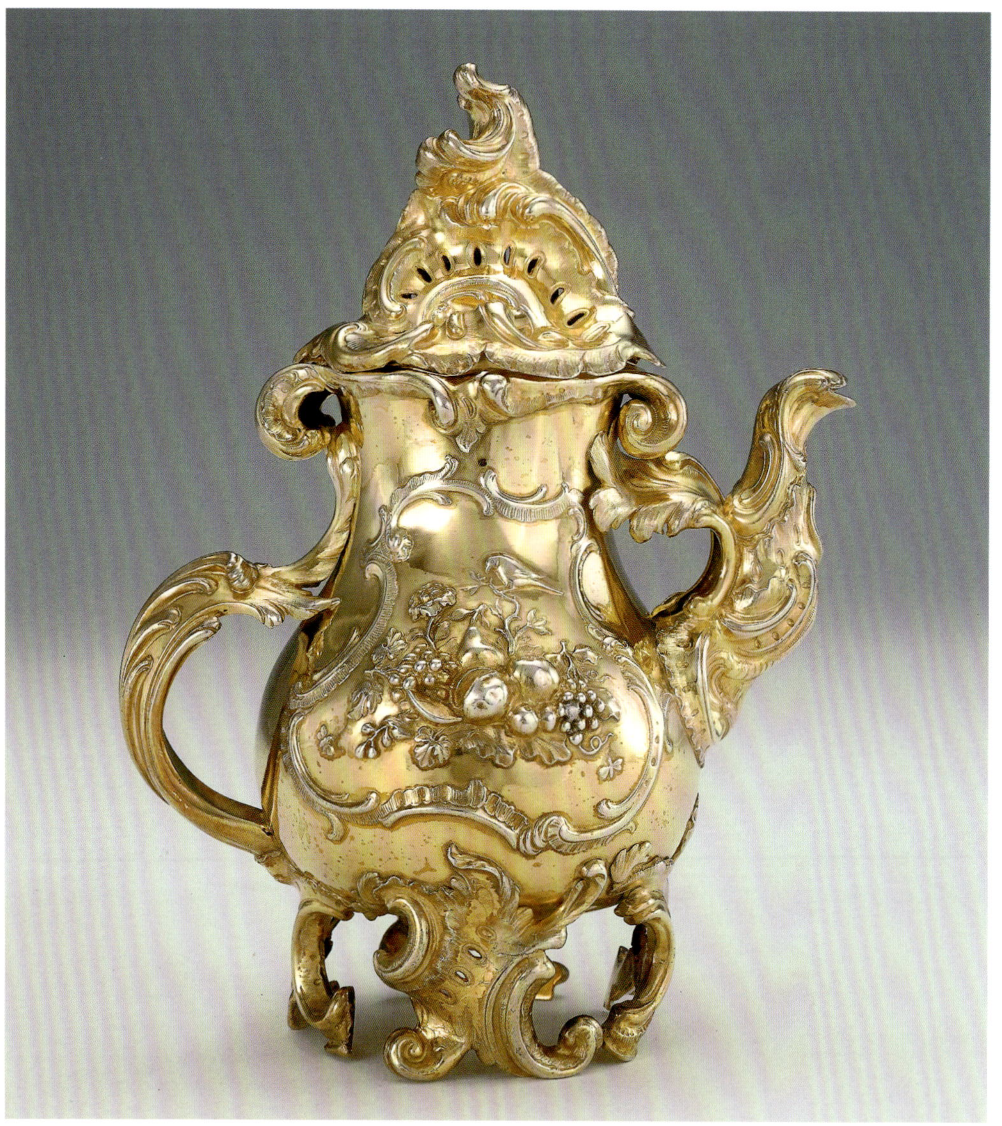

55. Coffee pot, silver, London, 1830/31, maker's mark of Paul Storr. The mixture of historical styles in this whimsical piece shows the eclecticism that became popular in the nineteenth century. Seventeenth-century auricular (literally, ear-shaped) contours mingle with rococo bat's-wing motifs taken from eighteenth-century German prints to make a startling appearance on the breakfast table.
Cat. no. 84

to drawing on Roman classicism for inspiration. The tea urn (figure 53, p. 58) is typical of the Egyptomania that took England by storm in the early years of the nineteenth century. *Voyage dans la Basse et la Haute Egypte pendant les campagnes du Général Bonaparte*, the book of views of Egyptian antiquities published in Paris in 1802 by Baron Vivant Denon, Napoleon's cultural arbiter, was one of several books which provided models for Egyptian decoration in English silver. Rundell's designers happily blended these with Greek and Roman motifs to come up with a style that was both exotic and monumental, and provided models for the tea table as well as the dining room. Similar winged paw feet are found on salts, sauceboats, and candelabra. The draftsman responsible for providing these designs to Rundell's was probably Jean-Jacques Boileau, a French artist who came to London in the 1790s to work at Carlton House, the sumptuous palace the Prince of Wales was decorating in London. His success lay in creating a style that was at once imposing and elegant. The crisp stiff foliage of the borders on the tea urn provides a pleasing contrast to the burnished plain surfaces of the body.

Other styles jostled for a place on the table-top. The rococo was being revived as early as 1810, and naturalistically cast and chased foliage and animals were a popular motif. The large salver (figure 56) continues the tradition of large display pieces, the broad expanse of silver providing a background for the depiction of the owner's armorials. But here, the engraving is

56. Salver, silver, London, 1823/24, maker's mark of Paul Storr. Like the magnificent dish and its two ewers of over a century earlier (figure 4), this salver is purely for display; the chased decoration in relief on its surface would preclude its use as a serving piece.
Cat. no. 73

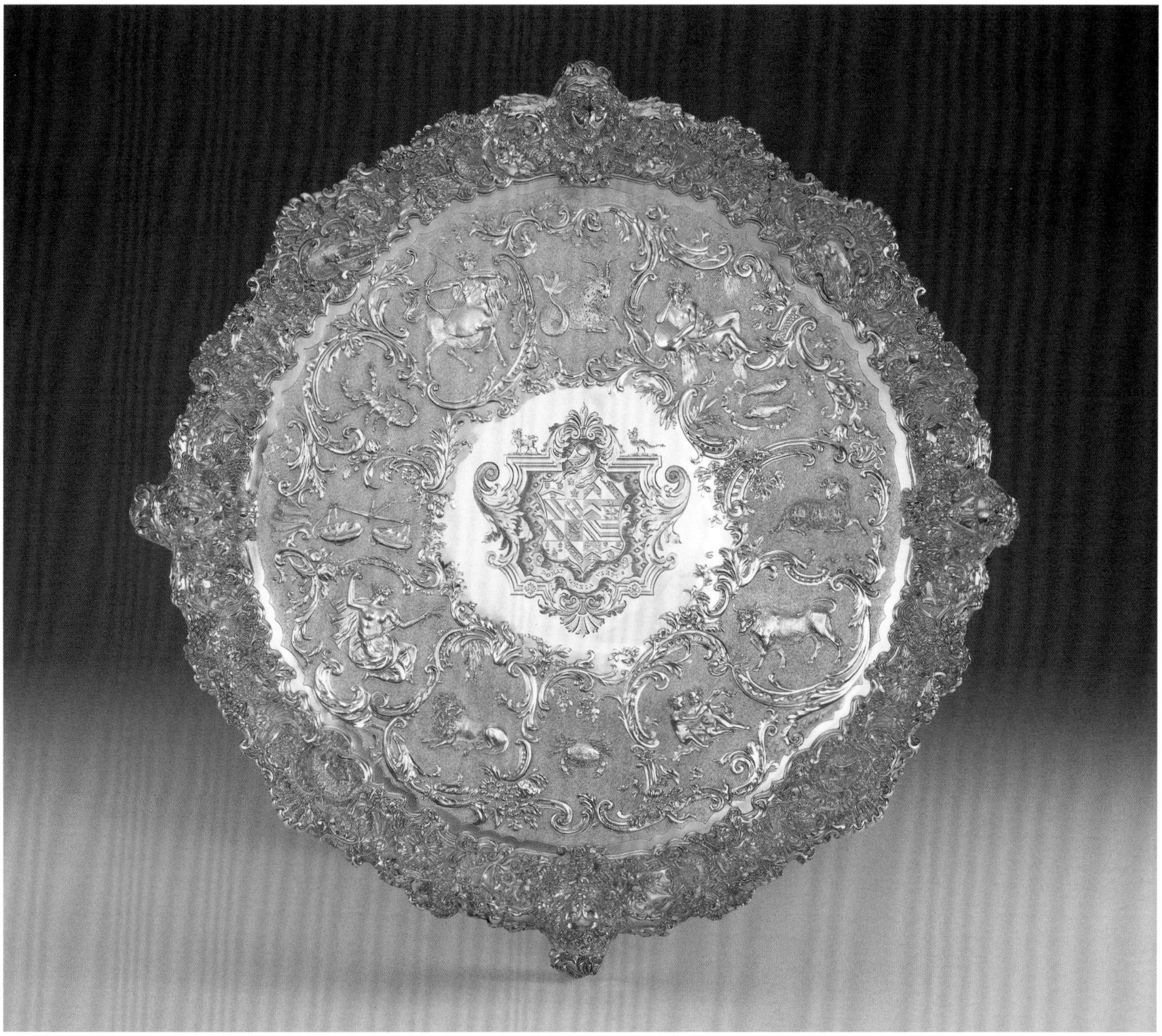

57. Bowl, silver, London, 1836/37, maker's mark of Paul Storr. Extravagant rococo and *Régence* motifs commingle on pieces in the extensive service commissioned by Robert Henry Herbert, 12th Earl of Pembroke, in the 1830s, shortly after he had moved to Paris. A noted *bon vivant*, Pembroke was visited there in 1837 by Lord Malmesbury, who noted that he "lives in great state … and is as famous for his cook as for his horses."
Cat. no. 88

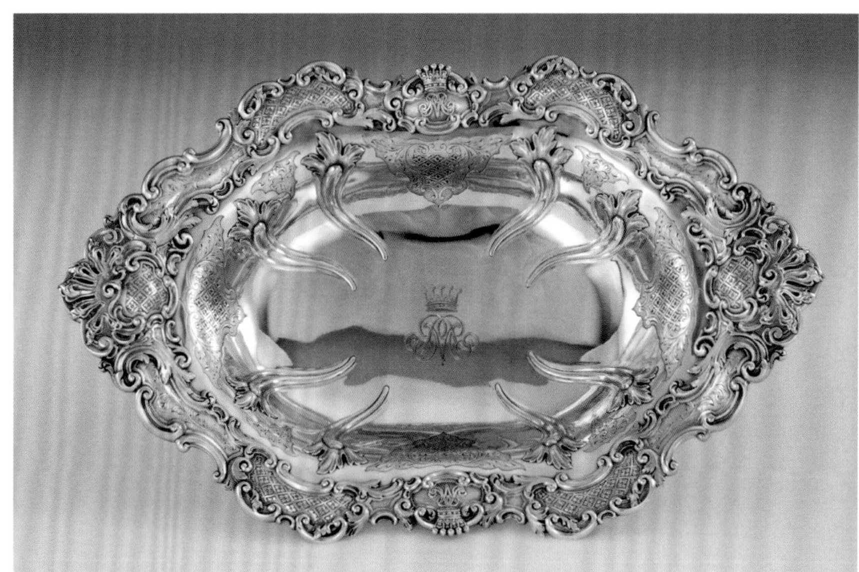

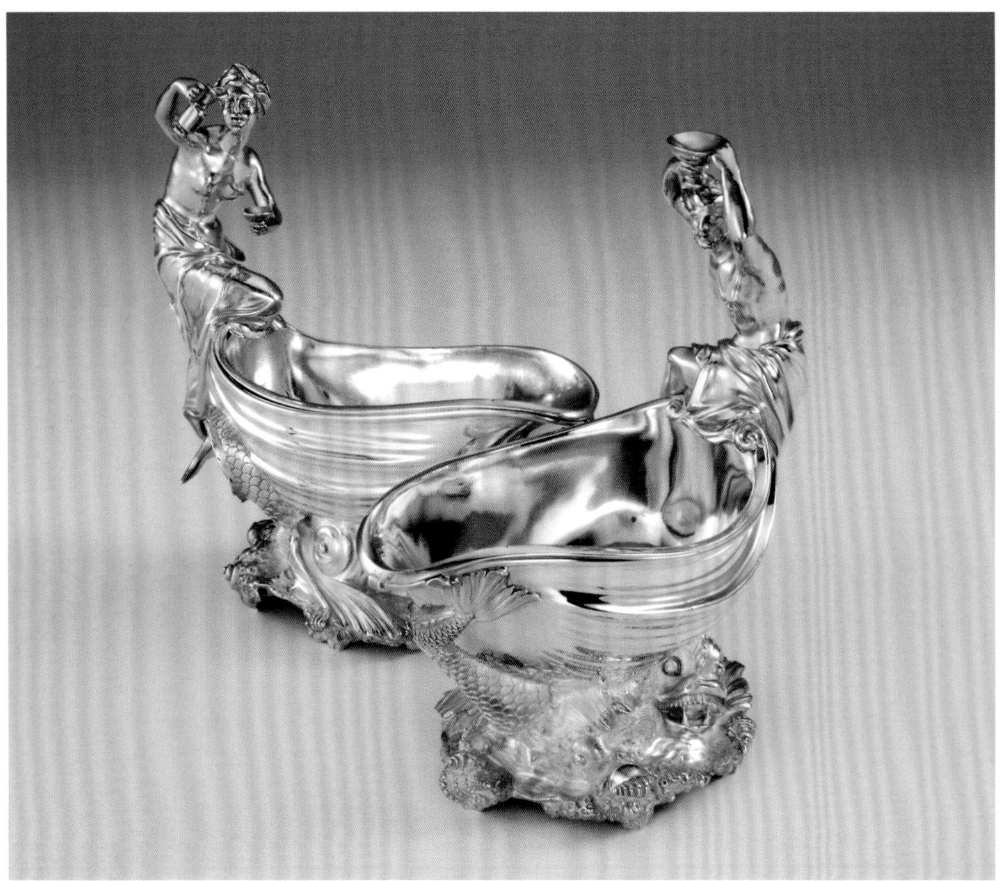

58. Pair of sauceboats, silver, London, 1824/25, maker's mark of Robert Garrard II. Based on examples made by Nicolas Sprimont for Frederick, Prince of Wales, in the 1740s, these sauceboats show the historicism of the early nineteenth century, when all styles of the past were either copied or used as inspiration for new creations.
Cat. no. 74

59. Set of four vegetable dishes, covers, and stands, silver, London, 1828/29, maker's mark of Robert Garrard II. Vestiges of the old service *à la française* remained, shown by these impressive vegetable dishes on warming stands, which would have held side dishes on the crowded table as servants passed roast meats around in service *à la russe*.
Cat. no. 80

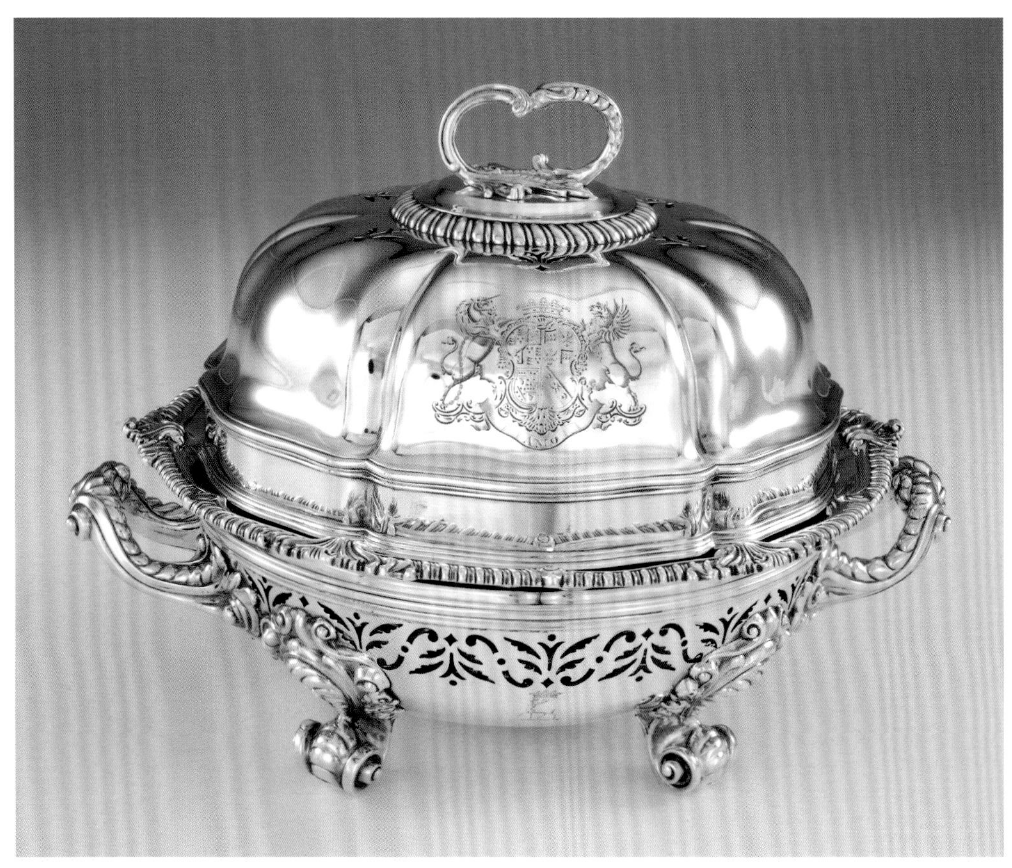

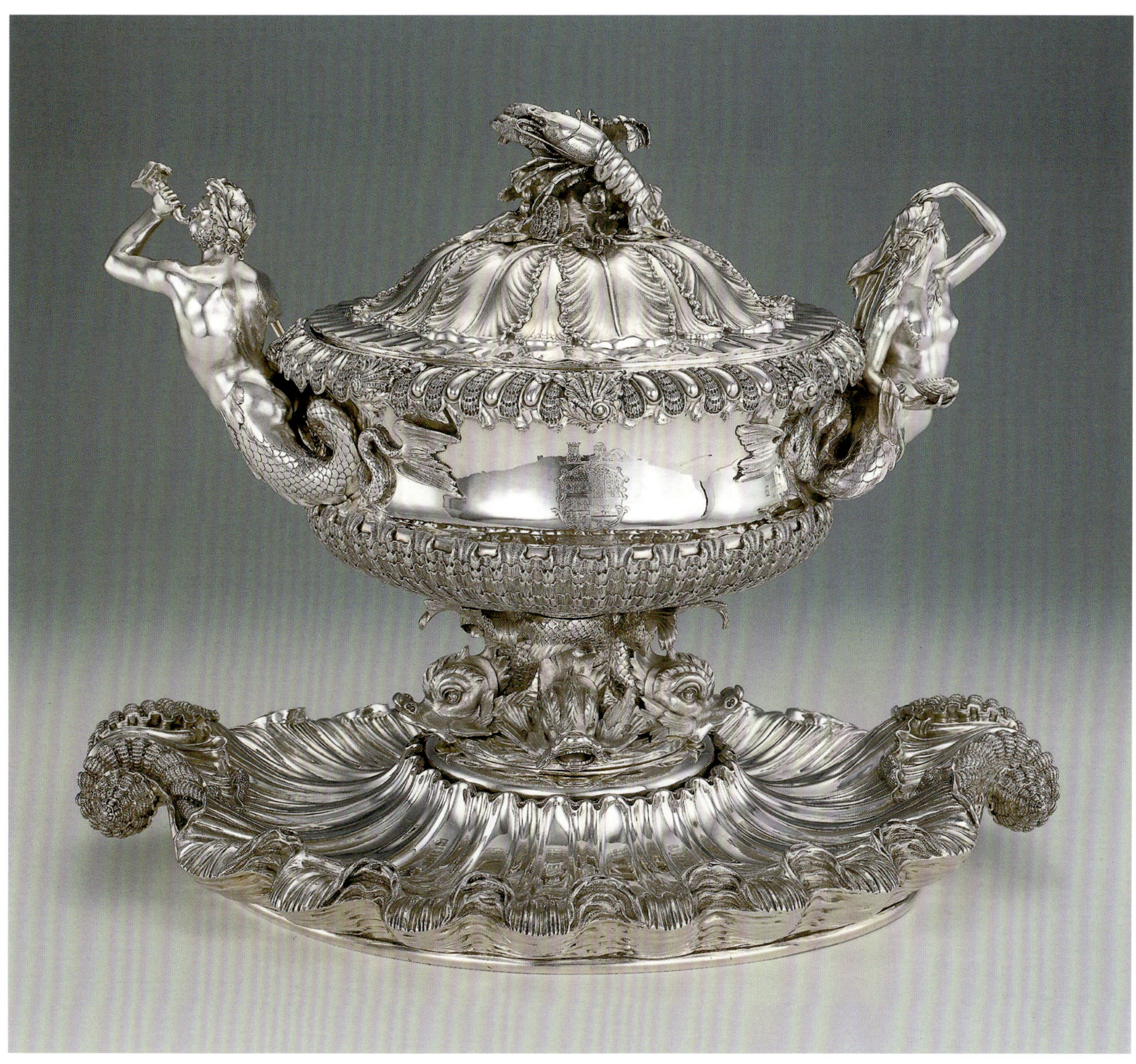

60. Soup tureen, cover and stand, silver, London, 1827/28, maker's mark of Robert Garrard II. How could anything but rich seafood be served from such a spirited evocation of the deep? Turtle soup—not only the richest dish but also the most costly—was an essential ingredient of formal banquets well into the nineteenth century.
Cat. no. 77

surrounded by the signs of the zodiac chased in relief within elaborate rococo foliate scrolls. The heavy cast border also abounds with rococo motifs. One of a series done by Storr's workshop in the 1820s, this salver shows the eclecticism of style that had taken over during the previous twenty years. The cohesiveness of design that characterized the early years of the century was gone.

At the forefront of promoting this new eclecticism on the dining table was the firm of Robert Garrard, rivals to Rundell's and ultimately, in the 1830s, to succeed them as royal goldsmiths and the leading suppliers of silver and silver-gilt plate. Garrard had taken over the business started by George Wickes in 1722 and, as in the case of the salver marked by Edward Wakelin in 1759/60 (figure 36, p. 45), much of Garrard's work can be traced from manufacturer to customer in the firm's surviving business ledgers.

The Garrard sauceboats of 1824/25 (figure 58) are based on examples supplied to Frederick, Prince of Wales by Nicolas Sprimont, which were part of a service of silver decorated with marine themes. Equally naturalistic is the soup tureen and stand of 1827/28 (figure 60) with its swept edges reminiscent of foaming brine. Yet it is a naturalism that is also a synthesis of various periods and styles: the crayfish clambering over mussel shells that forms the finial is worthy of Paul de Lamerie and the greatest creations of the rococo such as his soup tureen of 1736/37

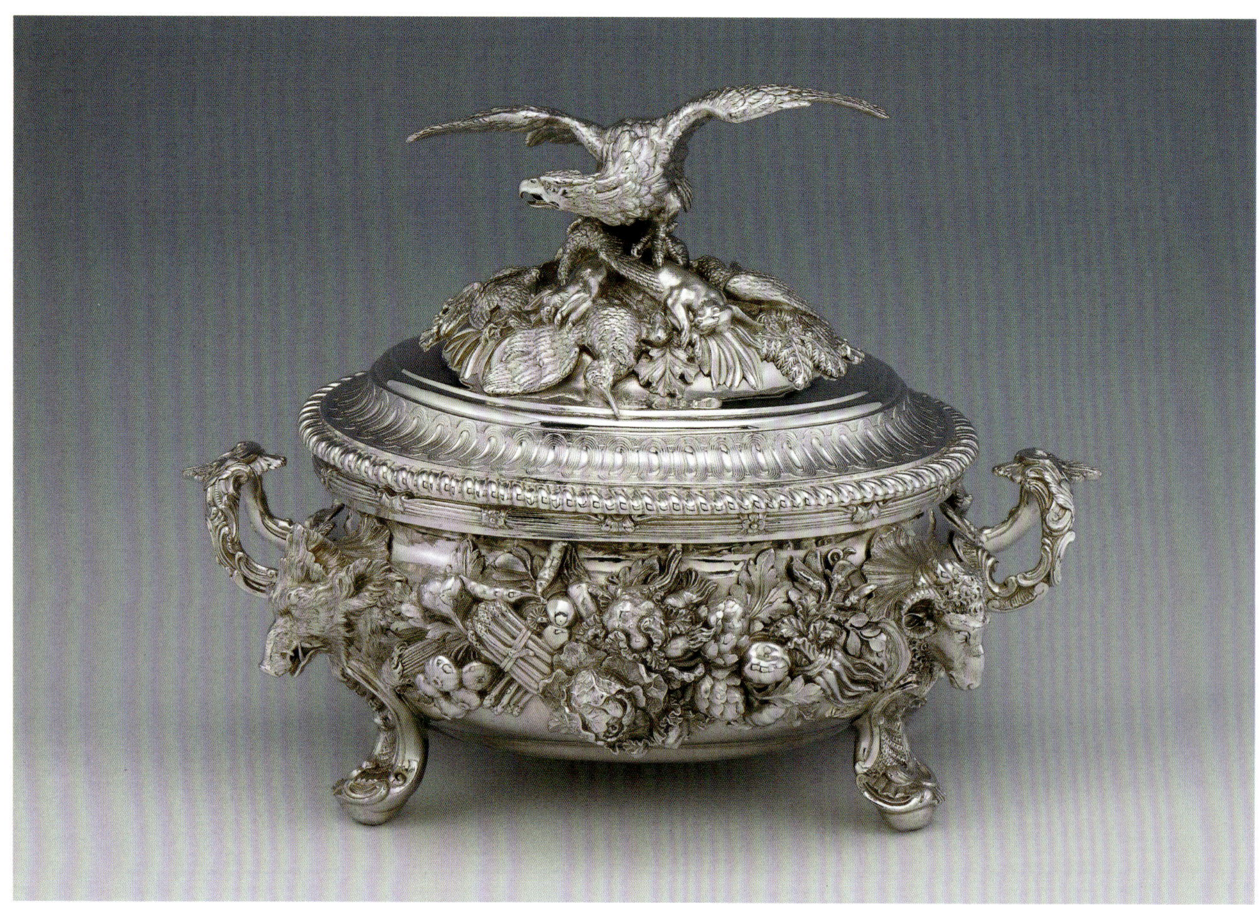

61. Soup tureen and cover, silver, London, 1831/32, maker's mark of Robert Garrard II. Inspired by rococo tureens of the 1740s, this example is a riot of naturalistically cast animals and vegetables.
Cat. no. 85

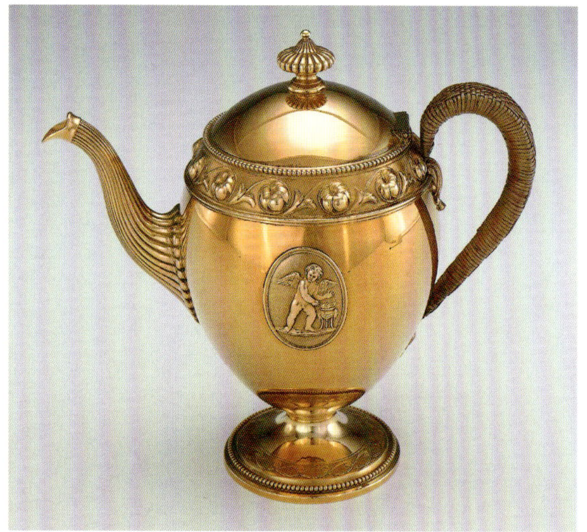

62. Teapot, gold and wicker, London, 1867/68, maker's mark of Robert Garrard II. Garrard's named this pattern "Flaxman" after the noted English neoclassical sculptor John Flaxman, who designed oval medallions similar to the ones that are applied to the body of this teapot for Wedgwood in the late eighteenth century. Neoclassicism was one of many styles revived during the Victorian era.
Cat. no. 99

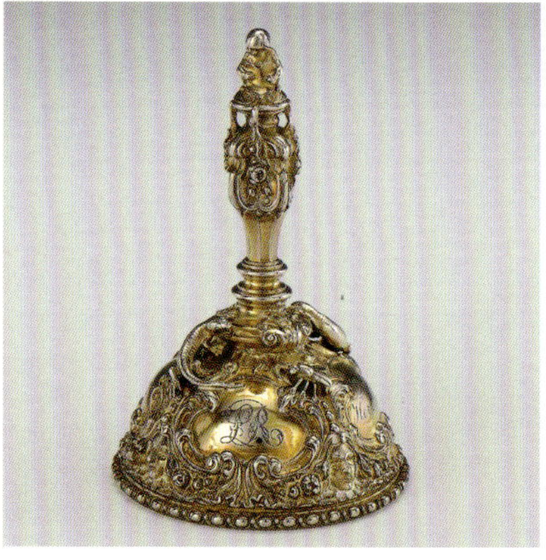

63. Bell, silver, parcel-gilt, London, 1849/50, maker's mark of Robert Garrard II. Historicism, in which styles and forms from the past are revived, enjoyed great popularity in the nineteenth century. This bell combines naturalistic elements typical of the work of the German Renaissance master Wenzel Jamnitzer (1508–1585) with rococo and neoclassical elements. An identical bell was exhibited by Garrard's at the Great Exhibition in 1851.
Cat. no. 94

(figure 13, p. 27) but the entwined dolphins that support the bowl are firmly rooted in the baroque, and the gadrooning around the edge is based on early eighteenth-century German prototypes. Much of this use of seemingly disparate motifs stemmed from the new interest in silverware from the past; a market for old silver had developed that was not only historically interesting, but startlingly different in its style. Rundell's as well as Robert Garrard copied old silver that passed through their hands, and copied components from it for use in their own imaginative creations. Garrard's soup tureen of 1831/32 (figure 61) represents the high point of this historicist style. Its crowded surfaces exemplify the consummate skills of the caster and modeler and recall the great works of the French rococo, but it is essentially a piece of baroque sculpture, with its symmetry and ponderousness. And, unlike the creations of de Lamerie's workshop, it neither conveys a message of love, nor even evokes an Arcadian paradise; instead, it merely depicts profusion.

The dining table, thronged with candelabra, tureens, and centerpieces, had been transformed into an altar to abundance. As one diarist remarked, "Nowadays hospitality is a means of revenge." Chefs vied with each other to create ever more complex dishes, and critics bemoaned the demise of the simple fare of Britain's glorious past. The boast of the owner of Brambleton Hall in Smollett's *The Expedition of Humphrey Clinker* of 1771, that "my table is, in a great measure, furnished from my own ground," was becoming a thing of the past, as people became more distanced from the sources of their food. By the middle of the nineteenth century, most of the well-to-do were eating food that they had bought, rather than grown or reared themselves, and the greater part of what they purchased was imported.

In spite of the formality that reigned supreme at a full-blown Victorian dinner, whimsy still lingered on the dining table. The delightful salts in the form of young boys and girls (figure 65, p. 66) from Robert Garrard's workshop hark back to the sculpted sugar figures that had adorned dining tables in the seventeenth century. The wheel had come full circle.

64. Richard Doyle (1824–1883), *A State Party*, engraving by the Brothers Dalziel from *Bird's Eye Views of Society*, London, 1864. In this print, dinner is served *à la russe* by a battalion of servants from the sideboard, although the host continues the old English custom of carving at the table. The table is crowded with decanters, fruit, and floral arrangements. *Private Collection.*

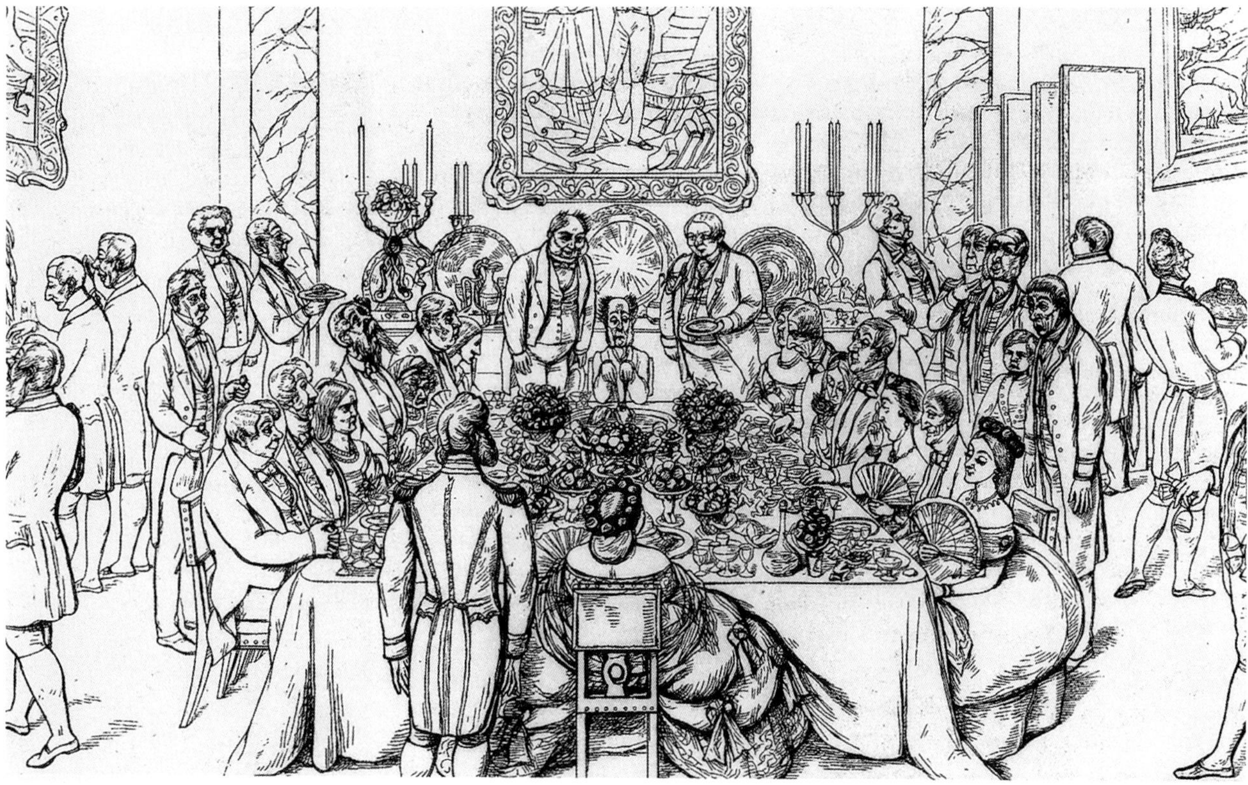

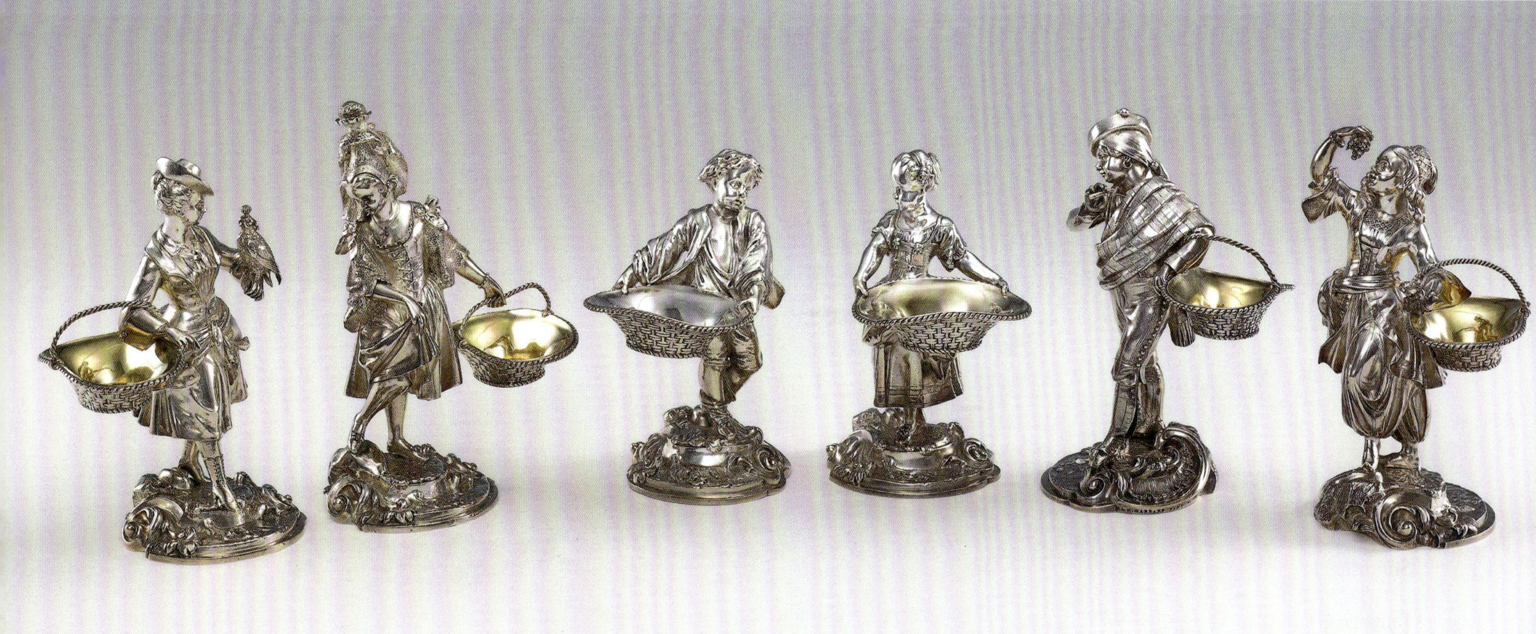

65. Six salts, silver, parcel gilt, London, 1861/62 and 1863/64, maker's mark of Robert Garrard II. The tradition of sugar table sculptures in the form of male and female figures dates from the early seventeenth century. The idea was taken up by Garrard's in the middle years of the nineteenth century with these figural salts, each depicting a young man or woman representing a different European country.
Cat. no. 97

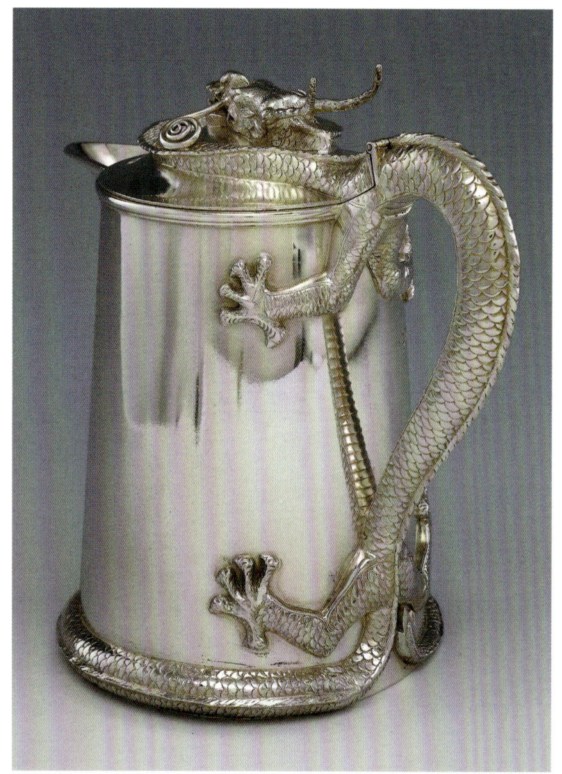

66. Jug, silver, London, 1875/76, maker's mark of Robert Hennell IV. Exoticism in the form of Asian motifs had been a popular feature on silver since the seventeenth century. By the second half of the nineteenth century, the arts of China and Japan provided the models as well as the decoration for many utilitarian objects, such as this pitcher for water or lemonade.
Cat. no. 100

FURTHER READING

Eating and Drinking

Peter B. Brown and Marla H. Schwartz, *Come Drink the Bowl Dry: Alcoholic Liquors and Their Place in 18th Century Society*, York Civic Trust, 1996

Robin Butler, *The Book of Wine Antiques*, Antique Collectors' Club, 1986

Sarah D. Coffin, ed., *Feeding Desire: Design and the Tools of the Table, 1500–2005*, Cooper-Hewitt, National Design Museum, Smithsonian Institution, New York, 2006

Philippa Glanville, ed., *The Art of Drink*, Victoria & Albert Museum Publications, 2007

Philippa Glanville and Hilary Young, eds., *Elegant Eating*, Victoria & Albert Museum Publications, 1997

Barbara Ketcham Wheaton, *Savoring the Past: The French Kitchen and Table from 1300 to 1789*, University of Pennsylvania Press, 1983

Gilly Lehmann, *The British Housewife: Cookery Books, Cooking and Society in Eighteenth-Century Britain*, Prospect Books, 1999

Maxime McKendry, *Seven Hundred Years of English Cooking*, Treasure Press, 1985

Sarah Paston-Williams, *The Art of Dining*, National Trust Enterprises, 1993

Maguelonne Toussaint-Samat, *A History of Food*, translated by Anthea Bell, Blackwell, 1992

Silver and Silversmiths

Ellenor M. Alcorn, *English Silver in the Museum of Fine Arts, Boston*, vol. I: *Silver before 1697*, Museum of Fine Arts, Boston, 1993, and vol. II: *Silver from 1697*, Museum of Fine Arts, Boston, 2000

——, *Beyond the Maker's Mark: Paul de Lamerie Silver in the Cahn Collection*, John Adamson, 2006

Vanessa Brett, ed., *Rococo Silver in England and Its Colonies* (Papers from a symposium at Virginia Museum of Fine Arts, Richmond, in 2004), The Silver Society, 2006

Philippa Glanville, *Silver in England*, Holmes & Meier, 1987

——, ed., *Silver*, Victoria & Albert Museum Publications, London, 1999

Alain Gruber, *Silverware*, Rizzoli, 1982

Christopher Hartop, *The Huguenot Legacy: English Silver 1680–1760 from the Alan and Simone Hartman Collection*, Thomas Heneage Ltd., 1996

——, *Royal Goldsmiths: The Art of Rundell & Bridge 1797–1842*, John Adamson, 2005

——, *British and Irish Silver in the Fogg Art Museum, Harvard University Art Museums*, Harvard University Press, 2007

Timothy Schroder, *The National Trust Book of English Domestic Silver 1500–1900*, National Trust Enterprises, 1988

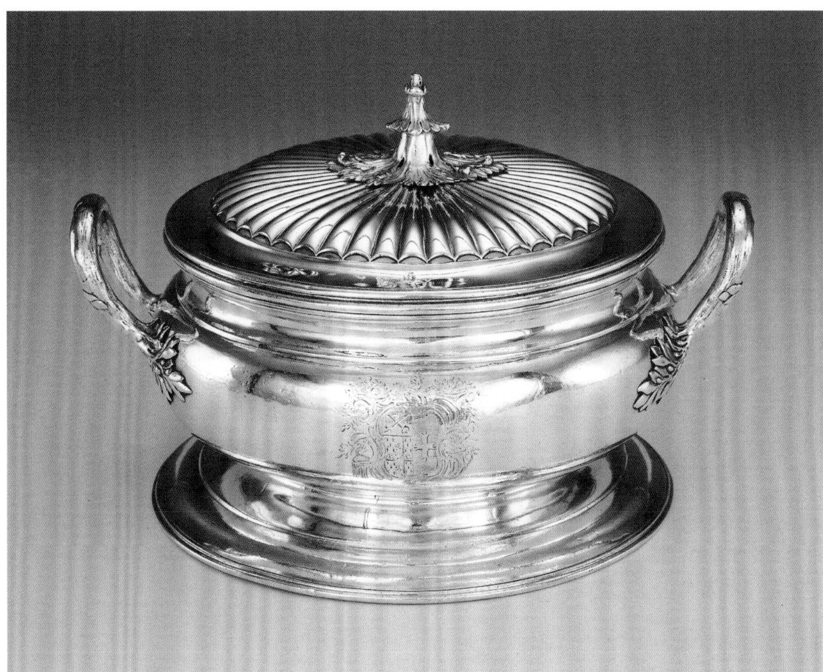

67. Chamber pot and cover, silver, London, 1818/19, maker's mark of Robert Garrard II. Engraved with the armorials of Richard York of Wighill Park, Yorkshire, who was Mayor of Leeds and later High Sheriff of Yorkshire. Family tradition has it that this chamber pot was at his disposal in the mayoral coach.
Cat. no. 66

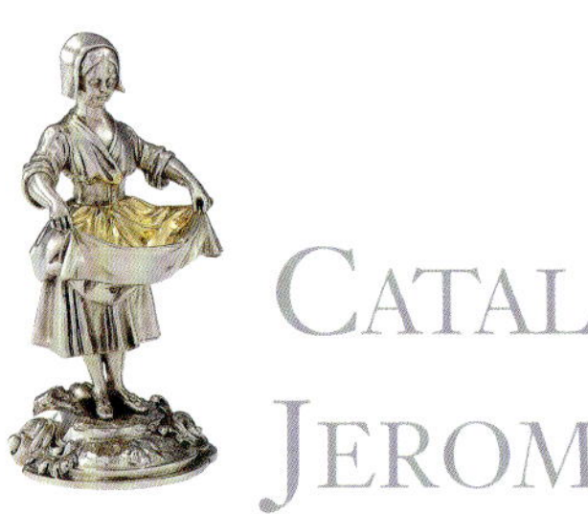

Catalogue of the Jerome and Rita Gans Collection

In England, the silver standard was sterling (925 parts pure silver per thousand) until 1697 when the legal (hallmarked) standard was raised to the Britannia standard (958/1000). In 1720 the sterling standard was resumed but the Britannia standard remained optional.

Specific dates of objects are provided by hallmarks, whenever present. The date letter did not change with the calendar. For example, in London, up to 1660, the date letter was usually changed in May of each year; from 1660 to 1975 it was changed on May 29. Dates are therefore given thus: 1665/66.

In this catalogue the term "maker's mark" denotes the mark stamped on an object by the person who submitted it for assay at Goldsmiths' Hall, or at a provincial assay office. This is not necessarily the same person as the one who made the object, and in fact most silver articles made during the period covered by this catalogue were the work of more than one individual. However, it has been decided to retain the term that has traditionally been used.

The size of all objects is given in inches. The equivalent in centimeters (to one decimal place) is given in parentheses. Weights are given in troy ounces and pennyweights, the traditional way of weighing silverware. There are 20 pennyweights (dwt.) in a troy ounce (oz.). Where there is a wooden handle, such as on a coffee pot, a "gross weight" is given. A scratch weight is an engraved indication of weight expressed in ounces and pennyweights, done, usually in the eighteenth century, for inventory purposes. It is shown here as it appears on the piece.

The following abbreviations are used: Diam. diameter; H. height; L. length; W. width; Wt. weight.

Provenance includes documented owners; engraved armorials are listed separately. A comma between the names of two owners indicates that the piece passed directly from the first to the second; a semi-colon indicates a gap in documentation.

• 1 •

CHALICE
Silver gilt
c. 1500
Marks: none
Maker's mark: none
Inscription: *Calicem Salutaris Accipiam et Nomen Domini Invocabo*

Provenance: Possibly Herbert Herries, 1st Lord Herries (d. 1506), by descent to the Lady Herries of Terregles, Everingham Park, Yorkshire, S.J. Shrubsole Corp., New York

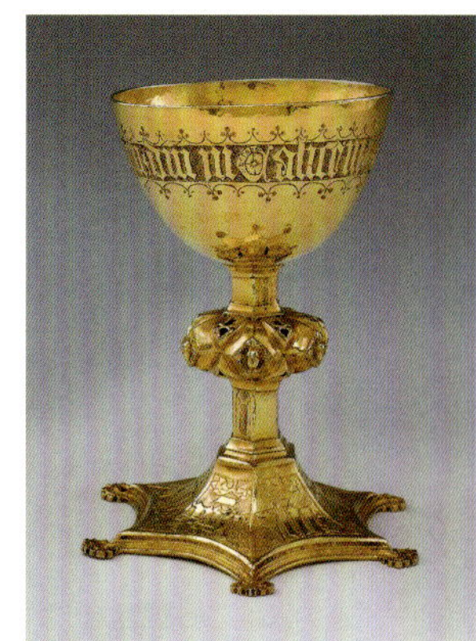

H. 6 5/16 in. (16 cm)
Wt. 12 oz. 9 dwt. (388 g)
Accession no.: 2006.582

• 2 •

PAIR OF LIVERY POTS
Silver gilt
Marks: Sterling, London, 1602/3
Maker's mark: *TE in monogram, pellet below* (Jackson, p. 109, line 11)

Provenance: Durlacher, London, purchased in 1871 by Baron Meyer de Rothschild, Mentmore, Buckinghamshire, by descent to the Rosebery Trust, sale, Sotheby's, London, February 11, 1999, lot 64, S.J. Shrubsole Corp., New York
Published: Jones, 1928a, pp. 21–22; Jones, 1928b, pl. XXXII, pp. 81 and 115

H. 13 1/2 in. (34 3 cm)
Wt. 99 oz. (3079 g)
Accession no.: 2006.580.1-.2

• 3 •

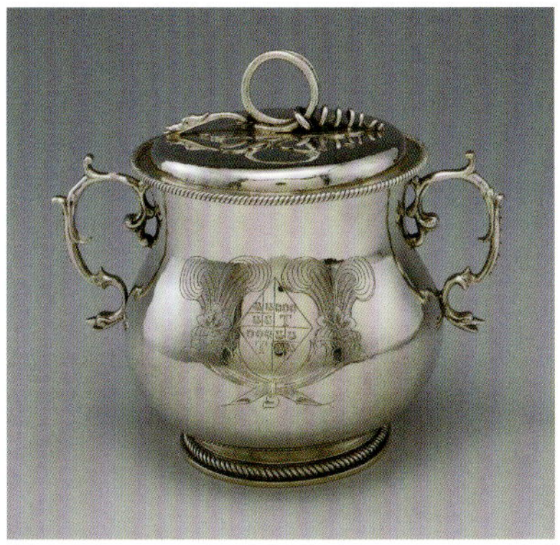

TWO-HANDLED CUP AND COVER
Silver
Marks: Sterling, London, 1661/62
Maker's mark: Robert Smythier (Jackson, p. 126, line 2)

Heraldry: Engraved arms of Burton quarterly with Tanke
Provenance: S.J. Shrubsole Corp., New York

H. $6\,^{7}/_{16}$ in. (16.4 cm)
Wt. 25 oz. 13 dwt. (798 g)
Accession no.: 2006.590a-b

• 5 •

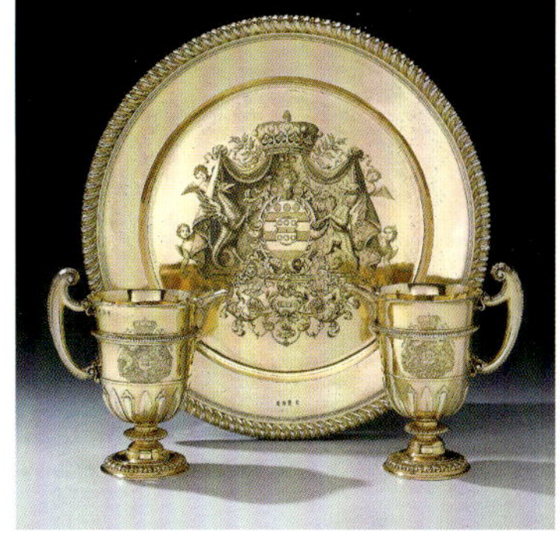

ROSEWATER DISH
AND
A PAIR OF EWERS
Silver gilt
Marks: Britannia, London, 1699/1700
Maker's mark: Benjamin Pyne (Grimwade, no. 2245)

Provenance: Anthony Grey, 11th Earl of Kent (1645–1702), by descent to Henry Grey, 12th Earl of Kent (1671–1740), who in 1710 was created Duke of Kent, by descent to the Trustees of the De Grey Silver Settlement, sale, Christie's, London, March 24, 1982, lot 95; S.J. Shrubsole Corp., New York
Exhibited: London, 1929a, nos. 663 and 665 (lent by Lord Desborough); London, 1929b, nos. 393 and 418 (lent by Lord Desborough)
Published: London, 1929a, nos. 663 and 665, pl. nos. LVII, LIX; London, 1929b, nos. 393, p. 47 and 418 (one of the pair), p. 49; Grimwade, 1988, p. 86; Shrubsole, 1999, pp. 50–52

Dish: diam. $24\,^{1}/_{2}$ in. (62.2 cm)
Ewers: H. 11 and $11\,^{1}/_{4}$ in. (28 and 28.6 cm)
Gross wt. 312 oz. 5 dwt. (9712 g)
Accession no.: 2001.226.1–.3

• 4 •

GINGER JAR
Silver
Marks: Sterling, London, 1693/94
Maker's mark: Anthony Nelme (Grimwade, no. 68)
Engraved under base: *NO. 1. 12. P. 94. 3*

Provenance: John Dunn-Gardner, Esq., London, sale, Christie's, London, April 29–30, 1902; lot 261; J.P. Morgan, the estate of the late J.P. Morgan, sale, Parke Bernet, New York, October 30–November 1, 1947, lot 478; Sotheby's, London, October 20, 1966, lot 165, purchased by Brissenden; Sotheby's, London, June, 13, 1983, lot 17, S.J. Phillips, Ltd., London
Exhibited: London, 1989a
Published: Jones, 1908, pp. XXXI–XXXII, p. 31, pl. XXVII; Brett, no. 551, p. 148; *Art and Auction*, September 1989, p. 178; *Grosvenor House Antiques Fair, 1989, Handbook*, p. 63; Bliss, no. 1, pp. 10–13

H. $22\,^{3}/_{4}$ in. (57.8 cm)
Wt. 166 oz. 19 dwt. (5193 g)
Scratch wt.: "170-4"
Accession no.: 97.1a-b

• 6 •

THREE CASTERS
Silver gilt
Marks: Britannia, London, 1704/5
Maker's mark: David Willaume I (Grimwade, no. 3192)

Heraldry: Engraved arms of Gorges as probably borne by Henry Gorges of Eye and the Mynde, Herefordshire
Provenance: Henry Gorges (c. 1665–1718) of Eye and the Mynde, Herefordshire, who married Elizabeth, daughter and heir of Robert Pye; Garrard & Co., London, purchased December 24, 1878 by Archibald, 5th Earl of Rosebery, by descent to the Rosebery Family Trust, sale, Sotheby's, London, February 11, 1999, lot 24, M.P. Levene, London

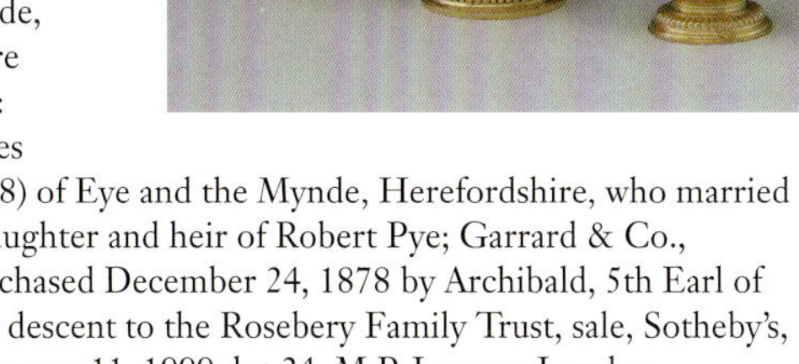

H. 10 in.; two are $7\,^{1}/_{8}$ in. (25.4; 18.1 cm)
Wt. 42 oz. 11 dwt. (1323 g)
Accession no.: 2006.589.1a-b, .2a-b, .3a-b

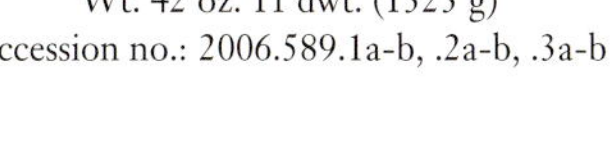

• 7 •

CASTER
Silver
Marks: Britannia, London, 1719/20
Maker's mark: Paul de Lamerie (Hare, no. 2)
Initial G pricked under base

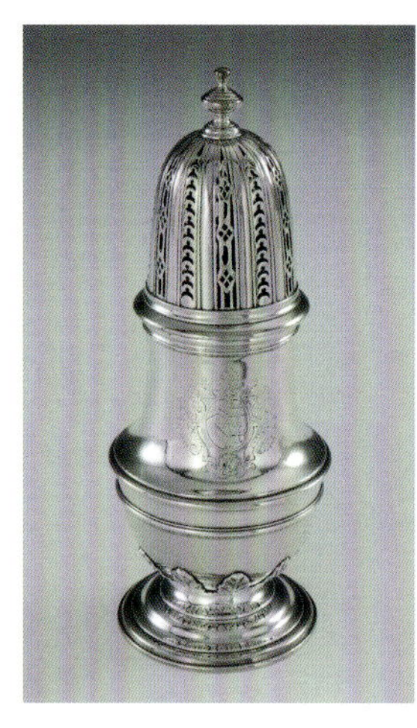

Heraldry: Engraved arms of Brougham of Brougham, Westmorland, quartering Vaux of Catterlan, Vaux of Tryermayne, and Delamore, probably for Henry Brougham of Scales Hall, Cumberland
Provenance: Probably Henry Brougham of Scales Hall, Cumberland; Mabel Brady Garvan, New York, sale, Sotheby Parke Bernet, New York, June 6, 1980, lot 107
Published: Bliss, 1990a, p. 8, Bliss, no. 2, pp. 16–17

H. 8 $^{3}/_{4}$ in. (22.2 cm)
Wt. 18 oz. 4 dwt. (566 g)
Accession no.: 97.2a-b

• 9 •

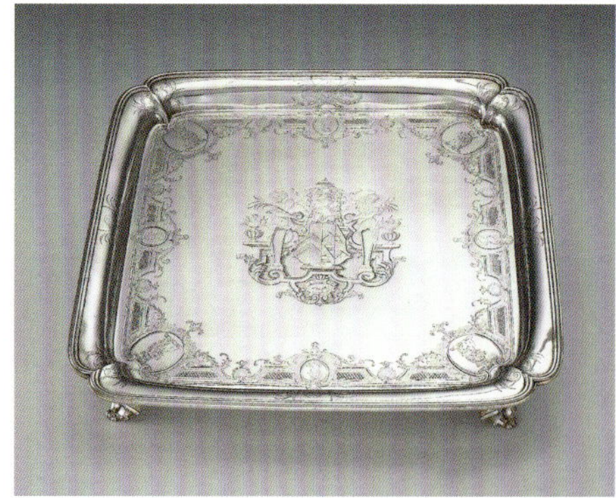

SALVER
Silver
Marks: Britannia, London, 1727/28
Maker's mark: Paul de Lamerie (Hare, no. 3)

Heraldry: Engraved arms of Reynardson of Plymouth, Devon, impaling Farnaby of Kent, for Lady Frances Reynardson, née Farnaby, widow of Sir Jacob Reynardson, who had died in 1719
Provenance: Tessiers, Ltd., London, 1935
Published: Phillips, p. 85, plate lv; Bliss, no. 4, pp. 20–21

W. 13 $^{1}/_{4}$ in. (33.6 cm)
Wt. 65 oz. 15 dwt. (2045 g)
Accession no.: 97.4

• 8 •

CUP AND COVER
Silver
Marks: Britannia, London, 1724/25
Maker's mark: Paul de Lamerie (Hare, no. 3)

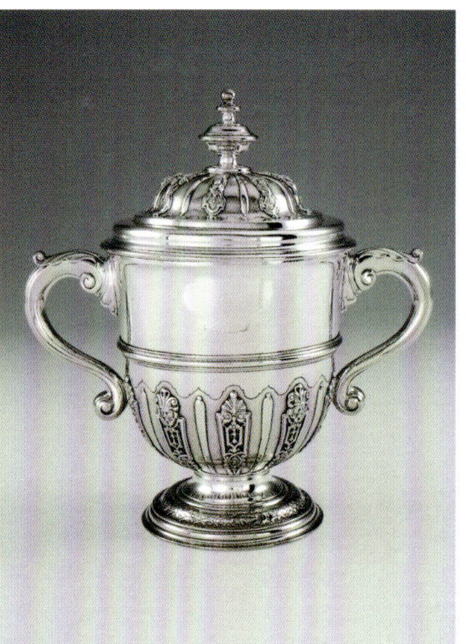

Provenance: Lady Islington, sale, Christie's, London, June 19, 1957, lot 46, D. Black, London; Donald S. Morrison, New Jersey, sale, Sotheby Parke Bernet, New York, June 6, 1980, lot 32 (gilt)
Exhibited: The Brooklyn Museum, Brooklyn, New York, 1958–1980 (on extended loan, L.58.4.2 a & b); Princeton, 1966
Published: Schwartz, p, 574; Princeton, no. 27; Hare, p. 55; Bliss, no. 3, pp. 18–19

H. 11 $^{7}/_{8}$ in. (30.2 cm)
Wt. 84 oz. (2613 g)
Accession no.: 97.3a-b

• 10 •

CHAMBER CANDLESTICK, WICK TRIMMER AND EXTINGUISHER
Silver gilt, steel
Marks: Sterling, London, 1731/32
Maker's mark: Paul de Lamerie (Hare, no. 3); the wick trimmer, Simon Pantin II (Grimwade, no. 2607)

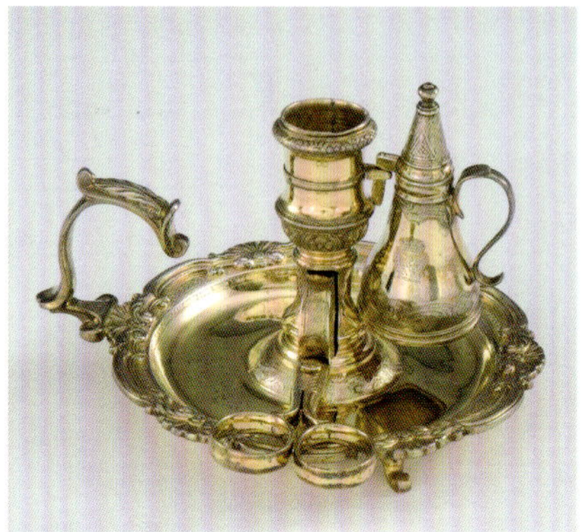

Heraldry: Later engraved crest and earl's coronet
Published: Bliss, no. 6, pp. 24–25

H. (of chamber candlestick) 3 $^{1}/_{2}$ in. (8.9 cm)
L. (of wick trimmer) 4 $^{11}/_{16}$ in. (11.9 cm)
H. (of extinguisher) 3 in. (7.6 cm)
Gross wt. 15 oz. 12 dwt. (485 g)
Accession no.: 97.6a-c

• 11 •

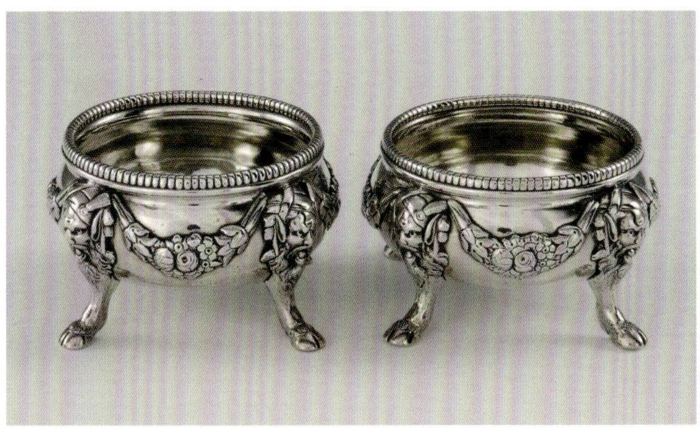

PAIR OF SALTS
Silver, gilt interiors
Marks: Britannia, London, 1731/32
Maker's mark: Paul de Lamerie (Hare, no. 3)

Heraldry: Engraved crest of Howard under an earl's coronet, for the Earl of Carlisle, the Earl of Suffolk and Berkshire, or the Earl of Stafford
Published: Bliss, no. 5, pp. 22–23

H. 2 in. (5.1 cm)
Wt. 7 oz. and 7 oz. 3 dwt. (218 and 222 g)
Accession no.: 97.5.1-.2

• 12 •

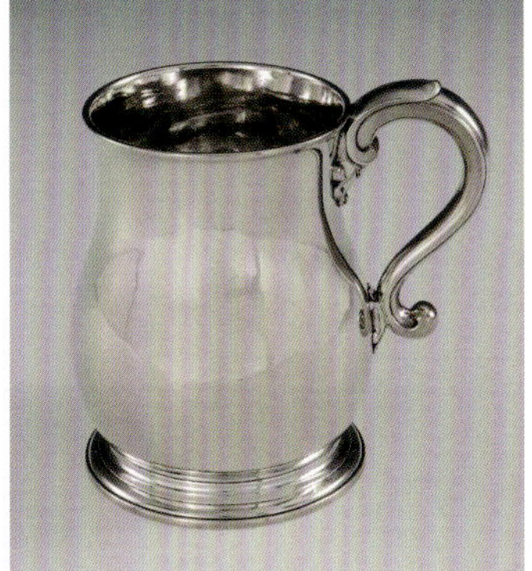

MUG
Silver
Marks: Sterling, London, 1733/34
Maker's mark: Paul de Lamerie (Hare, no. 4)

Provenance: Property of a Gentleman, sale, Christie's, London, June 16, 1931, lot 71, Crichton Brothers, London; "A Minneapolis Estate," sale, Sotheby Parke Bernet, New York, October 27, 1982, lot 382
Published: Bliss, 1990a, pp. 8–9; Bliss, no. 7, pp. 26–27

H. 6 1/4 in. (15.9 cm)
Wt. 23 oz. 4 dwt. (721 g)
Accession no.: 97.7

• 13 •

PAIR OF SHELL DISHES
Silver
Marks: Sterling, London, 1734/35
Maker's mark: Paul de Lamerie (Hare, no. 4)

Heraldry: Engraved crest of Selwin or Selwyn of Sussex and Essex
Provenance: Reverend Alfred Duane Pell (1864–1924), New York, 1894, by descent to "A Collector," sale, Christie's, New York, October 22–23, 1984, lot 336
Published: *Christie's Review of the Season, 1985*, p. 317; Müller, 1986, pp. 60–61, n. 3; Bliss, 1990a, p. 9; Bliss, no. 8, pp. 28–29

W. 5 3/16 in. (13.2 cm)
Wt. 7 oz. 6 dwt. and 6 oz. 12 dwt. (227 and 205 g)
Accession no.: 97.8.1-.2

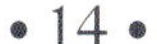

• 14 •

EWER AND DISH
Silver gilt
Marks: Sterling, London; ewer 1736/37; dish 1737/38
Maker's mark: Paul de Lamerie (Hare, no. 4)

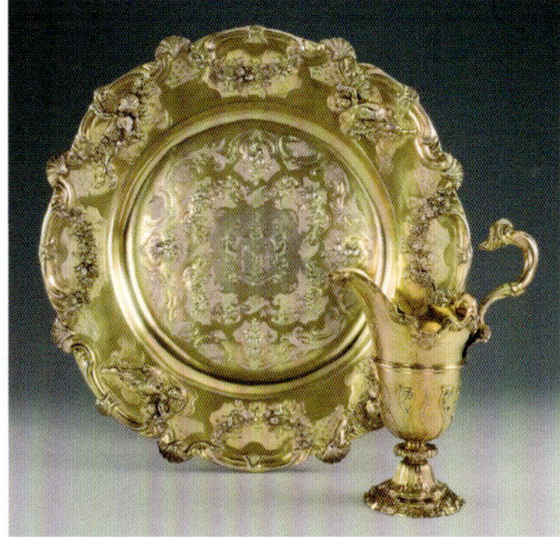

Heraldry: Engraved arms of Darell impaling Tierney for the Reverend Sir William Lionel Darell, 4th Bt., who married in 1843 Harriet Mary, only daughter of Sir Edward Tierney, Bt.
Provenance: Reverend Sir William Lionel Darell (1817–1883), by descent to Major Sir Lionel Darell, 6th Bt. (1876–1954), sale, Christie's, London, May 13, 1920, lot 67 (unsold), Sir Jeffrey Lionel Darell, 8th Bt., London, S.J. Phillips Ltd., London, J. Paul Getty, Sutton Place, Surrey, 1970, J. Paul Getty Museum, Malibu (de-accessioned 1982)
Published: Wenham, pl. XXX; Bliss 1990a, pp. 9–10; *The J.Paul Getty Museum Journal*, vol. 19, 1991, p. 163; Bliss, no. 9, pp. 30–33

H. of ewer 15 1/8 in. (38.4 cm)
Diam. of dish 25 3/4 in. (65.4 cm)
Wt. of ewer 68 oz. 18 dwt. (2143 g); Wt. of dish 175 oz. 11 dwt. (5460 g)
Scratch wt.: "244.00"
Accession no.: 97.9.1-.2

• 15 •

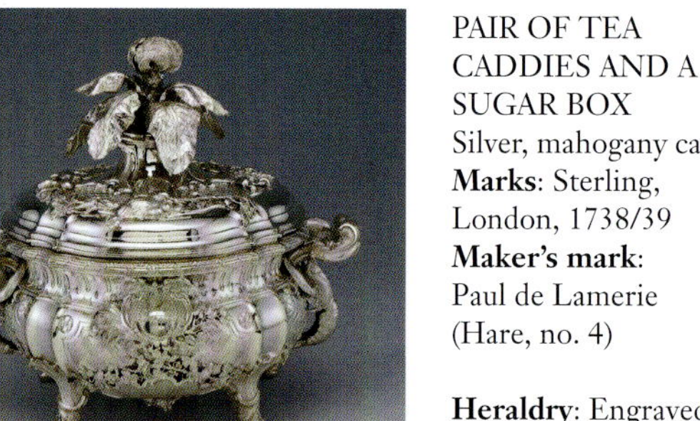

SOUP TUREEN AND COVER
Silver
Marks: Britannia, London, 1736/37; the liner, sterling, 1736/37
Maker's mark: Paul de Lamerie (Hare, no. 4); the liner, Paul Crespin (Grimwade, no. 2143a)

Heraldry: Engraved arms of Drury-Lowe impaling Steer for William Drury-Lowe of Denby and Locko Park, Derbyshire
Provenance: Possibly Philip, 4th Earl of Chesterfield (1694–1773), part of his official plate allowance, subsequently returned to the Jewel House and sold c. 1800; William Drury-Lowe (1753–1827), by descent to "An English Private Collection," sale, Sotheby's, London, June 2, 1992, lot 186; Titus Kendall, London, Jaime Ortiz-Patiño, sale, Sotheby's, London, June 4, 1998, lot 223, A.M. Marks Ltd., London
Exhibited: Bristol, 1965; London, 1978; London, 1984; London, 1990
Published: Bristol; London, 1978; *Rococo*, no. G2, p. 107; Hare, no. 82, p. 127

W. handle to handle 14 $^{1}/_{16}$ in. (35.7 cm)
Wt. 186 oz. 8 dwt. (5797 g)
Accession no.: 2006.591a-c

• 16 •

COFFEE POT
Silver, fruitwood
Marks: Sterling, London, 1738/39
Maker's mark: Paul de Lamerie (Hare, no. 4)

Heraldry: Later engraved unidentified arms
Provenance: S.J. Phillips, Ltd., London, 1954, "An Anonymous Collector, Europe," sale, Sotheby Parke Bernet, New York, October 13–15, 1981, lot 327
Published: Brett, no. 717; p. 176; Bliss, no. 10, pp. 34–35

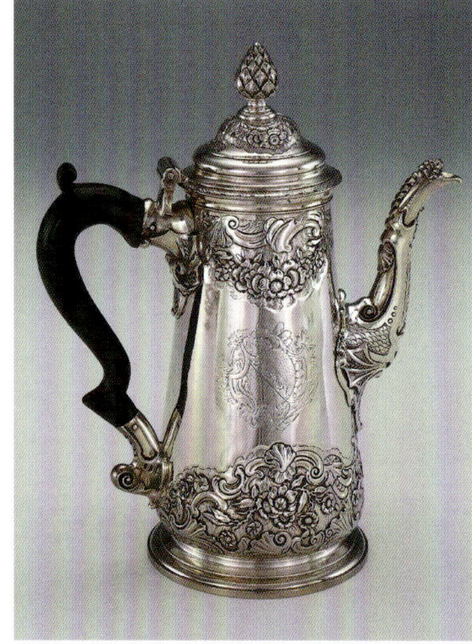

H. 9 $^{1}/_{8}$ in. (23.2 cm)
Gross wt. 25 oz. 15 dwt. (801 g)
Scratch wt.: "25:15"
Accession no.: 97.10

• 17 •

PAIR OF TEA CADDIES AND A SUGAR BOX
Silver, mahogany case
Marks: Sterling, London, 1738/39
Maker's mark: Paul de Lamerie (Hare, no. 4)

Heraldry: Engraved lozenge of arms of Moore impaling Long as borne by Lady Catharina Maria Moore, widow of Sir Henry Moore
Provenance: Lady Catharina Maria Moore (1727–1812); Sotheby's, London, March 18, 1982, lot 124
Published: *Art and Auction*, May 1982, pp. 48–49; *Art at Auction: The Year at Sotheby's 1981–1982*, p. 253; Bliss, 1990a, p. 10; Bliss, no. 11, pp. 36–39

H. of tea caddies 4 $^{1}/_{4}$ in. (10.8 cm)
H. of sugar box with handle raised 5 $^{3}/_{16}$ in. (13.2 cm)
Gross wt. without case 31 oz. 8 dwt. (977 g)
Accession no.: 97.11.1a-b-.2a-b, .3a-b

• 18 •

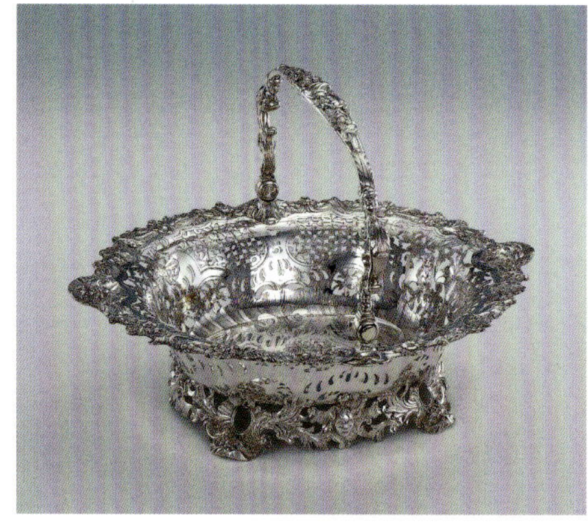

BASKET
Silver
Marks: Sterling, London, 1739/40
Maker's mark: Paul de Lamerie (Hare, no. 5)

Heraldry: Later engraved unidentified coat of arms
Published: Bliss, 1990a, pp. 8–9; Bliss, no. 14, pp. 46–49

H. with handle raised 9 $^{3}/_{4}$ in. (24.8 cm)
Wt. 55 oz. 15 dwt. (1734 g)
Scratch wt.: "55:17"
Accession no.: 97.14

• 19 •

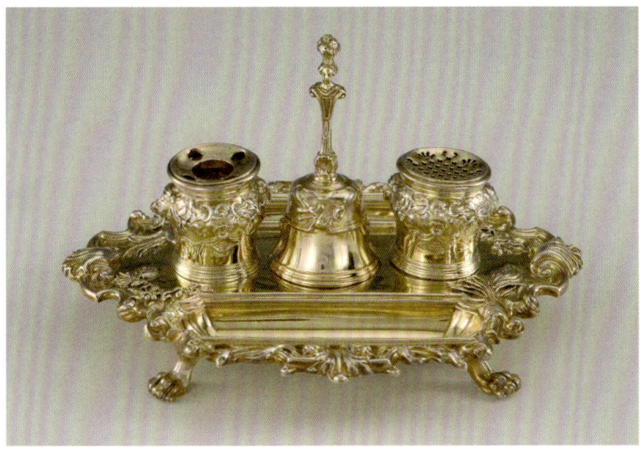

INKSTAND
Silver gilt
Marks: Sterling, London, 1739/40
Maker's mark: Paul de Lamerie (Hare, no. 5)
Inscription: Engraved monogram GMA

Published: Bliss, no. 13, pp. 44–45

L. 9 1/4 in. (23.5 cm)
Gross wt. 34 oz. 19 dwt. (1087 g)
Accession no.: 97.13.1, .2a-b, .3a-b, .4

• 21 •

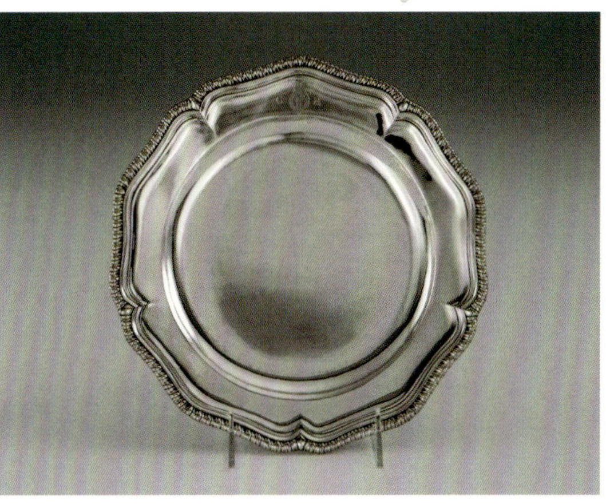

TWELVE DINNER PLATES
Silver
Marks: Sterling, London, 1741/42
Maker's mark: Paul de Lamerie (Hare, no. 5)

Heraldry: The royal badge enclosed by the motto of the Order of the Garter, crown, and initials of George II
Published: Bliss, no. 15, pp. 50–51

Diam. 9 5/8 in. (24.4 cm)
Wt. 189 oz. 11 dwt. (5896 g)
Accession no.: 97.15.1–.12

• 20 •

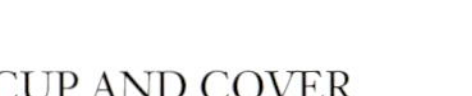

FOUR SAUCEBOAT STANDS
Silver
Marks: Sterling, London, 1739/40
Maker's mark: Paul de Lamerie (Hare, no. 5)

Heraldry: Engraved armorials of Anson quartering Carrier as borne by Admiral George Anson, 1st Baron Anson
Provenance: George, 1st Baron Anson (1697–1762), by descent to Thomas, 3rd Earl of Lichfield (1856–1982), "The Collection of Plate made for George, Lord Anson (The Celebrated Admiral) by Paul Lamerie [*sic*]," sale, Christie's, London, June 8, 1893, lots 15–18; three stands purchased by Captain Rawes, lots 15–17; M.P. Levene, Ltd., London, 1986; the fourth stand, lot 18, purchased by Duveen; Mrs. R.M. Robertson, Cambridge, Ontario, sale, Christie's, New York, October 27, 1987, lot 429
Exhibited: London, 1990 (one of the four)
Published: Hare, p. 81, no. 70; p. 114 (one of the four); Bliss, 1990a, p. 8; Bliss, no. 12, pp. 40–43; Hartop, 1994, p. 857, pl. X (one of the four)

L. 10 1/2 in. (26.6 cm)
Wt. 22 oz. 11 dwt. (701 g), 22 oz. 13 dwt. (705 g), 22 oz. 10 dwt. (700 g) and 22 oz. 15 dwt. (708 g)
Accession no.: 97.12.1–.4

• 22 •

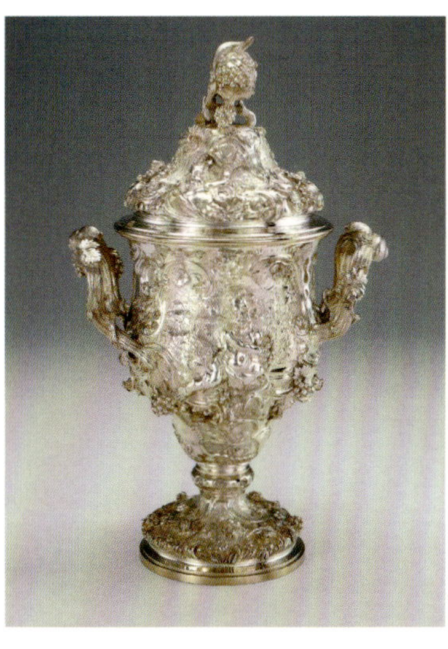

CUP AND COVER
Silver
Marks: Sterling, London, 1742/43
Maker's mark: Paul de Lamerie, (Hare, no. 5)

Provenance: Hunt and Roskell, London, 1862; William H. Green, sale, Sotheby's, London, May 19, 1955, lot 3
Exhibited: London, 1862
Published: Robinson, 1863, no. 5840, p. 495; Houston, no. 53; Carver and Casey, 1978, p. 22; *Virginia Museum of Fine Arts Annual Report 1987–88*, p. 6; *Virginia Museum of Fine Arts Bulletin*, vol. 48, no. 4, March/April, 1988, cover, p. 11; Minneapolis, p. 64; Bliss, 1990a, pp. 9–11; Bliss, no. 17, pp. 54–57; Wees, p. 81; *Rococo Silver*, p. 62, fig. 78; p. 122, figs. 176.1–3

H. 15 1/8 in. (38.4 cm)
Wt. 99 oz. 9 dwt. (3093 g)
Accession no.: 97.17a-b

• 23 •

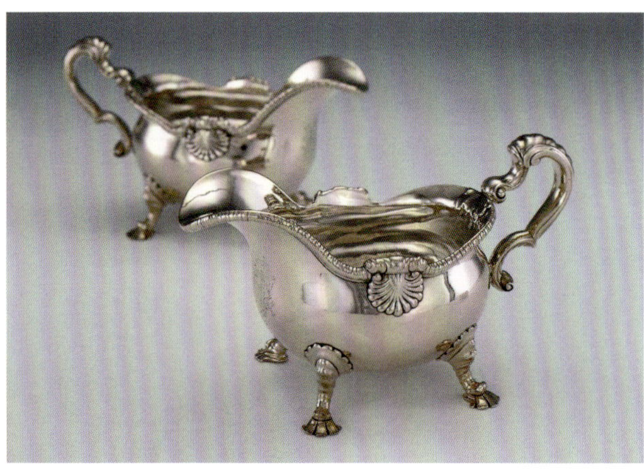

PAIR OF SAUCEBOATS
Silver
Marks: Sterling, London, 1742/43
Maker's mark: Paul de Lamerie (Hare, no. 5)

Heraldry: Engraved arms of Jodrell impaling Vanderplank
Published: Bliss, no. 16, pp. 52–53

H. 5 1/8 in. (13 cm)
Wt. 21 oz. 1 dwt. (654 g) and 20 oz. 10 dwt. (638 g)
Accession no.: 97.16.1-.2

• 24 •

PAIR OF CANDELABRA
Silver
Marks: Sterling, London, 1743/44
Maker's mark:
Paul de Lamerie (Hare, no. 5)

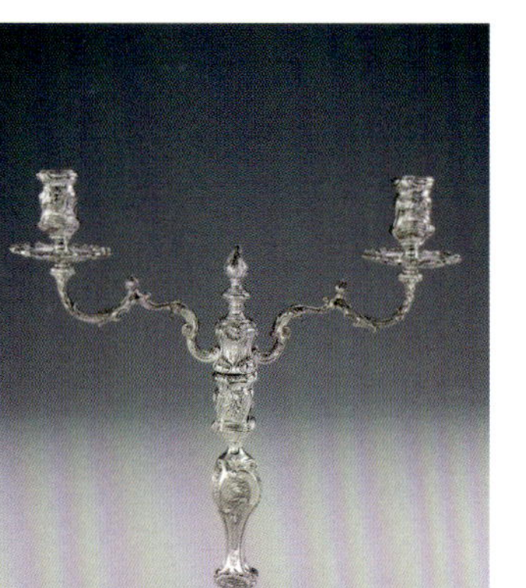

Heraldry: Unidentified engraved crest of a lion's jamb [leg] issuing from a mural crown
Provenance: Christie's, London, April 13, 1905, lot 70, Letts; Mrs. John E. Rovensky (formerly Mrs. Morton F. Plant), New York, sale, Parke Bernet, New York, January 19, 1957, lot 903
Published: Hackenbroch, pp. 92–93; Bliss, no. 18, pp. 58–59

H. 16 in. (40.6 cm)
Wt. 58 oz. 9 dwt. (1818 g) and 59 oz. 17 dwt. (1862 g)
Accession no.: 97.18.1a-f-.2a-f

• 25 •

SALVER
Silver
Marks: Sterling, London, 1743/44
Maker's mark:
Paul de Lamerie (Hare, no. 5)

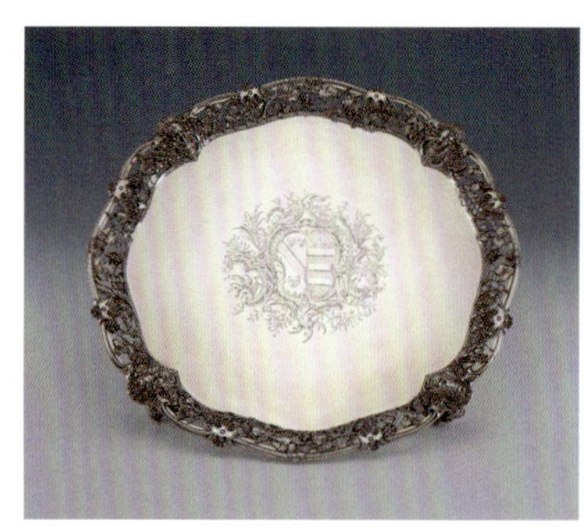

Heraldry: Engraved arms of Waldo impaling Wakefield, as borne by Edward Wakefield Meade-Waldo
Provenance: Edward Wakefield Meade-Waldo (1792–1858), by descent to E.G.B. Meade-Waldo, sale, Christie's, London, November 15, 1933, lot 114, Permain, London; William Randolph Hearst; Bryan Jenks Esq., sale, Christie's, London, June 16, 1965, lot 32, Thomas Lumley Ltd., London; Donald S. Morrison, New Jersey, sale, Sotheby Parke Bernet, New York, June 6, 1980, lot 26
Exhibited: Princeton, 1966; The Brooklyn Museum, Brooklyn, New York, 1958–1980 (on extended loan, L66. 18.9); London, 1990
Published: Princeton, no. 49; *Art at Auction: The Year at Sotheby's, 1979–1980*, p. 475; Schroder, 1983, p. 18; Clayton, 1985b, p. 171, no. 8; Hare, no. 112, p. 165; Bliss 1990a, pp. 9, 11; Bliss, no. 19, pp. 60–63

Diam. 22 in. (55.9 cm)
Wt. 146 oz. 15 dwt. (4565 g)
Scratch wt.: "149 = 12"
Accession no.: 97.19

• 26 •

CREAM JUG
Silver
Marks: Sterling, London, 1744/45
Maker's mark:
Paul de Lamerie (Hare, no. 5)

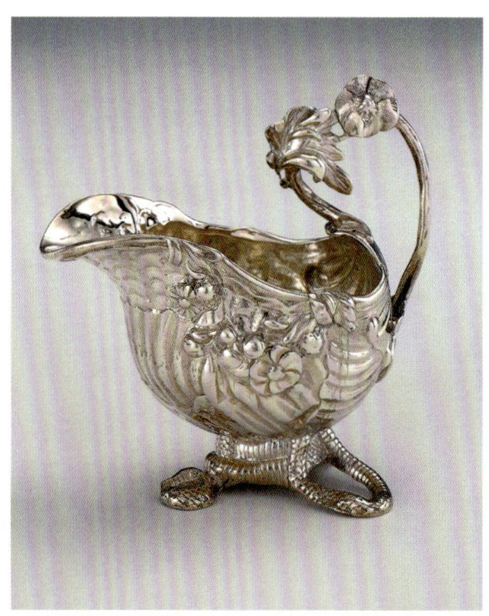

Provenance: Mrs. A. Hamilton Rice, Parke Bernet, New York, May 6, 1965, lot 68, I. Freeman & Son, Ltd., London
Published: Bliss, 1990a, p. 11; Bliss, no. 20, pp. 64–65; Hartop, 2007, no. 126, n. 1

H. 4 5/8 in. (11.7 cm)
Wt. 7 oz. 11 dwt. (235 g)
Accession no.: 97.20

• 27 •

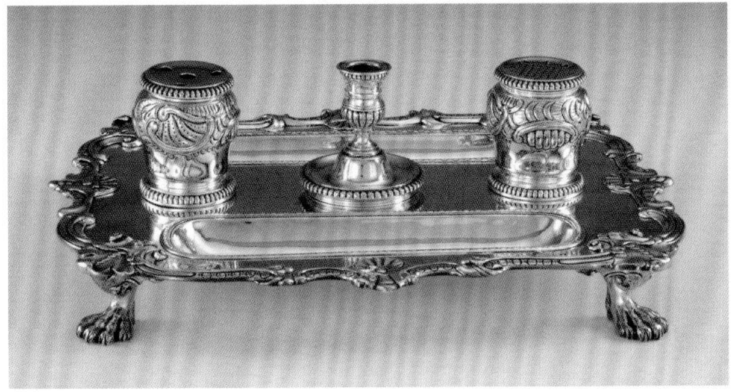

INKSTAND
Silver
Marks: Sterling, London, 1745/46
Maker's mark: Paul de Lamerie (Hare, no. 5)

Published: Bliss, no. 22, pp. 70–71

L. 26 3/4 in. (67.9 cm)
Wt. 72 oz. 18 dwt. (2268 g)
Accession no.: 97.22.1, .2, .3a-b, .4a-b

• 28 •

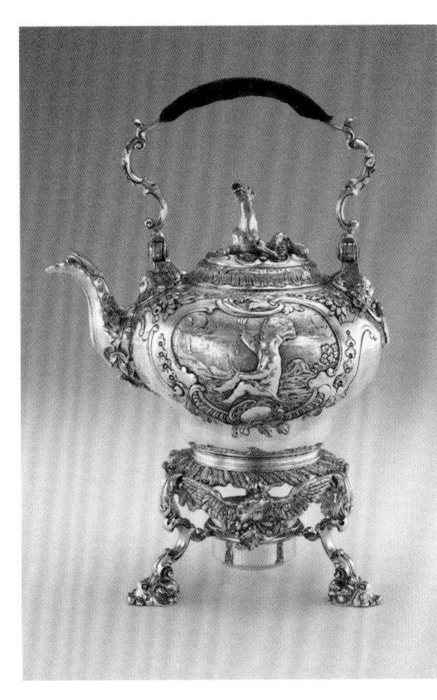

TEA KETTLE, STAND, AND LAMP
Silver, leather
Marks: Sterling, London, 1745/46; lamp 1741/42
Maker's mark: Paul de Lamerie (Hare, no. 5)

Provenance: Christie's, London, October 5, 1949, lot 99, purchased by Crouch; William A. McMahon, New York, sale, Christie's, London, March 28, 1973, lot 122; Arthur S. Leidesdorf, New York, sale, Sotheby Parke Bernet, New York, June 4, 1974, lot 69; "A Private Collector," sale, Sotheby's, New York, April 6, 1989, lot 158
Exhibited: London, 1973
Published: *Weltkunst*, June 1, 1989, p. 1664; *Art and Auction*, June 1989, pp. 192–93; *Art and Auction*, September 1989, pp. 178–79; Bliss, no. 21, pp. 66–69

H. of kettle with handle raised 15 in. (38.1 cm)
Gross wt. 95 oz. 3 dwt. (2959 g)
Scratch wt.: kettle "58 = 3," stand "37 = 17"
Accession no.: 97.21a-d

• 29 •

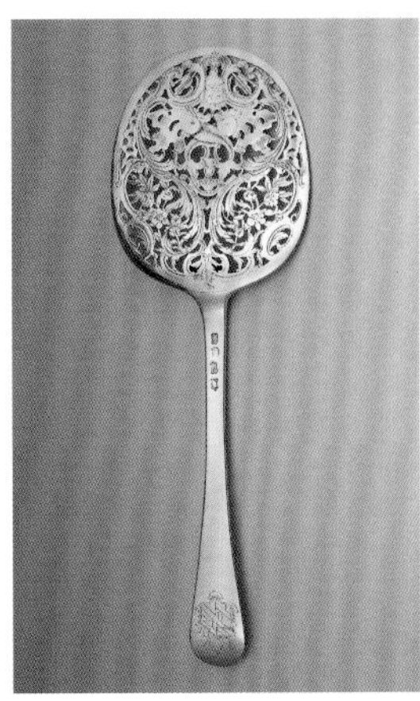

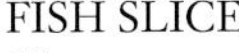

FISH SLICE
Silver
Marks: Sterling, London, 1746/47
Maker's mark: Paul de Lamerie (Hare, no. 5)

Heraldry: Engraved coat of arms of Anson quartering Carrier as borne by Admiral George Anson, 1st Baron Anson
Provenance: George, 1st Baron Anson (1697–1762), by descent to Thomas, 3rd Earl of Lichfield (1856–1982), "The Collection of Plate made for George, Lord Anson (The Celebrated Admiral) by Paul Lamerie [*sic*]," sale, Christie's, London, June 8, 1893, lot 3, Vander, London; Montagu Samuel, 1st Baron Swaythling (1832–1911), "The Swaythling Collection," sale, Christie's, London, May 6, 1924, lot 7; Christie's, New York, October 27, 1987, lot 420; Jaime Ortiz-Patiño, sale, Sotheby's, New York, April 22, 1998, lot 30, M.P. Levene, Ltd., London
Exhibited: London, 1902; London, 1990, no. 71
Published: *Christie's Review of the Season 1988*, p. 309; *Octagon*, vol. XXVII, no. 1, Spring, 1990, p. 13; Hare, no. 71, p. 115; Rabinovitch, pp. 40–41, fig. 1d; Hartop, 1994, p. 854, pl. vi

H. 13 3/4 in. (34.9 cm)
Wt. 7 oz. 14 dwt. (240 g)
Accession no.: 2006.585

• 30 •

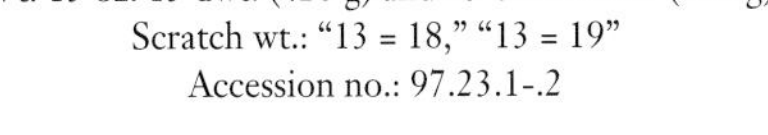

PAIR OF WAITERS
Silver
Marks: Sterling, London, 1747/48
Maker's mark: Paul de Lamerie (Hare, no. 5)

Heraldry: Engraved armorials of Anson quartering those of Carrier as borne by Admiral George Anson, 1st Baron Anson
Provenance: George, 1st Baron Anson (1697–1762), by descent to Thomas, 3rd Earl of Lichfield (1856–1982), sale, "The Collection of Plate made for George, Lord Anson (The Celebrated Admiral) by Paul Lamerie [*sic*]," Christie's, London, June 8, 1893, lots 9–10 (purchased by Charles Davis) or lots 11–12 (purchased by S.J. Phillips, Ltd., London); Montagu Samuel, 1st Baron Swaythling (1832–1911), anonymous sale [Lord Swaythling], Christie's, London, June 21, 1910, lot 41, Letts; Miss M.S. Davies, sale, Christie's, London, June 30, 1954, lot 139, Davidson; Bryan Jenks Esq., sale, Christie's, London, June 16, 1965, lot 30, Garrard and Company, Ltd., London; the Trustees of the 7th Earl of Radnor's Marriage Settlement, sale, Christie's, London, November 24, 1971, lot 78, S.J. Phillips, Ltd., London
Exhibited: London, 1902
Published: London, 1902, nos. 7 and 10, p. 15; Gardner, pl. 111, no. 3; *Christie's Review of the Year, 1964–1965*, p. 124; Schroder, 1988a, p. 222; Bliss, no. 23, pp. 72–75

Diam. 7 in. (17.8 cm)
Wt. 13 oz. 15 dwt. (428 g) and 13 oz. 17 dwt. (431 g)
Scratch wt.: "13 = 18," "13 = 19"
Accession no.: 97.23.1-.2

• 31 •

PAIR OF FIGURAL CANDLESTICKS WITH A PAIR OF TWO-LIGHT BRANCHES
Silver
Marks: Candlesticks: Sterling, London, 1748/49; branches: Sleeve of one struck with lion passant, leopard's head and London date letter for 1736/37, the other unmarked; all drip pans struck with the 1729–39 lion passant
Maker's mark: Candlesticks: Paul de Lamerie (Hare, no. 5)
Inscriptions: Undersides of candlestick branches engraved with the initial J

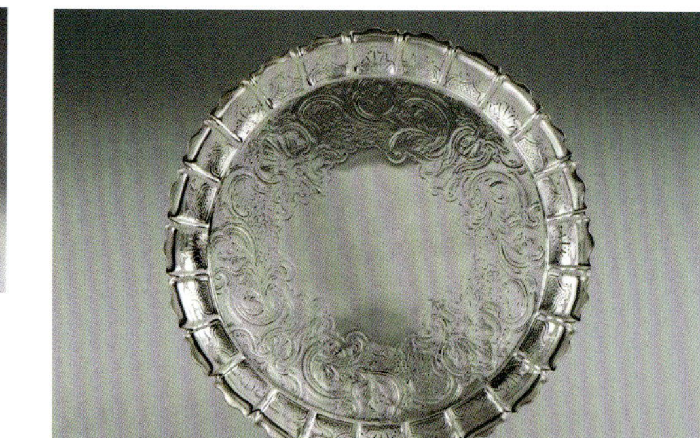

Heraldry: Engraved arms of Jenkinson on female caryatid stem
Marks: Sleeve of one struck with lion passant, leopard's head and London date letter for 1736/37; all drip pans struck with the 1729–39 lion passant
Provenance: Probably Charles Jenkinson (1693–1750) of Burford Lawn Lodge, Whichwood, Oxfordshire, by descent to Edward, 5th Earl of Liverpool, sale, Christie's, London, June 26, 1973, lot 32, Sir George Dowty (1901–1975), The Dowty Collection, sale, Christie's, New York, April 22, 1993, lot 61
Exhibited: Cheltenham, 1983, no. 15; London 1990, no. 115
Published: Schroder, 1983, p. 21; Hare, p. 168; Hartop, 1993, p. 3; Culme, 1999, pp. 36–41; *Rococo Silver*, p. 104, fig. 162

H. overall 17 in. (40.8 cm), W. of branches 7 5/8 in. (19.4 cm)
Wt. 80 oz. (2488 g) and 80 oz. (2489 g)
Accession no.: 97.91.1a-c-.2a-c

• 32 •

PAIR OF CANDLESTICKS
Silver
Marks: Sterling, London, 1748/49
Maker's mark: Paul de Lamerie (Hare, no. 5)

Provenance: Sotheby's, London, February 9, 1984, lot 201
Published: Bliss, no. 24, pp. 76–77

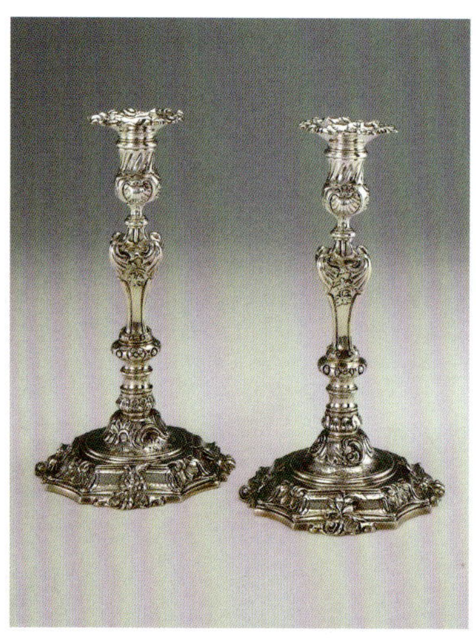

H. 9 3/4 in. (24.8 cm)
Wt. 23 oz. 8 dwt. (728 g) and 24 oz. 4 dwt. (753 g)
Scratch wt.: "97 oz. the 4"
Accession no.: 97.24.1a-b-.2a-b

• 33 •

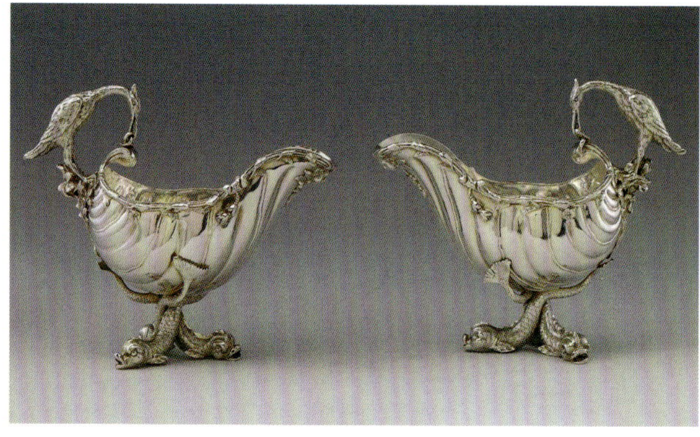

DISH OR SALVER
Silver
Marks: Sterling, London, 1748/49
Maker's mark: Paul de Lamerie (Hare, no. 5)

Provenance: Sotheby's, New York, April 7, 1987, lot 152
Published: Bliss, no. 25, pp. 78–79

Diam. 10 1/2 in. (26.7 cm)
Wt. 22 oz. 16 dwt. (709 g)
Scratch wt.: "24: 15," "28: 14: 75"
Accession no.: 97.25

• 34 •

PAIR OF SAUCEBOATS
Silver
Marks: Sterling, London, 1749/50
Maker's mark: William Cripps (Grimwade, no. 3057)

Provenance: Louis Huth Esq. of Possingworth, Hawkhurst, and 28 Hertford Street, Mayfair, sale, Christie's, London, May 26, 1905, lot 25; How of Edinburgh, London; S.J. Shrubsole Corp., New York
Published: Jackson, 1911, p. 822, fig. 1060; Grimwade, 1974, pl. 34C; Clayton, 1985a, no. 484, p. 244

H. 8 1/8 and 8 1/16 in. (20.6 and 20.5 cm)
Wt. 59 oz. 15 dwt. (1858 g)
Accession no.: 2006.594.1-.2

• 35 •

COFFEE JUG
Silver, raffia
Marks: Sterling, London, 1749/50
Maker's mark: Paul de Lamerie (Hare, no. 5)

Heraldry: Engraved arms of Hyde
Provenance: The late Colonel S.J.L. Hardie, sale, Sotheby's, London, December 4, 1969, lot 231, B. Schreiber; anonymous sale, Christie's, New York, October 26, 1992, lot 379
Published: Culme, 1999, no. 1, pp. 30–35

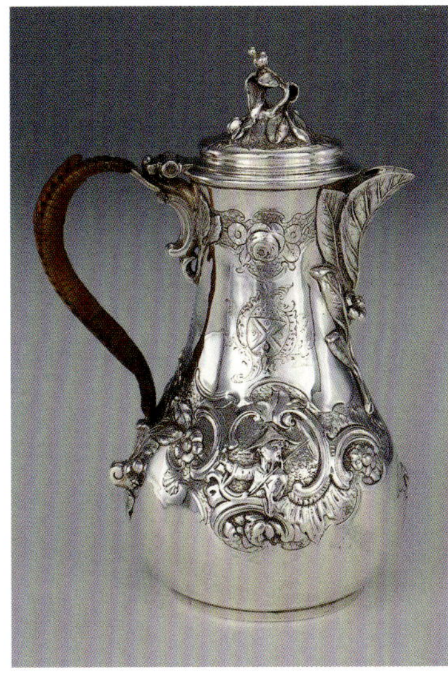

H. 7 5/8 in. (19.4 cm), W. 5 3/8 in. (13.6 cm)
Gross wt. 14 oz. 5 dwt. (443 g)
Accession no.: 97.90

• 37 •

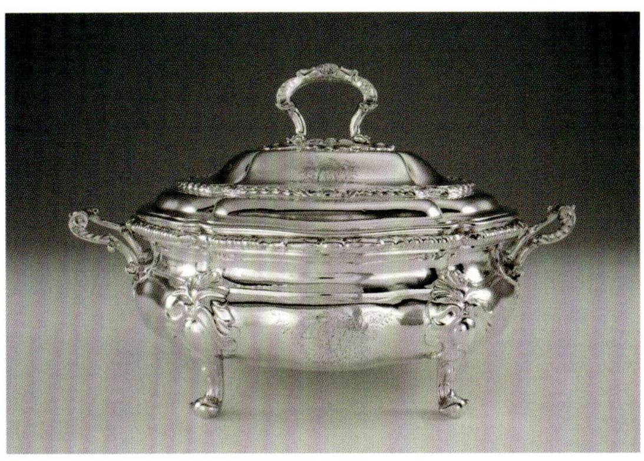

SOUP TUREEN AND COVER
Silver
Marks: Sterling, London, 1749/50
Maker's mark: Paul de Lamerie (Hare, no. 5)

Heraldry: Engraved arms of Trinity College, Dublin
Provenance: Sotheby's, London, May 17, 1973, lot 176; De Mello, sale, Christie's, Geneva, April 27, 1976, lot 226
Published: *Art at Auction: The Year at Sotheby's 1972–1973*, pp. 288–89; Bliss, no. 26, pp. 80–81

L. 17 1/2 in. (44.4 cm)
Wt. 126 oz. 12 dwt. (3938 g)
Accession no.: 97.26a-b

• 36 •

PAIR OF DISH COVERS
Silver
Marks: Sterling, London, 1749/50
Maker's mark: Paul de Lamerie (Grimwade, no. 2204)

Heraldry: Engraved armorials of Anson quartering Carrier as borne by Admiral George Anson, 1st Baron Anson
Provenance: George, 1st Baron Anson (1697–1762), by descent to Thomas, 3rd Earl of Lichfield (1856–1982), "The Collection of Plate made for George, Lord Anson (The Celebrated Admiral) by Paul Lamerie [*sic*]," sale, Christie's, London, June 8, 1893, lot 37 (with dishes), Vander, London; Flora Whitney Miller, sale, Sotheby's, New York, April 7, 1987, lot 158
Exhibited: London, 1990
Published: Hare, no. 72, p. 116; Bliss, no. 27, pp. 82–83

L. 9 in. (22.9 cm)
Wts. 20 oz. 4 dwt. (629 g) and 20 oz. 6 dwt. (632 g)
Scratch wts.: "20:14 1/2," "20: 16 1/2"
Accession no.: 97.27.1-.2

• 38 •

TEA KETTLE, STAND, AND LAMP
Silver, ivory
Marks: Sterling, London, 1749/50
Maker's mark: James Shruder (Jackson, p. 194)

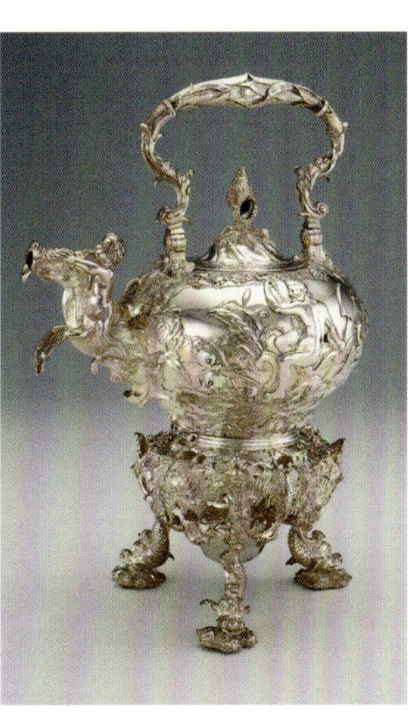

Heraldry: Engraved arms of Okeover impaling Nichol for Leake Okeover, who in 1730 married Mary, daughter of John Nichol of Colney Hatch, Middlesex, and various crests
Provenance: Leake Okeover (1701–1765), by descent to Colonel Sir Ian Walker-Okeover, Bt., sale, Christie's, London, June 25, 1975, lot 108; Garrard and Company, Ltd., London; Simon Kaye, Ltd., London; I. Freeman and Son, Inc., New York
Published: *Connoisseur*, September 1975, p. 31 (advertisement); *Rococo*, p. 118; Clayton, 1985b, no. 9, p. 165; Schroder, 1988b, p. 302; Bliss, 1990a, p. 11; Bliss, no. 29, pp. 88–92; *Rococo Silver*, frontispiece

H. of kettle with handle raised 16 1/4 in. (41.3 cm)
Gross wt. of kettle 112 oz. 11 dwt. (3500 g)
Scratch wts.: "110 =12," "62 = 2," "48 = 10"
Accession no.: 97.29a-d

• 39 •

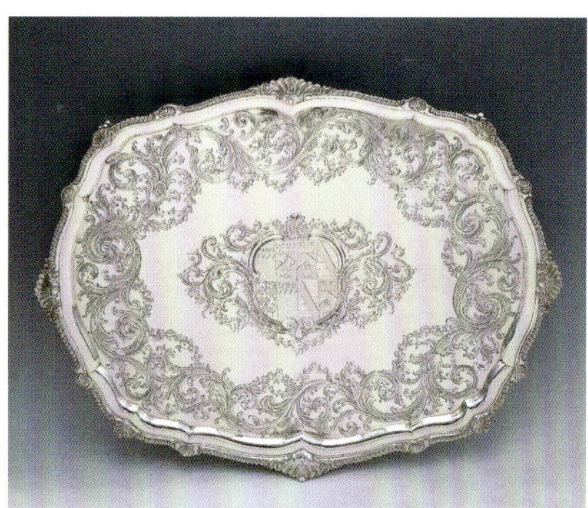

TRAY
Silver
Marks: Sterling
London 1749/50
Maker's mark:
Edward Wakelin
(Grimwade, no. 656)

Heraldry: Engraved arms of Harvey quartering Dycer, Williamson and Parker and impaling Skynner quartering Remington, as borne by William Harvey of Rolls Park, Chigwell, Essex, who married Emma, eldest daughter of Stephen Skynner of Walthamstow, in 1750
Provenance: William Harvey (d. 1763), by descent to Sir Eliab Harvey (d. 1830), then by descent probably to his eldest daughter Louisa, who married William Lloyd of Aston Hall, Shropshire; Major General E.H. Goulburn, D.S.O., sale, Christie's, London, April 2, 1952, lot 167, S.J. Shrubsole, London, private American collection, S.J. Shrubsole Corp., New York
Published: Grimwade, 1974, pp. 39 and 67, plate 19b

W. 29 $^{5}/_{8}$ in. (75.2 cm)
Wt. 238 oz. 16 dwt. (7428 g)
Accession no.: 2006.579

• 41 •

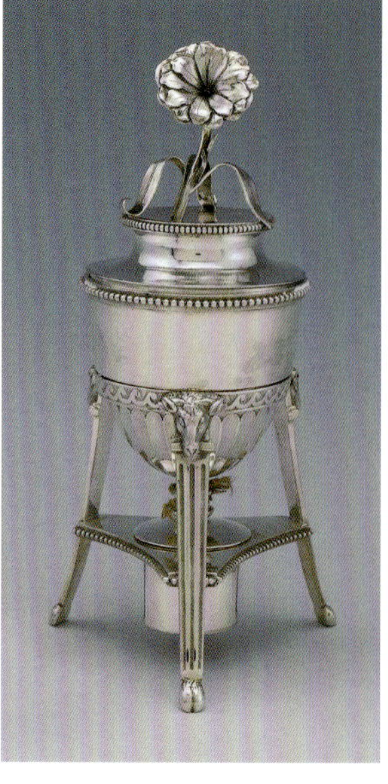

PERFUME BURNER
Silver
Marks: Sterling, London, 1785/86
Maker's mark: Andrew Fogelberg and Stephen Gilbert (Grimwade, no. 36)

Provenance: Sale, Sotheby's, London, December 6, 1979, lot 184; Richard Jarvis, London
Published: Brett, no. 1030, p. 232

H. 6 $^{11}/_{16}$ in. (17 cm)
Wt. 8 oz. (249 g)
Accession no.: 2006.593a-e

• 40 •

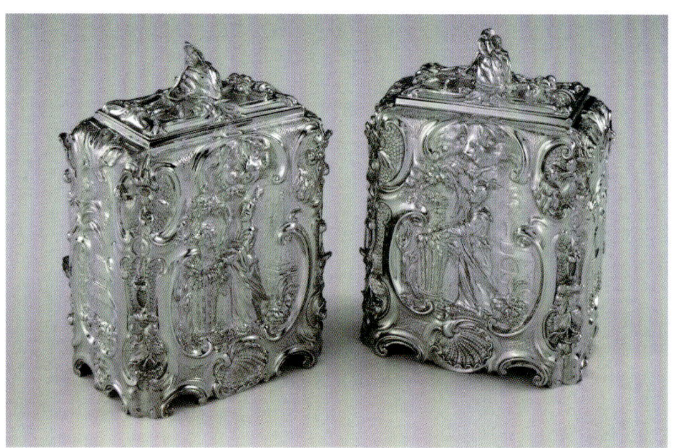

PAIR OF TEA CADDIES
Silver
Marks: Sterling, London, 1751/52
Maker's mark: Paul de Lamerie (Hare, no. 5)

Provenance: Sotheby's, London, April 28, 1977, lot 184
Published: Brett, no. 735, p. 179; Bliss, no. 28, pp. 84–86

H. 5 $^{3}/_{4}$ in. (14.6 cm)
Wt. 15 oz. 2 dwt. (470 g) and 14 oz. 10 dwt. (451 g)
Scratch wts.: "47: 21," "47: 23"
Accession no.: 97.28.1-.2

• 42 •

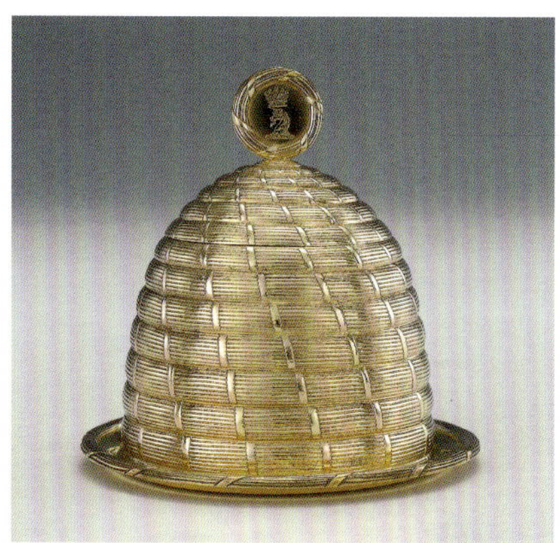

HONEY POT AND STAND
Silver gilt
Marks: Sterling, London, 1798/99
Maker's mark: Paul Storr (Grimwade, no. 2234)

Heraldry: Engraved crest of Ramsay, Earls of Dalhousie, under an earl's coronet
Published: Bliss, no. 30, pp. 94–95

H. on stand 4 $^{5}/_{16}$ in. (10.9 cm)
Wt. 11 oz. 8 dwt. (355 g)
Accession no.: 97.30a-c

• 43 •

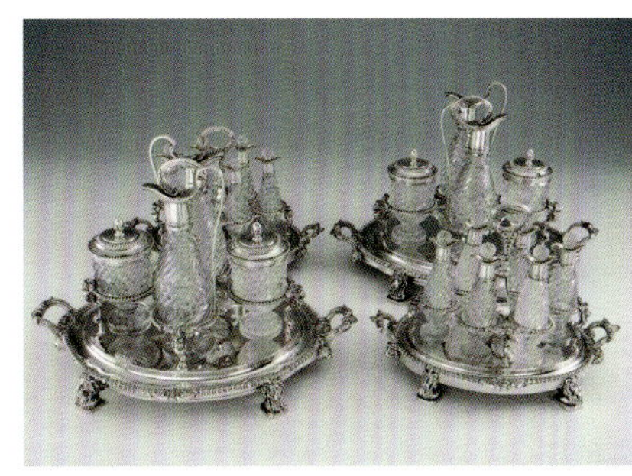

CRUET SERVICE WITH TWO LARGE AND TWO SMALL FRAMES
Silver, partially gilt mounts, cut glass
Marks: Sterling, London, 1806/7
Maker's mark: Paul Storr (Grimwade, no. 2234)

Heraldry: Engraved arms of Hamilton quartering Arran and Douglas, borne by Alexander, 10th Duke of Hamilton and Brandon
Provenance: Alexander, 10th Duke of Hamilton and 7th Duke of Brandon (1767–1854) by descent to the 15th Duke of Hamilton and 12th Duke of Brandon, sale, Sotheby's, London, June 20, 1988, lot 216
Published: Bliss, no. 32, pp. 98–99

L. of smaller stands 13 1/4 in. (33.7 cm)
L. of larger stands 17 1/2 in. (44.4 cm)
Gross wt. 107 oz. 6 dwt.; 106 oz. 18 dwt.; 194 oz. 17 dwt.; 191 oz. 18 dwt. (3338; 3325; 6060; 5969 g)
Accession nos.: 97.32.1.1, .2a-b–.7a-b; 97.32.2.1, .2a-b–.7a-b; 97.32.3.1, .2a-b-.3a–b, .4-.5; 97.32.4.1, .2a-b, .3a-b, .4-.5

• 44 •

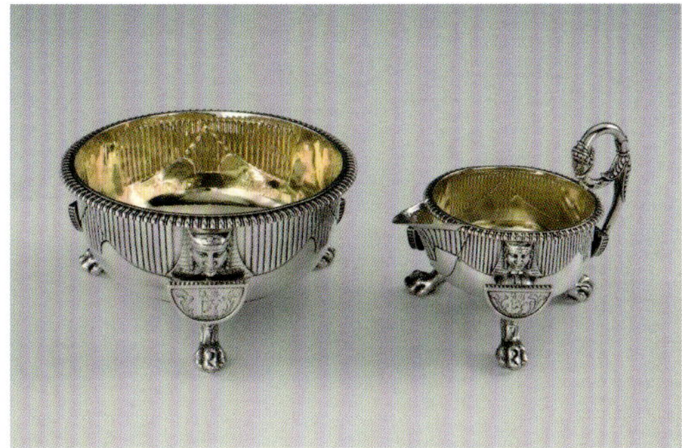

SUGAR BOWL AND CREAM JUG
Silver, gilt interiors
Marks: Sterling, London, 1806/7
Maker's mark: Paul Storr (Grimwade, no. 2235)

Heraldry: Engraved arms of Stracey with Brooksbank in pretence, for Edward Hardinge John Stracey (1768–1851), who married Ann, daughter and sole heir of William Brooksbank
Provenance: Lillian and Morrie Moss, Memphis, Tennessee, David Orgell, Inc., Beverly Hills
Published: Moss, 1968, p. 10; Moss, 1972, pp. 204–5, pl. 144; Bliss, no. 31, pp. 96–97

H. 3 3/4; 3 in. (9.5; 7.6 cm)
Wt. 16 oz. 11 dwt.; 11 oz. 9 dwt. (515; 356 g)
Accession no.: 97.31.1-.2

• 45 •

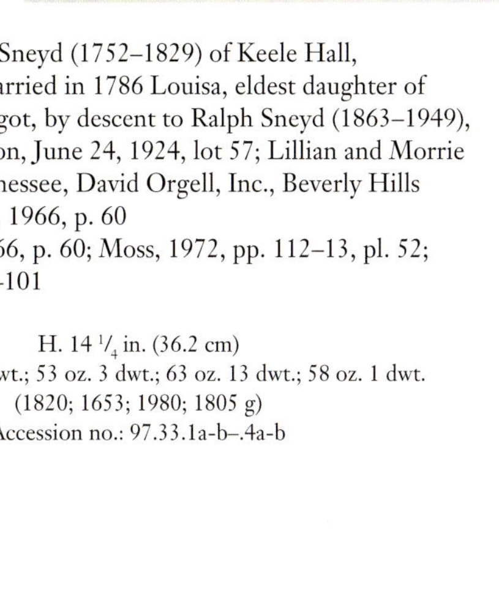

FOUR CANDLESTICKS
Silver gilt
Marks: Sterling, London, 1808/9
Maker's mark: Paul Storr (Grimwade, no. 2235)

Heraldry: Engraved coats of arms of Sneyd and of Bagot

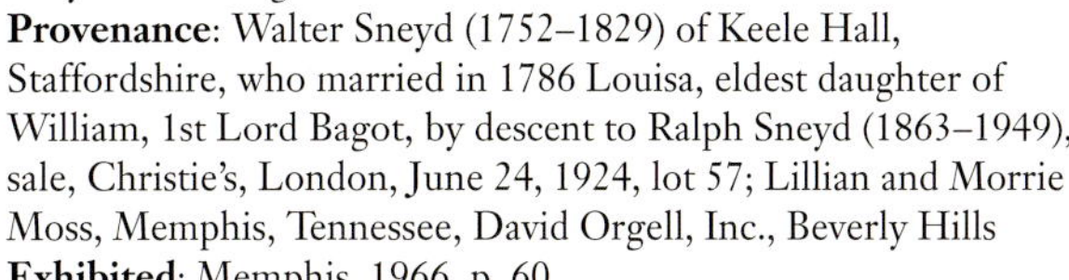

Provenance: Walter Sneyd (1752–1829) of Keele Hall, Staffordshire, who married in 1786 Louisa, eldest daughter of William, 1st Lord Bagot, by descent to Ralph Sneyd (1863–1949), sale, Christie's, London, June 24, 1924, lot 57; Lillian and Morrie Moss, Memphis, Tennessee, David Orgell, Inc., Beverly Hills
Exhibited: Memphis, 1966, p. 60
Published: Moss, 1966, p. 60; Moss, 1972, pp. 112–13, pl. 52; Bliss, no. 33, pp. 100–101

H. 14 1/4 in. (36.2 cm)
Wt. 58 oz. 10 dwt.; 53 oz. 3 dwt.; 63 oz. 13 dwt.; 58 oz. 1 dwt. (1820; 1653; 1980; 1805 g)
Accession no.: 97.33.1a-b–.4a-b

• 46 •

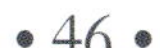

PAIR OF CUPS AND COVERS
Silver gilt
Marks: Sterling, London, 1809/10
Maker's mark: Robert Garrard I (Grimwade, no. 2320)

Heraldry: Engraved crest of Willoughby, Barons Willoughby de Eresby, probably for Peter Robert, 21st Baron Willoughby de Eresby
Provenance: Peter Robert, 21st Baron Willoughby de Eresby (1782–1865), by descent to 3rd Earl of Ancaster, sale, Christie's, London, June 29, 1955, lot 121, Carrington & Co. Ltd., London; Lady Beaverbrook (d. 1994), the estate of the late Lady Beaverbrook, sale, Sotheby's, London, November 9, 1995, lot 199
Published: Culme, 1999, no. 4, pp. 46–47

H. 16 1/8 in. (40.9 cm), D. 6 13/16 in. (17.3 cm)
Wt. 112 oz. 11 dwt. (3501 g) and 113 oz. 17 dwt. (3541 g)
Accession no.: 97.86.1a–b-.2a–b

• 47 •

EWER
Silver
Marks: Sterling, London, 1809/10
Maker's mark: Paul Storr (Grimwade, no. 2235)

Provenance: Christie's, London, April 17, 1928, lot 81
Published: Penzer, p. 262; Bliss, no. 34, pp. 104–5

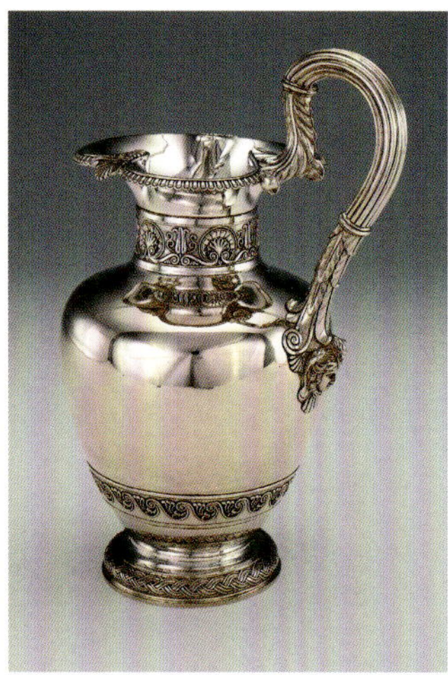

H. 12 $^{3}/_{4}$ in. (32.4 cm)
Wt. 65 oz. 2 dwt. (2025 g)
Accession no.: 97.34

• 48 •

PAIR OF SOUP TUREENS, COVERS, AND STANDS
Silver
Marks: Sterling, London, 1810/11
Maker's mark: Robert Garrard I (Grimwade, no. 2320)
Interiors of tureens and covers stamped *1*, *2*

Heraldry: Engraved arms of Sneyd impaling Bagot, borne by Walter Sneyd of Keele Hall, who married in 1786 Louisa, daughter of William, 1st Lord Bagot
Provenance: Walter Sneyd (1752–1829) of Keele Hall, Staffordshire, by descent to Ralph Sneyd (1863–1949), sale, Christie's, London, June 24, 1924; William Randolph Hearst, sale, Parish-Watson & Co., New York, 1938; anonymous sale, Sotheby Parke Bernet, New York, June 10–11, 1975, lot 499, Sotheby's, New York, April 27, 1990; lot 382
Published: *Art at Auction: The Year at Sotheby's, 1974–75*, p. 270; Ogilvy, p. 68; Bliss, no. 67, pp. 192–95

L. of stands 21 $^{1}/_{4}$ in. (54 cm)
Wt. 158 oz.; 160 oz. 3 dwt. (4914; 4981 g)
Scratch wts.: "158 = 8," "160 = 18"
Accession no.: 97.67.1a-c-.2a-c

• 49 •

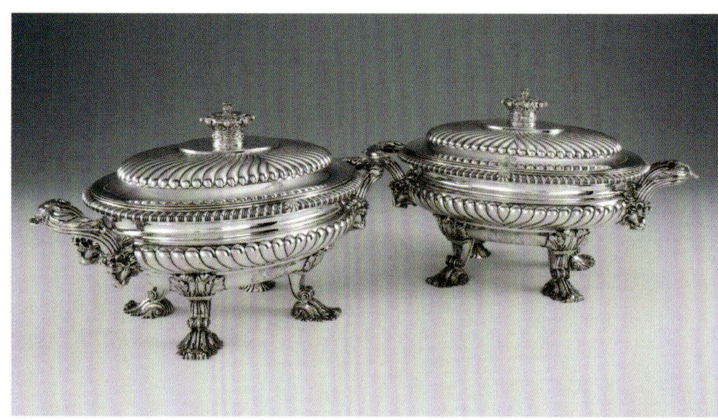

PAIR OF SOUP TUREENS AND COVERS
Silver
Marks: Sterling, London, 1810/11
Maker's mark: Paul Storr (Grimwade, no. 2235)
Stamped on one of the cover flanges and on both tureen borders: *555*, and numbered *1* and *2*

Heraldry: Engraved achievement of George, 9th Earl of Winchelsea and Nottingham
Provenance: George, 9th Earl of Winchelsea and Nottingham (1752–1826); Major James Hanbury, sale, Christie's, London, June 13, 1947, lot 73
Published: Penzer, p. 273; Bliss, no. 35, pp. 106–7

L. 17 $^{3}/_{4}$ in. (45 1 cm)
Wt. 163 oz. 14 dwt.; 158 oz. 18 dwt. (5092 and 4943 g)
Accession no.: 97.35.1a-c-.2a-c

• 50 •

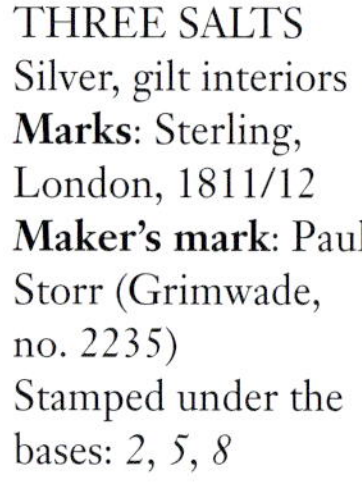

THREE SALTS
Silver, gilt interiors
Marks: Sterling, London, 1811/12
Maker's mark: Paul Storr (Grimwade, no. 2235)
Stamped under the bases: *2*, *5*, *8*

Published: Bliss, no. 37, pp. 112–13

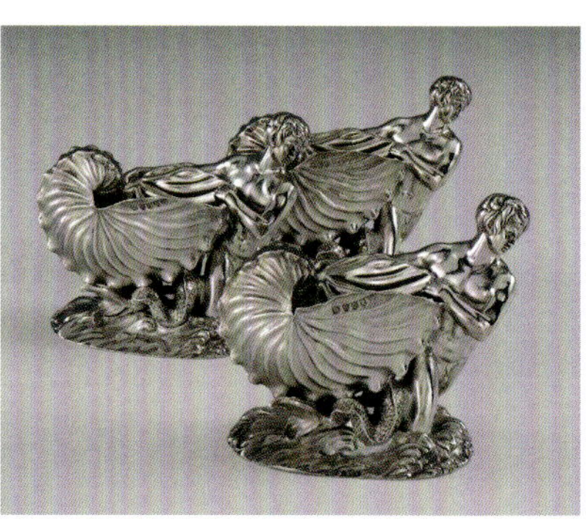

H. 4 in. (10.2 cm)
Wt. 20 oz. 18 dwt.; 20 oz. 3 dwt.; 20 oz. 7 dwt. (650, 626, 633 g)
Accession no.: 97.37.1–.3

• 51 •

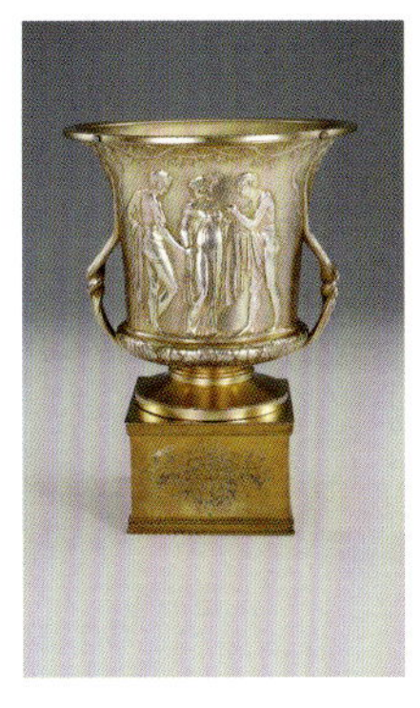

THEOCRITUS CUP
Silver gilt
Marks: Sterling, London, 1811/12
Maker's mark: Paul Storr (Grimwade, no. 2235)
Signature: Stamped on foot: *RUNDELL BRIDGE ET RUNDELL AURIFICES REGIS ET PRINCIPIS WALLIÆ LONDINI*
Inscription: Later engraved on plinth: *MADE IN LONDON A.D. 1811-12 BY PAUL STORR FOR H.R.H. PRINCE OF WALES AND PRESENTED BY HIM TO THE BISHOP OF WINCHESTER*
Stamped on the plinth: *606*

Heraldry: On plinth: engraved arms of Winchester College, the badge and motto of George, Prince of Wales, and an unidentified coat of arms
Provenance: William Stanley Goddard, Headmaster of Winchester College (1793–1810), Frederick G. Morgan, 1911; Lillian and Morrie Moss, Memphis, Tennessee, David Orgell, Inc., Beverly Hills
Exhibited: Memphis, 1968; Indianapolis, 1972; Dayton, 1972
Published: Jones 1911, p. 49; Moss, 1968, p. 5; Wark, 1970, p. 79; Moss, 1972, pp. 30, 56, 206–7, pl. 145; Indianapolis, no. 32, p. 12; Bury, 1979, p. 144; Clayton, 1985a, p. 428; Newman, 1987, p. 322; Bliss, no. 36, pp. 108–11

H. with stand 13 in. (33 cm)
Wt. 143 oz. 10 dwt. (4463 g)
Scratch wt.: "143.5"
Accession no.: 97.36a-b

• 52 •

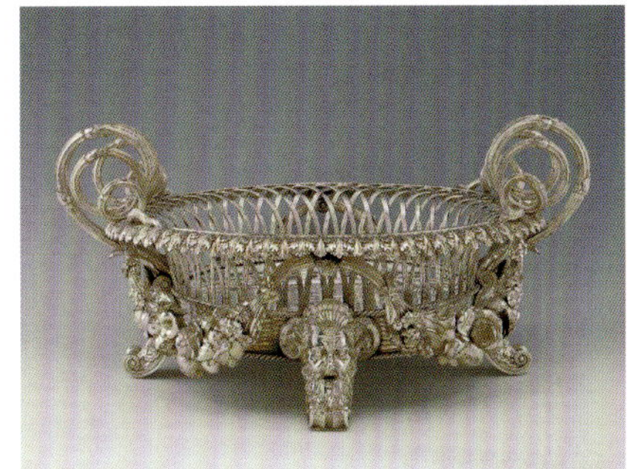

BASKET
Silver
Marks: Sterling, London, 1813/14
Maker's mark: Paul Storr (Grimwade, no. 2235)

Heraldry: Engraved arms of Wyndham quartering Hopton, as borne by George, 3rd Earl of Egremont and his wife Elizabeth, whom he married in 1801
Provenance: George, 3rd Earl of Egremont (1751–1837), by descent to John, 1st Baron Egremont, "The Executors of the late Lord Egremont," sale, Christie's, London, March 21, 1979, lot 36, Koopman Ltd., London, His Excellency Mohamed Mahdi Altajir, "Property of a Gentleman," sale, Christie's, London, June 11, 2003, lot 29, A.M. Marks Ltd., London
Exhibited: London, 1989b, no. 135
Published: Hawkins, pp. 136–37; Truman, 1989, no. 135, p. 175; Hartop, 2005, p. 66, fig. 56

Diam. 16 1/2 in. (41.9 cm)
Wt. 271 oz. 19 dwt. (8458 g)
Accession no.: 2006.586

• 53 •

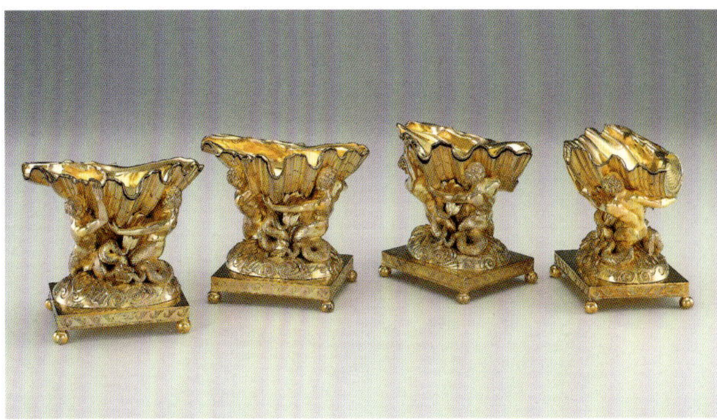

FOUR SALTS
Silver gilt
Marks: Sterling, London, 1813/14
Maker's mark: Paul Storr (Grimwade, no. 2235)
Signature: Base is stamped: *RUNDELL BRIDGE ET RUNDELL AURIFICES REGIS ET PRINCIPIS WALLIÆ REGENTIS BRITANNIAS*
Stamped under the bases and on liners: *1, 2, 3, 4*

Heraldry: Engraved unidentified crest
Published: Bliss, no. 38, pp. 114–17

H. 5 3/16 in. (13.2 cm)
Wt. 39 oz. 4 dwt.; 38 oz. 10 dwt.; 38 oz. 19 dwt.; 40 oz. 17 dwt.
(1219; 1197; 1211; 1271 g)
Accession no.: 97.38.1a-d–.4a-d

• 54 •

FOUR CANDLESTICKS
Silver gilt
Marks: Sterling, London, 1814/15
Maker's mark: Paul Storr (Grimwade, no. 2235)
Signature: Base is stamped: *RUNDELL BRIDGE ET RUNDELL AURIFICES REGIS ET PRINCIPIS WALLIÆ REGENTIS BRITANNIAS*
Inscription: On bases of one pair: *FROM THE DUKE OF CAMBRIDGE'S COLLECTION*
Stamped on wax pans: *4, 6, 7, 11*

Provenance: Pair 1: Adolphus Frederick, 1st Duke of Cambridge (1774–1850), seventh son of King George III, by descent to George, 2nd Duke of Cambridge (1819–1904), sale, Christie's, London, June 6, 1904, lot 202; Mary S. Harkness, Waterford, Connecticut and New York, sale, Parke Bernet, New York, January 17–20, 1951, lot 565, Arthur D'Espies, Short Hills, New Jersey, sale, Sotheby Parke Bernet, New York, April 12–13, 1977, lot 234
Published: Penzer, p. 248 (pair 1); Bliss, no. 40, pp. 122–23

H. 9 in. (22.9 cm)
Wt. 28 oz. 2 dwt.; 28 oz. 6 dwt.; 28 oz. 6 dwt.; 28 oz. 7 dwt.
(874; 880; 881; 882)
Accession no.: 97.40.1a-b, .2a-b, .3a-b, .4a-b

• 55 •

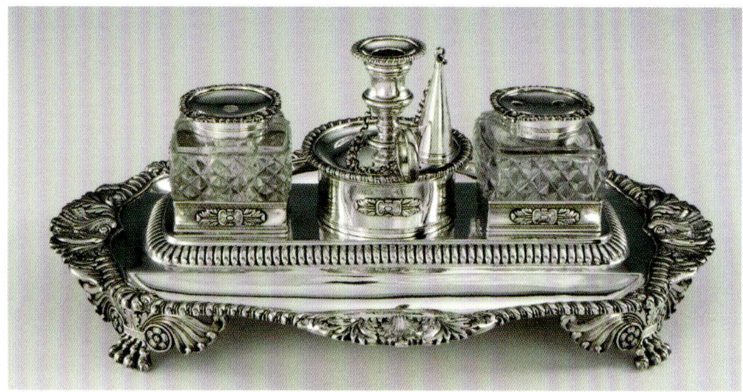

INKSTAND
Silver, cut glass
Marks: Sterling, London, 1814/15
Maker's mark: Paul Storr (Grimwade, no. 2235)

Provenance: Lillian and Morrie Moss, Memphis, Tennessee, David Orgell, Inc., Beverly Hills
Exhibited: Memphis, 1966
Published: Moss, 1966, p. 70; Moss, 1972, pp. 144–45, pl. 83; Bliss, no. 41, pp. 124–25

L. 13 1/4 in. (33.6 cm)
Gross wt. 59 oz. 3 dwt. (1839 g)
Accession no.: 97.41.1, .2a-c, .3a-d, .4a-d

• 56 •

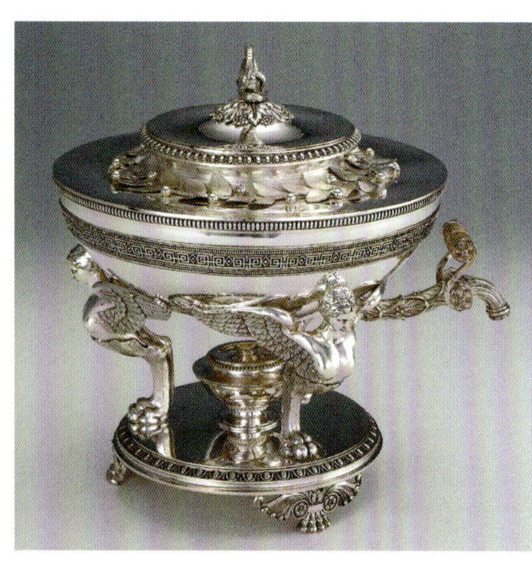

TEA URN
Silver, ivory
Marks: Sterling, London, 1814/15
Maker's mark: Paul Storr (Grimwade, no. 2235)

Provenance: Lillian and Morrie Moss, Memphis, Tennessee, David Orgell, Inc., Beverly Hills
Exhibited: Memphis, 1966
Published: Moss, 1966, p. 17; Moss, 1972, pp. 190–91, pl. 130; Bliss, no. 39, pp. 118–21

H. 13 1/8 in. (33.3 cm)
Gross wt. 201 oz. 4 dwt. (6258 g)
Scratch wt.: "202"
Accession no.: 97.39a-g

• 57 •

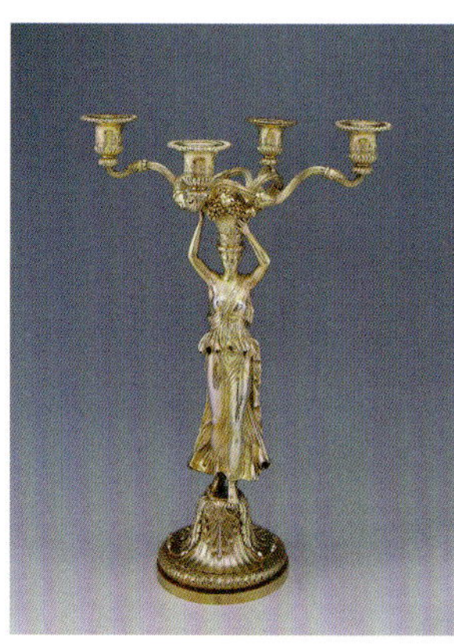

PAIR OF WINE COOLERS
Silver-gilt
Marks: Sterling, London, 1814/15, the square pedestal bases 1894/95 (not illustrated)
Maker's mark: Benjamin Smith II (Grimwade, no. 230), the bases, James Garrard
Signature: The foot rims engraved: *Philip Gilbert Regis aurifex fecit*

Heraldry: Engraved crest of the Marquess of Buckingham
Provenance: Richard, 2nd Marquess of Buckingham (1776–1839), created Duke of Buckingham in 1822, by descent to Richard 2nd Duke of Buckingham (1797–1861), sale, Stowe House, Christie's, September 6, 1848, lot 445, Town and Emanuel, London; John Deere, Chicago, sale, Sotheby's, New York, October 21, 1998, lot 252, M.P. Levene, Ltd., London
Published: Forster, p. 129, no. 445

H. without pedestals 14 7/16 in. (36.7 cm)
Wt. without pedestals 432 oz. (13437 g)
Accession no.: 2006.587.1a-c-.2a-c

• 58 •

FOUR-LIGHT CANDELABRUM
Silver gilt
Marks: Sterling, London, 1815/16
Maker's mark: Paul Storr (Grimwade, no. 2235)
Signature: Stamped on bases: *RUNDELL BRIDGE ET RUNDELL AURIFICES REGIS ET PRINCIPIS WALLIÆ REGENTIS BRITANNIAS*

Heraldry: Engraved crest of Russell as borne by Sir Henry Russell, chief of the Supreme Court of Bengal
Provenance: Sir Henry Russell (1751–1836); Neville Hamwee, sale, Christie's, London, May 18, 1966, lot 33; anonymous sale, Sotheby's, London, November 22, 1984, lot 105; anonymous sale, Christie's, New York, October 17, 1996, lot 259, S.J. Shrubsole Corp., New York
Published: Clayton, 1985b, p. 249, fig. 8

H. 20 3/8 in. (51.8 cm)
Wt. 143 oz. 7 dwt. (4459 g)
Accession no.: 2006.581a-i

• 59 •

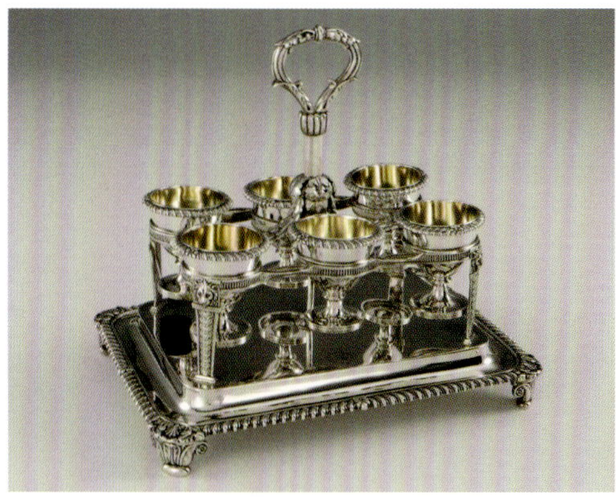

EGG STAND
Silver, gilt interiors
Marks: Sterling, London, 1815/16
Maker's mark: Paul Storr (Grimwade, no. 2235)
Stamped under base: *432*

Heraldry: Engraved crest and motto of Herbert of Llanarth, Monmouthshire
Provenance: Christie's, London, November 12, 1952, lot 142
Published: Penzer, p. 279; Bliss, no. 43, pp. 128–29

L. 9 1/2 in. (24 1 cm)
Wt. 39 oz. 3 dwt. (1218 g)
Accession no.: 97.43.1a-b, .2–.7

• 60 •

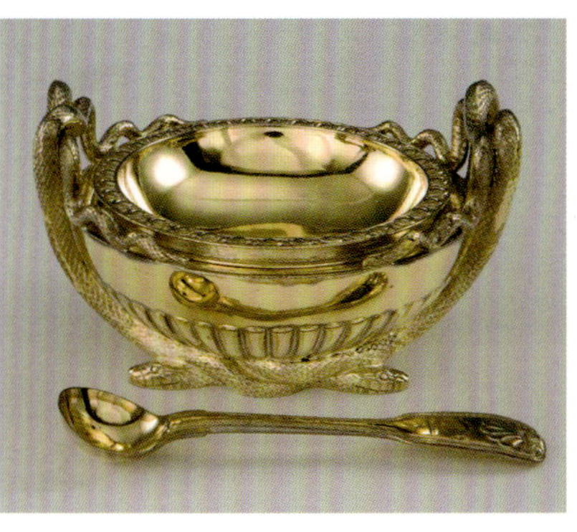

FOUR SALTS AND SPOONS
Silver gilt
Marks: Sterling, London, 1815/16; spoons 1812/13
Maker's mark: Paul Storr (Grimwade, no. 2235)
Stamped under bases and on liners: *390*

Heraldry: Engraved crest and motto of Molesworth on the spoons
Provenance: Christie's, London, January 9, 1946, lot 82; 7th Lord Camoys, sale, Christie's, London, March 21, 1979, lot 25
Published: Penzer, pp. 194–95, 264, pl. 58; Ramsay, 1960, pp. 212–17; *Christie's Review of the Season, 1979*, p. 282; Clayton, 1985b, p. 272, fig. 1; *Virginia Museum of Fine Arts Bulletin*, vol. 48, no. 4, March/April, 1988, p. 1; Bliss, no. 42, pp. 126–27

H. of salts 2 1/2 in. (6 4 cm)
L. of spoons 4 1/4 in. (10.8 cm)
Wt. 53 oz. 12 dwt. (1667 g)
Accession no.: 97.42.1a-c–.4a–c

• 61 •

FOUR WINE COASTERS
Silver, fruitwood, baize
Marks: Sterling, London, 1815/16
Maker's mark: Paul Storr (Grimwade, no. 2235)
Inscription: Stamped on base: *RUNDELL BRIDGE ET RUNDELL AURIFICES REGIS ET PRINCIPIS WALLIÆ REGENTIS BRITANNIAS*

Heraldry: Engraved arms of Bowes
Provenance: Claude Bowes-Lyon, 14th Earl of Strathmore and Kinghorne (1855–1944), Glamis Castle, Forfar, Angus, purchased by Catchpole and Williams, London, c. 1921, Henry G. Brengle, Philadelphia, Pennsylvania, donated by him to the Fly Club (formerly the ΑΔΦ Club), Harvard University, sale, Sotheby Parke Bernet, New York, December 4–5, 1974, lot 434
Published: Bliss, no. 44, pp. 130–31

H. 2 7/8 in. (7.3 cm)
Wt. 83 oz. 7 dwt. (2593 g)
Accession no.: 97.44.1–.4

• 62 •

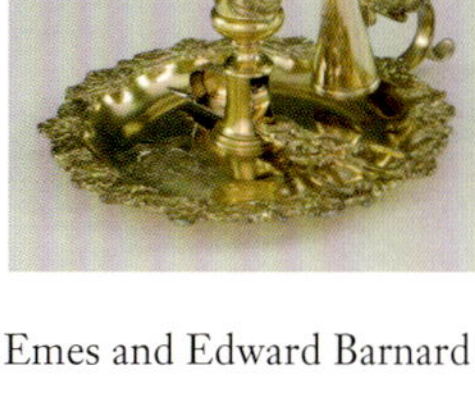

PAIR OF CHAMBER CANDLESTICKS, WICK TRIMMERS, AND EXTINGUISHERS
Silver gilt, steel
Marks: Sterling, London, 1816/17; one pair of trimmers 1815/16, the other pair is a modern copy
Maker's mark: Paul Storr (Grimwade, no. 2235); one pair of trimmers, Rebecca Emes and Edward Barnard I (Grimwade, no. 2309)
Stamped under bases: *749*
Inscription: Engraved (except Emes and Barnard trimmers) *E.A.Fs.* [Ernst August Fideikommiss (to faith entrusted)]

Heraldry: Engraved armorials on the candlesticks of Ernest Augustus, Duke of Cumberland, fifth son of George III; extinguishers and Emes and Barnard trimmers with royal badge, Garter motto and royal ducal coronet
Provenance: Ernest Augustus, 1st Duke of Cumberland (1771–1851), King of Hanover (reigned 1837–1851), by descent to Ernst August, Duke of Brunswick (1887–1953), sold privately 1924, Gluckselig, Vienna, Crichton Brothers, London
Published: Bliss, no. 46, pp. 136–37

H. of candlesticks 3 7/8 in. (9.8 cm)
L. of trimmers 5 1/16 in. (12.8 cm)
H. of extinguishers 3 3/8 in. (8.6 cm)
Gross wt. 40 oz. 16 dwt. (1268 g)
Accession no.: 97.46.1a-d-.2a-d

• 63 •

FOUR SUGAR VASES, TWO SIFTERS AND TWO LADLES
Silver gilt, glass
Marks: Sterling, London, 1816/17; the sifters and ladles 1817/18
Maker's mark: Paul Storr (Grimwade, no. 2235)
Stamped under bases and on covers: *2*, *4*, *5*, *8*

Heraldry: Engraved crest of Howard, borne by Bernard, 12th Duke of Norfolk
Provenance: Supplied by Rundell, Bridge & Rundell to Bernard, 12th Duke of Norfolk (1765–1842), by descent to Bernard Fitzalan-Howard, 16th Duke of Norfolk, sold privately c. 1956; Lillian and Morrie Moss, Memphis, Tennessee, David Orgell, Inc., Beverly Hills
Exhibited: Memphis, 1966; Indianapolis, 1972; Dayton, 1972
Published: Penzer, p. 26; Moss, 1966, p. 67; Moss, 1972, pp. 28, 192–93, pl. 132; Indianapolis, no. 49, p. 15; Bliss, no. 45, pp. 132–35

H. of vases 7 7/8 in. (20 cm)
L. of sifters and ladles 5 1/2 in. (14 cm)
Wt. without glass liners 153 oz. 3 dwt. (4764 g)
Accession no.: 97.45.1a-e–.4a-e

• 65 •

PAIR OF SAUCEBOATS
Silver, gilt interiors
Marks: Sterling, London, 1817/18
Maker's mark: Paul Storr (Grimwade, no. 2235)
Stamped under bases: *16*

Heraldry: Engraved unidentified arms
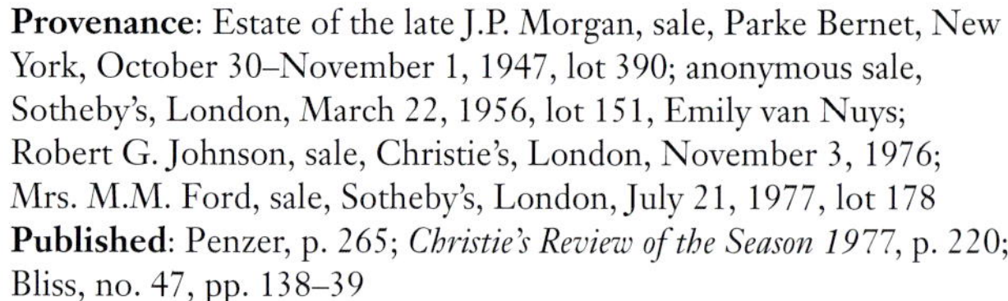
Provenance: Estate of the late J.P. Morgan, sale, Parke Bernet, New York, October 30–November 1, 1947, lot 390; anonymous sale, Sotheby's, London, March 22, 1956, lot 151, Emily van Nuys; Robert G. Johnson, sale, Christie's, London, November 3, 1976; Mrs. M.M. Ford, sale, Sotheby's, London, July 21, 1977, lot 178
Published: Penzer, p. 265; *Christie's Review of the Season 1977*, p. 220; Bliss, no. 47, pp. 138–39

H. 6 in. (15.2 cm)
Wt. 36 oz. 3 dwt.; 36 oz. 16 dwt. (1125; 1144 g)
Accession no.: 97.47.1-.2

• 64 •

PAIR OF ENTRÉE DISHES AND COVERS

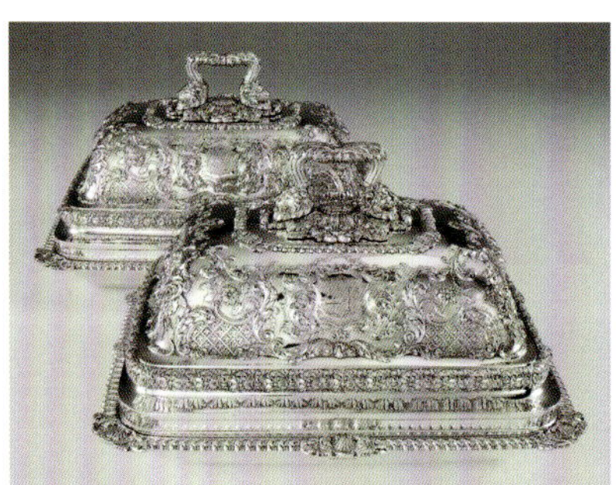

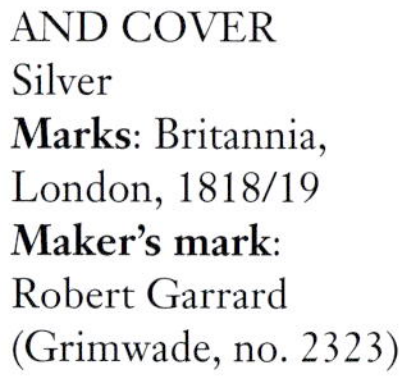

Silver
Marks: Sterling, London, 1817/18
Maker's mark: Paul Storr (Grimwade, no. 2235)
Stamped under bases and inside covers: *224*, stamped inside covers *1*, *2*
Inscription: Engraved underneath: *C. to E. DAVIDSON*

Heraldry: Engraved arms of Davidson, Curriehill, Scotland, impaling another
Provenance: George S. Heyer, Jr., Austin, Texas
Exhibited: Indianapolis, 1972; Dayton, 1972
Published: Indianapolis, no. 51, p. 15; Schroder, 1988a, p. 428; Bliss, no. 48, pp. 140–41

L. 12 3/4 in. (32.4 cm)
Wt. 98 oz. 16 dwt.; 97 oz. 4 dwt. (3073; 3024 g)
Accession no.: 97.48.1a–b-.2a–b

• 66 •

CHAMBER POT AND COVER

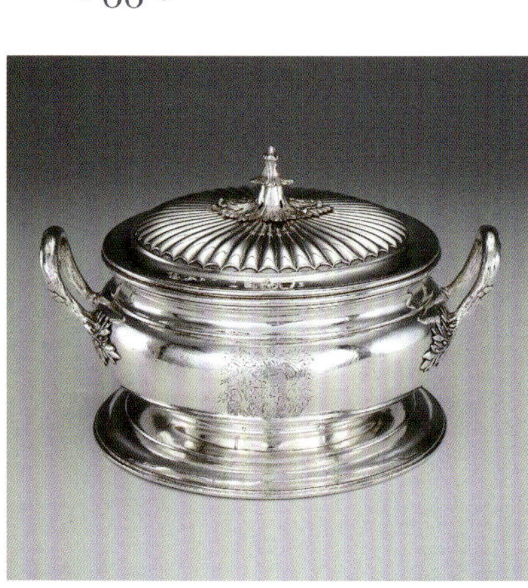

Silver
Marks: Britannia, London, 1818/19
Maker's mark: Robert Garrard (Grimwade, no. 2323)

Heraldry: Arms of York impaling Lascelles for Richard York of Wighill Park, Yorkshire, who married Mary Anne, daughter of Edward Lascelles, 1st Earl of Harewood, in 1801
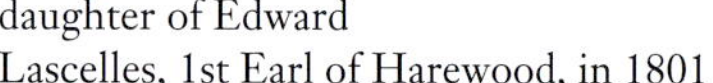
Provenance: Richard York (d. 1843) (High Sheriff of Yorkshire in 1832 and Mayor of Leeds) by descent to O.F. York, Esq., sale, Sotheby's, London, May 12, 1966, lot 12; Christie's, New York, April 22, 1993, lot 176
Published: Culme, 1999, no. 5, pp. 48–49

H. 7 7/8 in. (20 cm), W. 12 9/16 in. (31.9 cm), Diam. 9 7/8 in. (25.1 cm)
Wt. 90 oz. 5 dwt. (2807 g)
Accession no.: 97.92a-b

• 67 •

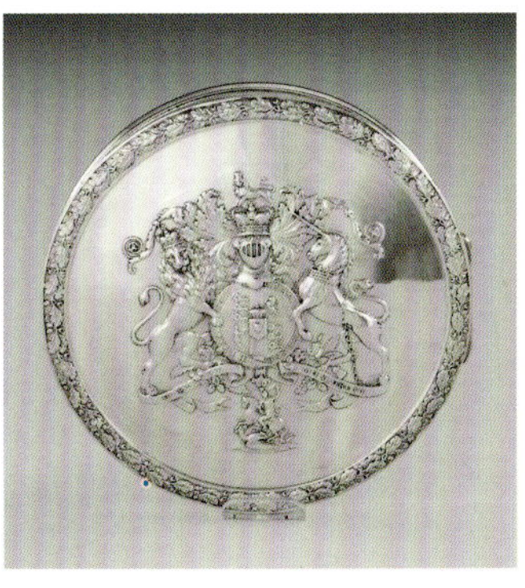

SKIPPET OR SEAL BOX
Silver
Marks: Sterling, London, 1818/19
Maker's mark: Paul Storr (Grimwade, no. 2235)
Stamped on interior: *57*

Heraldry: Chased royal arms of George III
Provenance: Presented by King Edward VII in 1903 to Sir Arthur Littleton-Annesley, K.C.B., K.C.V.O. (1837–1906) at a private investiture when Sir Arthur was made a Knight Commander of the Victorian Order on retiring as A.D.C. to the king, by descent to Mrs. Annesley Vachell, sale, Sotheby's, London, December 12, 1974, lot 20
Published: Banister, p. 1609; Waldron, p. 29; Bliss, no. 49, pp. 142–43

Diam. 6 3/4 in. (17.2 cm)
Wt. 21 oz. 1 dwt. (654 g)
Scratch wt.: "21:5"
Accession no.: 97.49

• 69 •

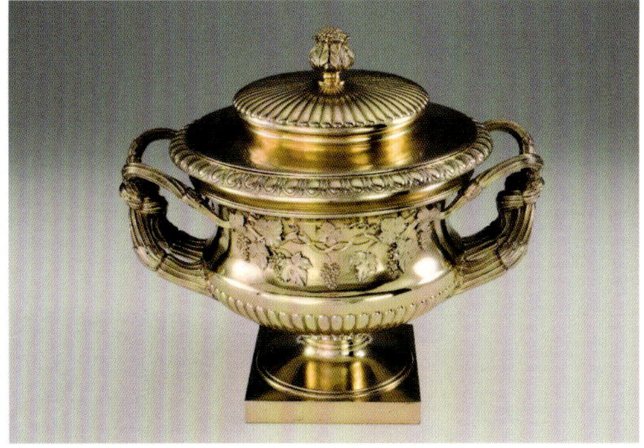

VASE AND COVER
Silver gilt
Marks: Sterling, London, 1819/20
Maker's mark: Paul Storr (Grimwade, no. 2235)
Signature: The cover flange engraved: *MAKEPEACE SON & HARKER FECER^{T}.*
Inscription: The foot engraved: *BURDEROP RACES 1821* and *IOHN BENETT ESQ^{R}. Steward.*

Published: Bliss, no. 50, pp. 144–47

H. 12 in. (30.5 cm)
Wt. 136 oz. 4 dwt. (4236 g)
Accession no.: 97.50a-b

• 68 •

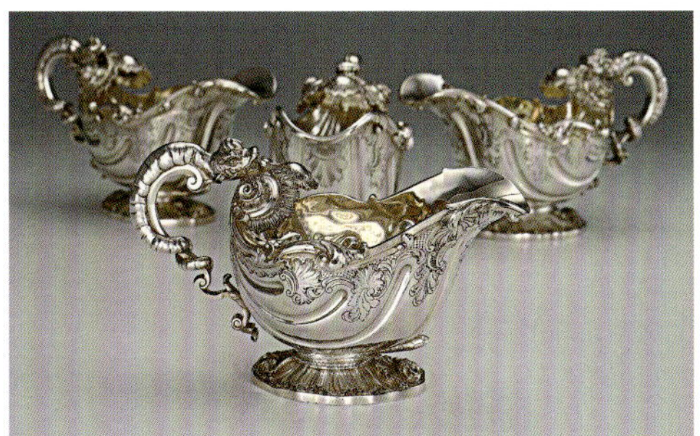

FOUR SAUCEBOATS
Silver
Marks: Sterling, London, 1819/20
Maker's mark: Paul Storr (Grimwade, no. 2235)

Heraldry: Engraved crest of Browne, Earls of Kenmare, under an earl's coronet
Provenance: Pair 1: Violet, Lady Beaumont, sale, Christie's, London, November 16, 1949, lot 129; the San Antonio Museum Association, sale, Christie's, New York, October 18, 1989, lot 163; pair 2: "A New York Collector," sale, Christie's, New York, April 9, 1992
Published: Penzer, p. 265; Bliss, no. 51, pp. 148–51

H. 6 in. (15.2 cm)
Wt. 33 oz. 13 dwt.; 35 oz.; 33 oz. 16 dwt.; 34 oz. 2 dwt.
(1046; 1088; 1052; 1060 g)
Accession no.: 97.51.1–.4

• 70 •

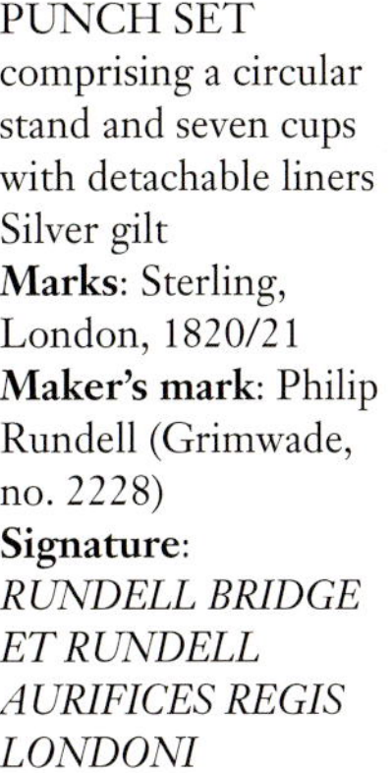

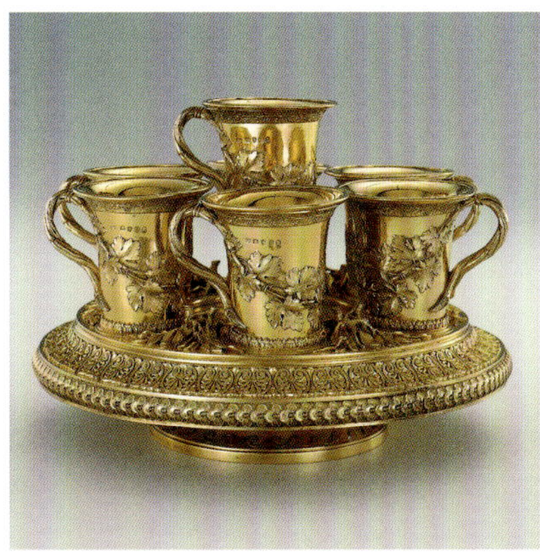

PUNCH SET
comprising a circular stand and seven cups with detachable liners
Silver gilt
Marks: Sterling, London, 1820/21
Maker's mark: Philip Rundell (Grimwade, no. 2228)
Signature: *RUNDELL BRIDGE ET RUNDELL AURIFICES REGIS LONDONI*
Base stamped: *3*, each component engraved: *6366*

Provenance: Christie's, New York, October 15, 1994, lot 287
Published: Culme, 1999, no. 3, pp. 42–45

H. of stand: 4 1/4 in. (10.2 cm), Diam. 10 1/8 in. (25.7 cm)
H. of stand with center cup: 6 7/8 in. (17.5 cm)
H. of each cup 2 5/8 in. (6.7 cm), Diam. at handle: 3 3/8 in. (8.6 cm)
Wt. of set: 99 oz. 8 dwt. (3092 g)
Accession no.: 97.89.1, .2a-b–.8a-b

• 71 •

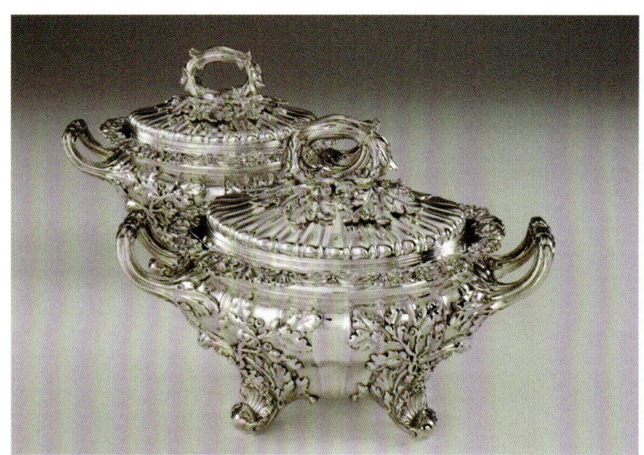

PAIR OF SAUCE TUREENS AND COVERS
Silver
Marks: Sterling, London, 1820/21
Maker's mark: Paul Storr (Grimwade, no. 2235)

Provenance: Lillian and Morrie Moss, Memphis, Tennessee, David Orgell, Inc., Beverly Hills
Exhibited: Memphis, 1966
Published: Moss, 1966, p. 32; Moss, 1972, pp. 88–89, pl. 29; Bliss, no. 52, pp. 152–53

H. 6 $^1/_2$ in. (16.5 cm)
Wt. 47 oz. 5 dwt.; 49 oz. 8 dwt. (1470; 1537 g)
Accession no.: 97.52.1a-b-.2a-b

• 72 •

CUP
Silver gilt
Marks: Sterling, London, 1821/22
Maker's mark: Paul Storr (Grimwade, no. 2235)

Heraldry: Engraved crest of France of Bostock, Cheshire and Oswestry, Shropshire
Provenance: Lillian and Morrie Moss, Memphis, Tennessee, David Orgell, Inc., Beverly Hills
Exhibited: Memphis, 1966
Published: Moss, 1966, p. 22; Moss, 1972, pp. 148–49, pl. 86; Bliss, no. 53, pp. 154–55

H. 7 $^1/_2$ in. (19 cm)
Wt. 29 oz. 6 dwt. (911 g)
Accession no.: 97.53

• 73 •

SALVER
Silver
Marks: Sterling, London, 1823/24
Maker's mark: Paul Storr (Grimwade, no. 2235)

Heraldry: Engraved arms of ffarington quarterly with Benson, Rufine, Bradshaw, Bradshaw (ancient), Aspull, Fitton, Carden, Malvoisin, Brereton, Nowell, and Hargreaves, as borne by Lieutenant Colonel William ffarington, High Sheriff of Lancashire in 1813
Provenance: Lieutenant Colonel William ffarington (1766–1837); "An Eastern Art Museum," sale, Parke Bernet, February 2–3, 1962, lot 229, Thomas Lumley Ltd., London; anonymous sale, Sotheby's, London, December 13, 1962, lot 91; W. Comyns and Sons, Ltd., Lillian and Morrie Moss, Memphis, Tennessee, David Orgell, Inc., Beverly Hills
Exhibited: Memphis, 1966, Indianapolis, 1972, Dayton, 1972
Published: Moss, 1966, p. 38; Moss, 1972, pp. 26–27, 160–61, pl. 103; Indianapolis; Skerry, p. 25; Bliss, no. 54, pp. 156–59

Diam. 26 $^7/_{16}$ in. (67.1 cm)
Wt. 249 oz. 4 dwt. (7751 g)
Accession no.: 97.54

• 74 •

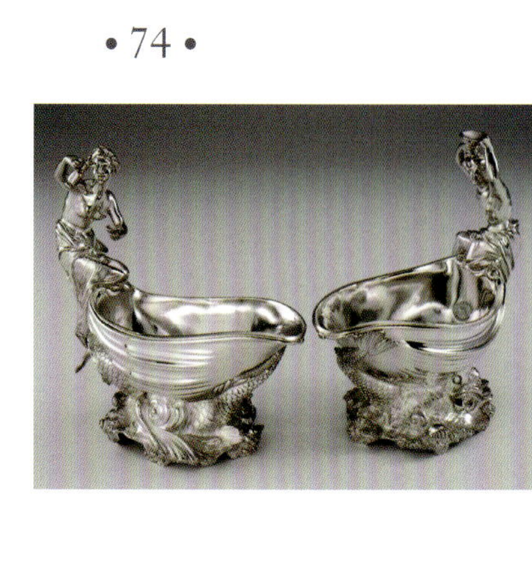

PAIR OF SAUCEBOATS
Silver
Marks: Sterling, London, 1824/25
Maker's mark: Robert Garrard II (Grimwade, no. 2322)
Stamped on bottom of the bases: *GARRARDS, PANTON STREET, LONDON*
Stamped on the liners: *3*, *5*; scratched on base: *3/01/13587*

Heraldry: Engraved unidentified crest under a baron's coronet
Provenance: Property of a lady, sale, Sotheby's, London, July 18, 1974, lot 84
Exhibited: London, 1991
Published: *Art at Auction, The Year at Sotheby's 1972–1973*, p. 292; Waldron, no. 450, p. 146; Ogilvy, no. 27, pp. 64–66; North, p. 353; Bliss, no. 68, pp. 196–99

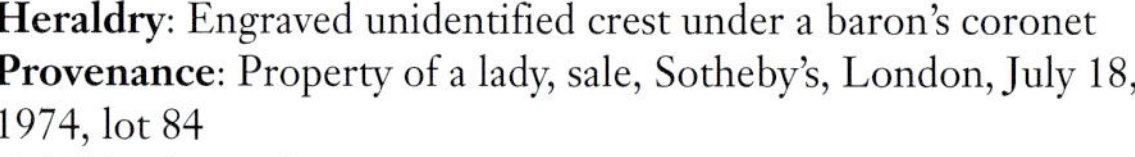

H. 9 in. (22.9 cm)
Wt. 56 oz. 12 dwt.; 55 oz. 19 dwt. (1761; 1740 g)
Accession no.: 97.68.1a-b-.2a-b

• 75 •

PAIR OF CANDELABRA
Silver
Marks: Sterling, London, 1825/26; branch sleeves and nozzles 1826/27
Maker's mark: Robert Garrard II (Grimwade, no. 2322)
Stamped on the branch sleeves: *1, 2;* stamped on the sockets, nozzles and drip-pans: *1, 2, 3, 4, 5, 6*
Signature: Stamped inside each base: *GARRARDS, PANTON STREET, LONDON*

Published: Bliss, no. 69, pp. 200–203

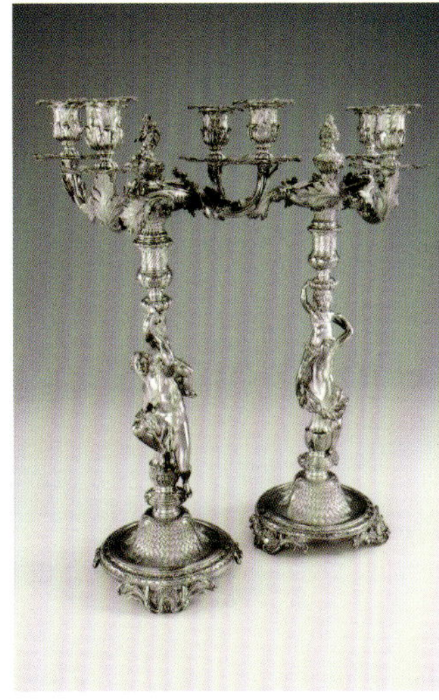

H. 23 1/8 in. (58.7 cm)
Wt. 161 oz. 5 dwt.; 160 oz. 4 dwt. (5016; 4983 g)
Accession no.: 97.69.1a-k-.2a-k

• 76 •

STIRRUP CUP
Silver, gilt interior
Marks: Sterling, London, 1826/27
Maker's mark: Paul Storr (Grimwade, no. 2235)
Inscription: Engraved around the lip: *MOSTYN HUNT. CUP WON 1826. BY MR. STEVEN'S GR. G. BY GRIMALDI.*

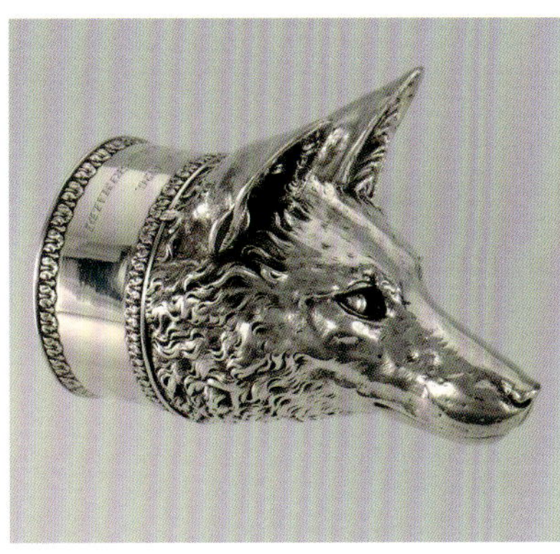

Provenance: Ormond Arthur Blyth, Esq., sale, Sotheby's, London, March 16, 1978, lot 171
Published: Bliss, no. 55, pp. 160–61

L. 5 9/16 in. (14.1 cm)
Wt. 12 oz. 5 dwt. (381 g)
Accession no.: 97.55

• 77 •

SOUP TUREEN, COVER, AND STAND
Silver
Marks: Sterling, London, stand 1827/28; body and cover 1829/30
Maker's mark: Robert Garrard II (Grimwade, no. 2322)
Signature: Stamped on foot: *GARRARDS, PANTON STREET, LONDON*
The base and stem stamped: *1;* the dolphin stamped: *1, 2, 3, 4*

Heraldry: Engraved arms of Higginson quarterly with Barneby Lutley, as borne by Edmund Barneby of Saltmarshe Castle, Herefordshire
Provenance: Edmund Barneby (1802–1871) of Saltmarshe Castle, Herefordshire; anonymous sale, Sotheby's, London, June 20, 1988, lot 222
Published: Bliss, no. 70, pp. 204–7

L. 21 1/4 in. (54 cm)
Wt. 511 oz. 8 dwt. (15907 g)
Scratch wt.: "512 17"
Accession no.: 97.70a-d

• 78 •

CUP AND COVER
Silver gilt
Marks: Sterling, London, 1827/28
Maker's mark: Paul Storr (Grimwade, no. 2235)

Provenance: Lillian and Morrie Moss, Memphis, Tennessee, David Orgell, Inc., Beverly Hills
Exhibited: Memphis, 1966
Published: Moss, 1966, p. 58; Moss, 1972, pp. 108–9, pl. 48; Bliss, no. 57, pp. 164–65

H. 15 1/8 in. (38.4 cm)
Wt. 121 oz. 4 dwt. (3769 g)
Scratch wt.: "121 05"
Accession no.: 97.57a-b

• 79 •

MUG
Silver
Marks: Sterling, London, 1827/28
Maker's mark: Paul Storr (Grimwade, no. 2235)
Engraved underneath: *F*

Published: Bliss, no. 56, pp. 162–63

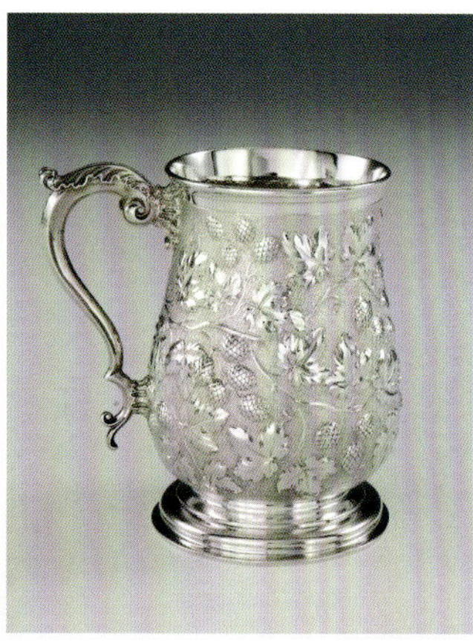

H. 5 1/4 in. (13.3 cm)
Wt. 11 oz. 8 dwt. (355 g)
Accession no.: 97.56

• 81 •

DRESSING SERVICE
Silver gilt, glass, steel, brass, ivory, enamel, rosewood, and velvet
Marks: Sterling, London, 1829/30
Maker's mark: Paul Storr (Grimwade, no. 2235)

Heraldry: Engraved arms of Bruce impaling Clifton, as borne by Sir Henry Hervey Bruce, who married Marianne Margaret, daughter of Sir J.G. Jukes Clifton, in 1842

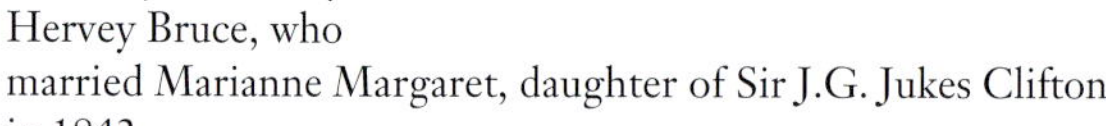

Provenance: Sir Henry Hervey Bruce (1820–1907)
Published: Armstrong, p. 72; Bliss, no. 60, pp. 172–73

L. of case 16 7/8 in. (42.9 cm)
Gross wt. of silver components 436 oz. 4 dwt. (13537 g)
Accession no.: 97.60.1-.27

• 80 •

FOUR VEGETABLE DISHES, COVERS, AND STANDS
Silver
Marks: Sterling, London, 1828/29
Maker's mark: Robert Garrard II (Grimwade, no. 2322)
Signature: Stamped on dishes, covers, and stands: *GARRARDS Panton Street, London*
Heater stands numbered 1 to 4; one hotplate an unmarked modern replacement; the remainder numbered 2 to 4; the covers numbered 5 to 8; the handles numbered 5 to 8

Heraldry: Engraved achievement of Walter Francis Montagu-Douglas-Scott, 5th Duke of Buccleuch
Provenance: Walter Francis Montagu-Douglas-Scott, 5th Duke of Buccleuch (1806–1884); Christie's, New York, April 22, 1993; lot 308
Published: Culme, 1999, no. 6, pp. 50–55

H. 9 1/4 in. (23.5 cm), Diam. 11 1/2 in. (29.2 cm),
W. of stands at handles 13 in. (33 cm)
Wt. 556 oz. 16 dwt. (17318 g)
Scratch wts.: On stands: "oz 83-14," "oz 83-0," "oz 83-14," "oz 83-18";
on dishes: "oz 29-19," "oz 30-17," "oz 31-,7" "oz 29-13";
on covers: "oz 32-14," "oz 32-12," "oz 31-19," "oz 32-9";
Accession no.: 97.88.1a-d–.3a-d, .4a-f

• 82 •

FIGURE OF HEBE
Silver
Marks: Sterling, London, 1829/30
Maker's mark: Paul Storr (Grimwade, no. 2235)

Provenance: "Property of a Gentleman," sale, Sotheby's, London, February 5, 1970, lot 92; Lillian and Morrie Moss, Memphis, Tennessee, David Orgell, Inc., Beverly Hills
Exhibited: Memphis, 1971
Published: Moss, 1971, pp. 12–13; Moss, 1972, pp. 39, 244–45, pl. 181; Brett, no. 1280, pp. 276–77; Bliss, no. 59, pp. 168–71

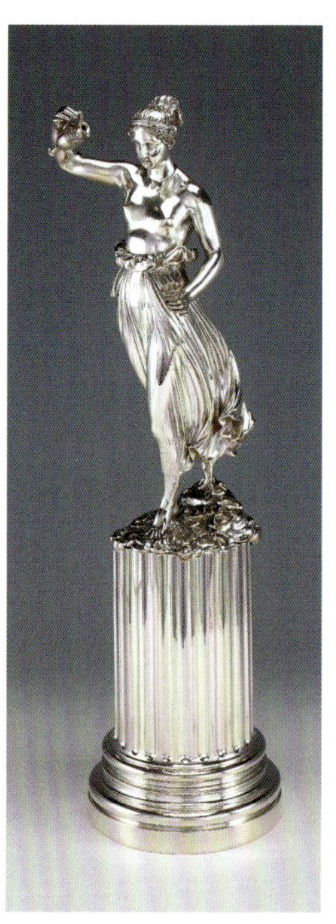

H. 35 in. (88.9 cm)
H. of pedestal 13 3/4 in. (34.9 cm)
Wt. 303 oz. 6 dwt. (9433 g)
Accession no.: 97.59a-b

• 83 •

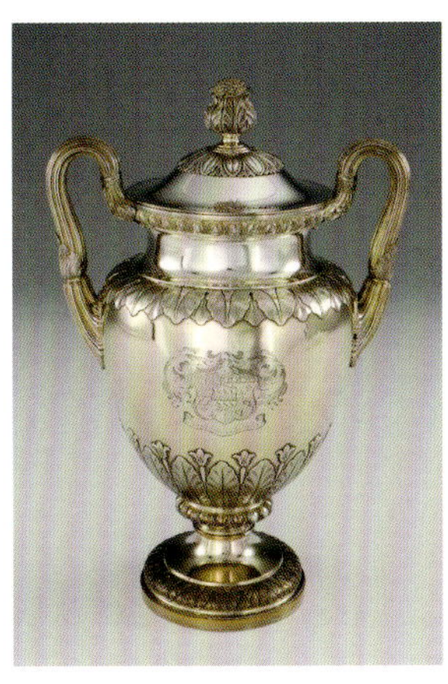

VASE AND COVER
Silver, partially gilt
Marks: Sterling, London, 1829/30
Maker's mark: Paul Storr (Grimwade, no. 2235)

Heraldry: On one side engraved with the arms of Granville with Onslow in pretence, as borne by Bernard Granville, who married Mathewana Sarah, daughter of Captain Matthew Onslow, in 1828; on the other side with those of Grave quarterly with five others
Provenance: Lillian and Morrie Moss, Memphis, Tennessee, David Orgell, Inc., Beverly Hills
Exhibited: Memphis, 1966
Published: Moss, 1966, p. 57; Moss, 1972, pp. 146–47, pl. 85; Bliss, no. 58, pp. 166–67

H. 13 $^7/_8$ in. (35.2 cm)
Wt. 66 oz. 17 dwt. (2080 g)
Accession no.: 97.58a-b

• 84 •

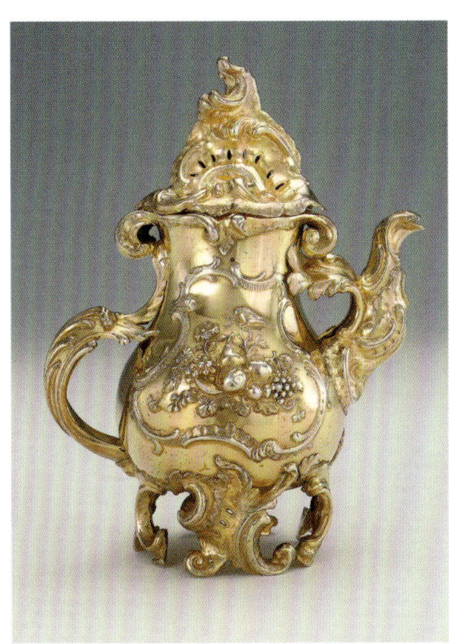

COFFEE POT
Silver gilt
Marks: Sterling, London, 1830/31
Maker's mark: Paul Storr (Grimwade, no. 2235)

Heraldry: Engraved crest, unidentified
Provenance: Lillian and Morrie Moss, Memphis, Tennessee, David Orgell, Inc., Beverly Hills
Exhibited: Memphis, 1966; Indianapolis, 1972, Dayton, 1972
Published: Moss, 1966, p. 13; Moss, 1972, pp. 104–5, pl. 44; Indianapolis, no. 68, p. 18; Bliss, no. 61, pp. 174–77

H. 10 $^3/_{16}$ in. (25.9 cm)
Wt. 31 oz. 13 dwt. (984 g)
Accession no.: 97.61a-b

• 85 •

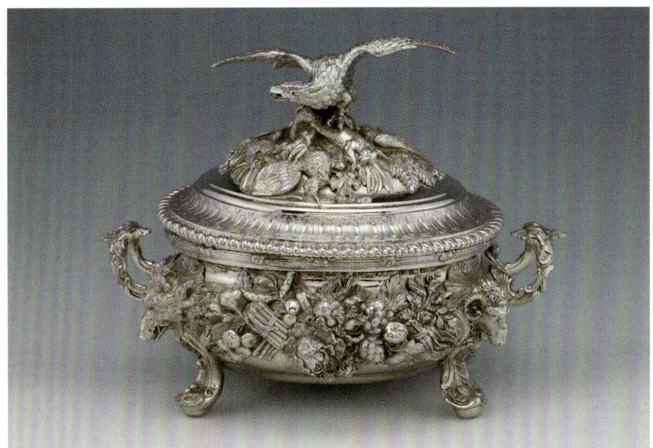

SOUP TUREEN AND COVER
Silver
Marks: Sterling, London, 1831/32
Maker's mark: Robert Garrard (Grimwade, no. 2322)

Provenance: S.J. Shrubsole Corp., New York

W. 10 $^3/_8$ in. (26.4 cm)
Wt. 183 oz. 18 dwt. (5720 g)
Accession no.: 2006.588a-c

• 86 •

COFFEE JUG
Silver, ivory
Marks: Sterling, London, 1833/34
Maker's mark: Paul Storr (Grimwade, no. 2235)
Signature: Stamped under base: *STORR AND MORTIMER* and *273*

Heraldry: Engraved arms of Quin impaling Spencer, as borne by George Quin, second son of Thomas, 1st Marquess of Headfort, who married Georgiana Charlotte, third daughter of 2nd Earl Spencer, in 1814
Provenance: George Quin (1792–1888)
Published: Bliss, no. 62, pp. 178–79

H. 11 in. (27.9 cm)
Gross wt. 30 oz. 12 dwt. (952 g)
Accession no.: 97.62

• 87 •

STIRRUP CUP
Silver, partially gilt interior
Marks: Sterling, London, 1834/35
Maker's mark: Paul Storr (Grimwade, no. 2235)

Published: Clayton, 1985a, p. 389; Newman, p. 302; Bliss, no. 63, pp. 180–81

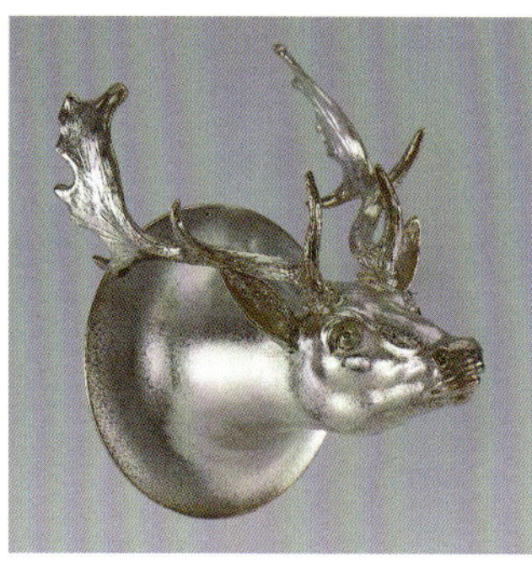

L. 6 1/2 in. (16.5 cm)
Wt. 16 oz. 18 dwt. (526 g)
Accession no.: 97.63

• 89 •

WRITING SET
Silver gilt, cut glass
Marks: Sterling, London, 1837/38; taper stick 1838/39
Maker's mark: Paul Storr (Grimwade, no. 2235)
Signature: Stamped under base of stand: *STORR & MORTIMER 219*; stamped on taperstick: *STORR & MORTIMER 178*
Stamped on top of stand: *1*

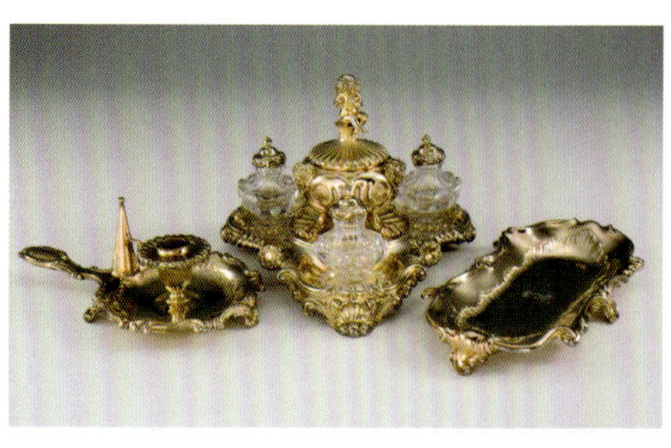

Heraldry: Engraved monogram of Charles, 4th Earl of Hardwicke, under an earl's coronet
Provenance: Charles, 4th Earl of Hardwicke (1799–1873); anonymous sale, Christie's, London, February 24, 1971, lot 166; I. Freeman, London; Lillian and Morrie Moss, Memphis, Tennessee, David Orgell, Inc., Beverly Hills
Exhibited: Memphis, 1972
Published: Moss, 1972, p. 44; pp. 262–63, pl. 194; Clayton, 1985b, p. 292; Bliss, no. 65, pp. 184–87

H. of inkstand 7 3/4 in. (19.7 cm)
H. of taper stick 4 in. (10.1 cm)
L. of pen tray 13 in. (33 cm)
Gross wt. 102 oz. 3 dwt. (3177 g)
Accession no.: 97.65.1, .2a-i, .3a-c

• 88 •

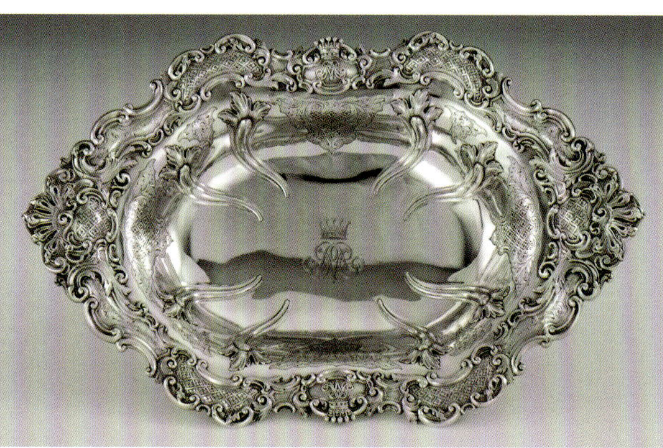

BASKET
Silver
Marks: Sterling, London, 1836/37
Maker's mark: Paul Storr (Grimwade, no. 2235)
Engraved underneath: *NO. 2* and *MP*

Heraldry: Engraved and chased monogram of Robert, 12th Earl of Pembroke and 9th Earl of Montgomery under an earl's coronet
Provenance: Robert, 12th Earl of Pembroke and 9th Earl of Montgomery (1791–1862)
Published: Bliss, no. 64, pp. 182–83

L. 16 1/4 in. (41.3 cm)
Wt. 43 oz. 12 dwt. (1356 g)
Accession no.: 97.64

• 90 •

CHRISTENING CUP AND COVER
Silver gilt
Marks: Sterling, London, 1840/41
Maker's mark: Edward Cornelius Farrell (Grimwade, no. 585)
Inscription: Engraved around the top of the cup: *TO THE HON. VICTOR ALEXANDER YORKE, FROM HIS GODMOTHER VICTORIA, R. 2: JUNE 1842.*

Published: Bliss, no. 78, pp. 228–31

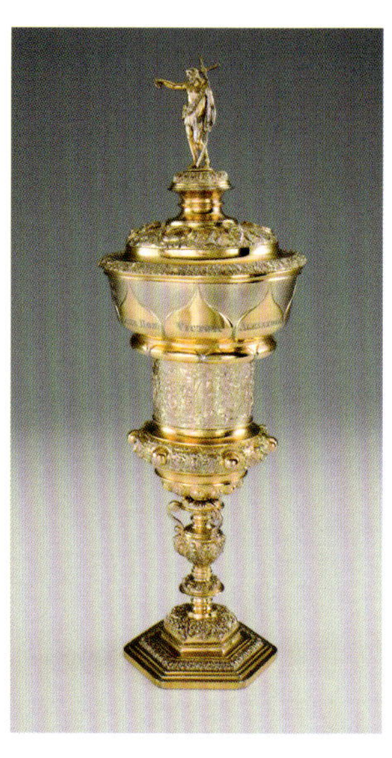

H. 18 3/4 in. (47.6 cm)
Wt. 65 oz. 17 dwt. (2048 g)
Accession no.: 97.85a-c

• 91 •

STANDING CUP AND COVER
Silver gilt
Marks: Sterling, London, 1843/44
Maker's mark: Robert Garrard II (Grimwade, no. 2322)

Published: Bliss, no. 71, pp. 208–11

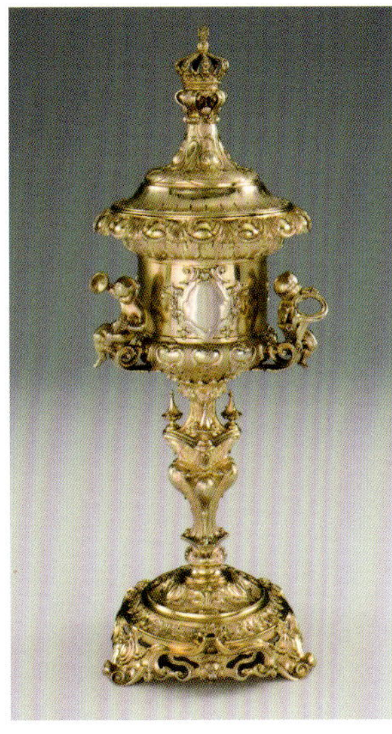

H. $16\,^{3}/_{4}$ in. (42.5 cm)
Wt. 53 oz. 13 dwt. (1668 g)
Accession no.: 97.71 a-c

• 92 •

TWO WINE COOLERS
Silver
Marks: Sterling, London, one vase: 1845/46; one vase and one collar and liner 1855/56; one liner 1837/38
Maker's mark: John S. Hunt (Jackson, no. 231); one collar and one liner: Paul Storr (Grimwade, no. 2235)
Signature: Stamped on one vase: *No. 2295 published as the Act directs by Hunt & Roskill 156 New Bond Street London Decr. 9 1846*
Stamped on one liner: *4*

Heraldry: Engraved crest of a stag trippant, which pertains to a number of families
Provenance: P.J. Dearden, Esq., sale, Sotheby's, London, November 12, 1970, lot 139; N. Bloom and Son, Ltd., London
Published: Culme, 1977, p. 105; Bliss, no. 66, pp. 188–90

H. $12\,^{5}/_{8}$ in. (32.1 cm)
Wt. 121 oz. 18 dwt.; 120 oz. 4 dwt. (3791; 3739 g)
Accession no.: 97.66.1a-c, .2a-c

• 93 •

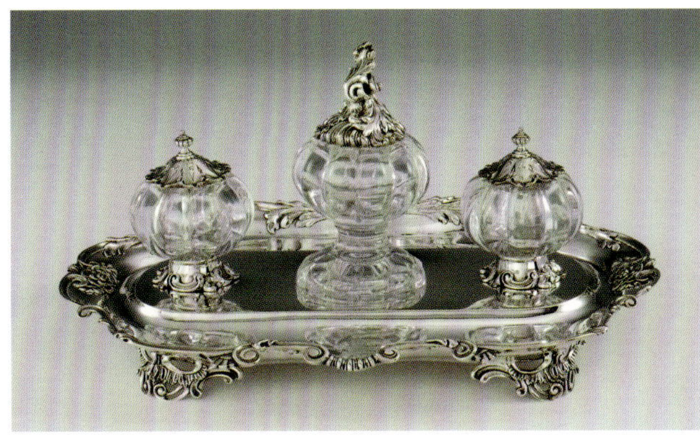

INKSTAND
Silver, cut glass
Marks: Sterling, London, 1849/50
Maker's mark: Robert Garrard II (Grimwade, no. 2322)
Signature: Stamped underneath the tray: *R. & S. GARRARD PANTON ST. LONDON.*

Heraldry: Engraved unidentified crests
Published: Bliss, no. 73, pp. 214–15

L. $13\,^{3}/_{4}$ in. (34.9 cm)
Gross wt. 77 oz. 10 dwt. (2410 g)
Accession no.: 97.73.1, .2a-b, .3a-b-.4a-b

• 94 •

TABLE BELL
Silver, partially gilt
Marks: Sterling, London, 1849/50
Maker's mark: Robert Garrard II (Grimwade, no. 2322)
Inscription: Engraved from cartouche to cartouche: *LR FROM HER MAJESTY VR XMAS 1855*

Exhibited: London, 1851
Published: Wyatt, pl. 46; Culme and Strang, p. 70; Bliss, no. 72, pp. 212–13

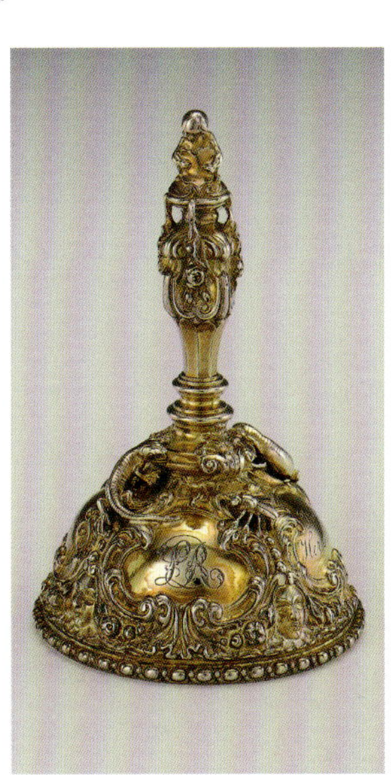

H. 5 in. (12.7 cm)
Wt. 10 oz. 17 dwt. (337 g)
Accession no.: 97.72

• 95 •

FIGURAL SALT
Silver gilt
Marks: Sterling, London, 1856/57
Maker's mark: Robert Garrard II (Grimwade, no. 2322)

Provenance: Christie's, Geneva, May 15, 1995, lot 7
Published: Culme, 1999, no. 7, pp. 56–57

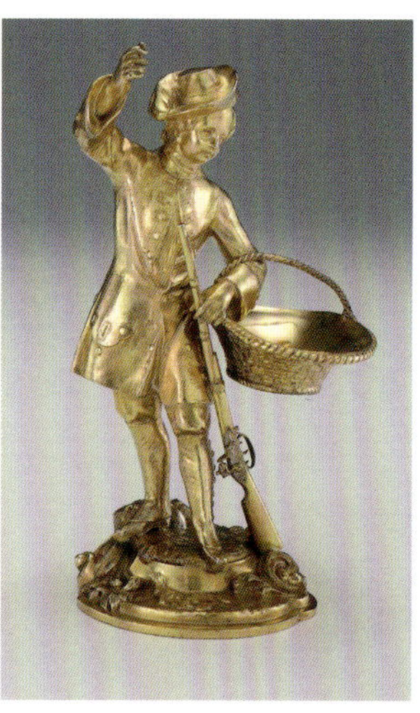

H. of boy huntsman 7 3/16 in. (18.2 cm)
Wt. 15 oz. 9 dwt. (481 g)
Accession no.: 97.87

• 97 •

SIX FIGURAL SALTS
Silver, four with baskets with gilt interiors
Marks: Sterling, London, 1863/64; Greek girl 1861/62; Irish lad and miss 1855/56
Maker's mark: Robert Garrard II (Grimwade, no. 2322)
Signature: Stamped near bottom edge of the stands: *R. & S. GARRARD PANTON ST., LONDON.*

Provenance: four: William Ward, 1st Earl of Dudley (1817–1885), by descent to William, 4th Earl of Dudley, sale, Sotheby's, London, February 6/11/20, 1986, lot 149
Published: Bliss, no. 76, pp. 222–23 (excluding Irish miss)

H. of Hungarian lass 6 11/16 in. (17 cm)
H. of French girl 7 1/8 in. (18.1 cm)
H. of Irish lad 7 in. (17.8 cm); H. of Irish miss 7 in. (17.8 cm)
H. of Spanish dandy 6 3/4 in. (17.2 cm); H. of Greek girl 6 7/8 in. (17.5 cm)
Wt. of Hungarian lass 16 oz. 2 dwt. (501 g)
Wt. of French girl 18 oz. 16 dwt. (585 g)
Wt. of Irish lad 15 oz. 5 dwt. (475 g); Wt. of Irish miss 15 oz. (466 g)
Wt. of Spanish dandy 15 oz. 13 dwt. (486 g)
Wt. of Greek girl 18 oz. 3 dwt. (565 g)
Accession nos.: 97.76, 97.77, 97.78, 97.79, 97.80, 97.81

• 96 •

PAIR OF FIGURAL SALTS
Silver, baskets with gilt interiors
Marks: Sterling, London, 1859/60
Maker's mark: Robert Garrard II (Grimwade, no. 2322)
Signature: Stamped along the base rim: *R. & S. GARRARD PANTON ST., LONDON.*

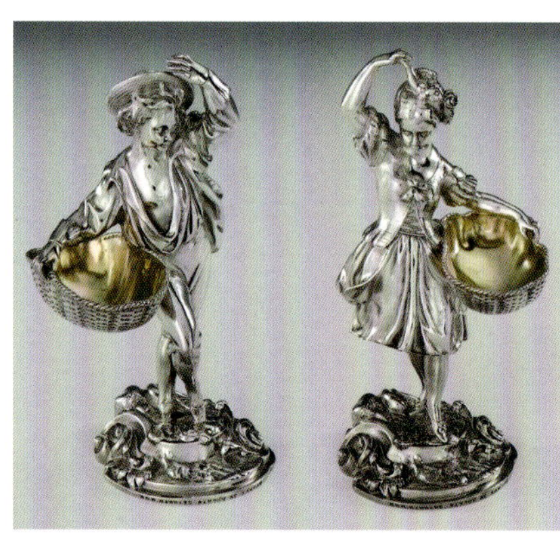

Provenance: Christie's, London, July 23, 1975, lot 79
Published: Bliss, no. 74, pp. 216–17

H. of English boy: 5 15/16 in. (15 cm)
H. of English girl: 5 7/8 in. (14.9 cm)
Wt. of boy: 15 oz. 2 dwt. (470 g)
Wt of girl: 15 oz. 2 dwt. (470 g)
Scratch wt. "31 oz."
Accession nos.: 97.74, 97.75

• 98 •

PAIR OF FIGURAL SALTS
Silver and silver gilt
Marks: Sterling, London, 1866/67
Maker's mark: Robert Garrard II (Grimwade, no. 2322)
Signature: Stamped along the base rim: *R & S. GARRARD PANTON ST., LONDON.*

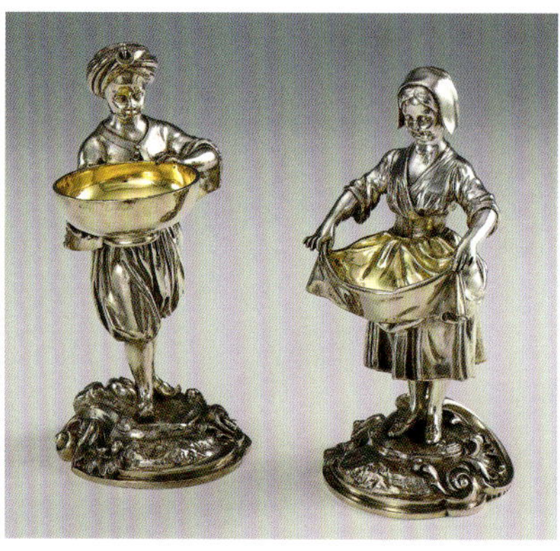

Published: Culme, 1999, no. 8, pp. 58–59

H. of blackamoor 6 3/4 in. (17.1 cm)
H. of Dutch girl 6 7/16 in. (16.3 cm)
Wt. of blackamoor 14 oz. 15 dwt. (458 g)
Wt. of Dutch girl 15 oz. 9 dwt. (480 g)
Accession nos.: 97.82, 97.83

• 99 •

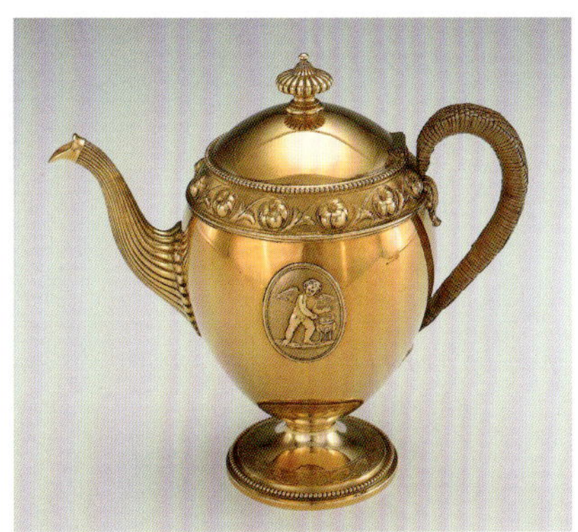

TEAPOT
Gold, wicker
Marks: 18 kt. standard, London, 1867/68
Maker's mark: Robert Garrard II (Grimwade, no. 2322)
Signature: Engraved around the rim of the foot: *R. & S. GARRARD. LONDON.*
Engraved under the base: *03.01.1827*

Exhibited: London, 1991
Published: Ogilvy, no. 44, p. 87; North, p. 353; Bliss, no. 77, pp. 224–26

H. 7 $^{5}/_{8}$ in. (19.4 cm)
Wt. 22 oz. 13 dwt. (704 g)
Accession no.: 97.84

• 100 •

LEMONADE JUG
Silver
Marks:
Sterling, London, 1875/76
Maker's mark:
Robert Hennell IV (Culme, no. 12139)

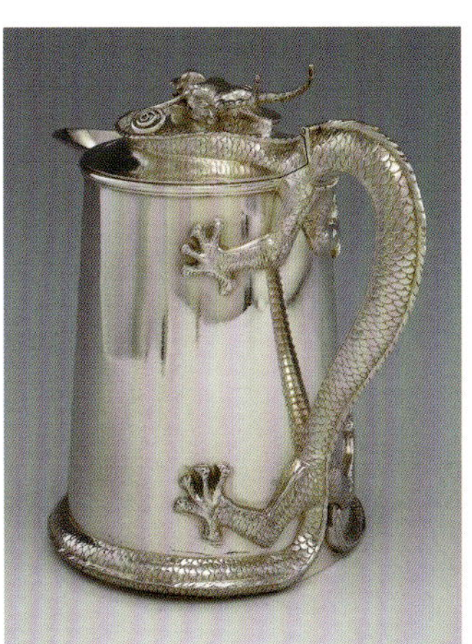

H. 8 $^{1}/_{2}$ in. (21.6 cm)
Wt. 34 oz., 17 dwt. (1084 g)
Accession no.: 2006.583

• 101 •

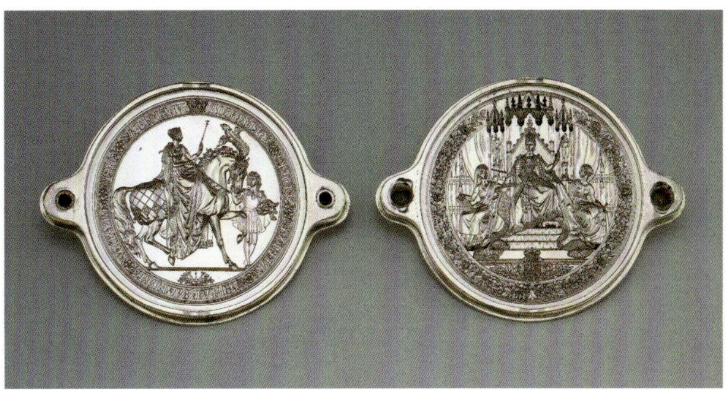

PAIR OF SEAL MATRICES:
THE GREAT SEAL OF ENGLAND
Silver
Together with a wax impression of the seal contained in a tinned iron box
Marks: Sterling, London, 1878/79
Maker's mark: Joseph Shepherd Wyon & Alfred Benjamin Wyon (Culme, no. 10113)

Heraldry: The royal arms are those of Queen Victoria (1818–1901)
Provenance: Morton & Eden, Ltd., London

W. 9 in. (22.9 cm)
Wt. 183 oz. 12 dwt. (5711 g)
Accession no.: 2006.584a-c

• 102 •

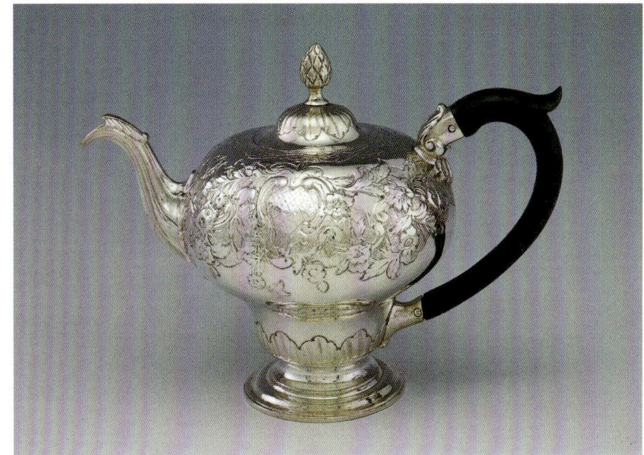

TEAPOT
Silver, fruitwood
New York, c. 1765
Maker's mark: Myer Myers of New York (Barquist, no. 9)

Provenance: S.J. Shrubsole Corp., New York
Exhibited: New Haven, Yale University Art Gallery, 2002,
Published: Barquist, pp. 164–65, no. 68; *Rococo Silver*, p. 100, fig. 157

W. 9 $^{3}/_{4}$ in. (24.8 cm)
Gross wt. 19 oz. 3 dwt. (595 g)
Accession no.: 2006.592

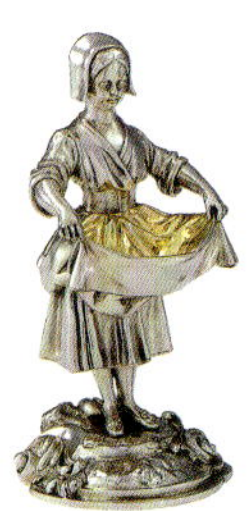

BIBLIOGRAPHY OF WORKS CITED

Armstrong
Nancy Armstrong, "Antiques for the dressing table," *Architectural Digest*, vol. 39, February 1982, pp. 72–77

Banister
Judith Banister, "Preserving a good impression, some silver seal boxes," *Country Life*, June 4, 1981, p. 1609

Barquist
David Barquist, *Myer Myers; Jewish Silversmith in Colonial New York*, exh. cat., Yale University Art Gallery, New Haven, 2001

Bliss
Joseph R. Bliss, *The Jerome and Rita Gans Collection of English Silver on Loan to the Virginia Museum of Fine Arts*, n.d. [1992]

Bliss, 1990a
Joseph R. Bliss, "Highlights by Paul de Lamerie from the Gans Collection of English Silver at the Virginia Museum," two parts, *Silver*, vol. 23, September/October, 1990, pp. 8–10 and November/December, 1990, pp. 8–11

Bliss, 1990b
Joseph R. Bliss, "Decorative arts from Byzantium to Edwardian Europe at the Virginia Museum," *The Magazine Antiques*, vol. CXXXVIII, August, 1990, pp. 270–77

Brett
Vanessa Brett, *The Sotheby's Directory of Silver, 1600–1940*, London, 1986

Bristol
English Silver, 1650–1800, exh. cat., City Art Gallery, Bristol, England, 1965

Carver and Casey
Beth S. Carver and Eileen M. Casey, *Silver by Paul de Lamerie at the Sterling and Francine Clark Art Institute*, exh. cat., Sterling and Francine Clark Art Institute, Williamstown, Massachusetts, 1976

Clayton, 1985a
Michael Clayton, *The Collector's Dictionary of the Silver and Gold of Great Britain and North America*, London, 1985

Clayton, 1985b
Michael Clayton, *Christie's Pictorial History of English and American Silver*, Oxford, 1985

Culme
John Culme, *The Directory of Gold & Silversmiths: Jewellers & Allied Traders 1838–1914 from the London Assay Office Registers*, 2 vols., Woodbridge, 1987

Culme, 1977
John Culme, *Nineteenth-Century Silver*, London, 1977

Culme, 1999
John Culme, *English Silver: The Jerome and Rita Gans Collection*, Richmond, Virginia, 1999

Culme and Strang
John Culme and John G. Strang, *Antique Silver and Silver Collecting*, London, 1973

Forster
Henry Rumsey Forster, ed., *The Stowe Catalogue Priced and Annotated*, London, 1848

Gardner
J. Starkie Gardner, *Old Silver-Work Chiefly English, from the XVth to the XVIIIth Centuries: A Catalogue of the Unique Loan Collection Exhibited in 1902 at St. James's Court, London, in Aid of the Children's Hospital, Gt. Ormond Street*, London, 1903

Grimwade
Arthur G. Grimwade, *London Goldsmiths and Their Marks*, rev. ed., London, 1990

Grimwade, 1974
Arthur Grimwade, *Rococo Silver, 1727–1765*, London, 1974

Grimwade, 1988
Arthur G. Grimwade, "The Master of George Vertue," *Apollo*, vol. 127, no. 312, 1988, pp. 83–89

Hackenbroch
Yvonne Hackenbroch, *English and other Silver in the Irwin Untermyer Collection*, rev. ed., New York, 1969

Hare
Susan Hare, ed., *Paul de Lamerie: At the Sign of The Golden Ball. An Exhibition of the Work of England's Master Silversmith (1688–1751)*, exh. cat., Goldsmiths' Hall, London, 1990

Hartop, 1991
Christopher Hartop, "Everything Solid, Liberal, Rich and English," *Christie's International Magazine*, vol. VIII, no. 1, pp. 14–15

Hartop, 1993
Christopher Hartop, "Paul de Lamerie: Virtuoso or Entrepreneur?" *Christie's International Magazine*, vol. X, no. 2, pp. 2–4

Hartop, 1994
Christopher Hartop, "Admiral George Anson and his de Lamerie Silver," *The Magazine Antiques*, vol. CXLV, no. 6, June 1994, pp. 850–57

Hartop, 2005
Christopher Hartop, *Royal Goldsmiths: The Art of Rundell & Bridge 1797–1843*, exh. cat., Koopman Rare Art, London, 2005

Hartop, 2007
Christopher Hartop, *British and Irish Silver in the Fogg Art Museum, Harvard University Art Museums*, Cambridge, Massachusetts, 2007

Hawkins
J.B. Hawkins, *The Al Tajir Collection of Silver and Gold*, London, 1983

Houston
Silver by Paul de Lamerie in America, exh. cat., Museum of Fine Arts, Houston, Texas, 1956

Indianapolis
Mark A. Clark, *Silver by Paul Storr in American Collections*, exh. cat., Indianapolis Museum of Art, Indianapolis, Indiana, 1972

Jackson, 1911
Charles James Jackson, *An Illustrated History of English Plate*, London, 1911

Jones, 1908
E. Alfred Jones, *Illustrated Catalogue of the Collection of Old Plate of J. Pierpont Morgan, Esquire*, London, 1908

Jones, 1928a
E. Alfred Jones, "Some Old English and Continental Silver in the Collection of Lord Dalmeny," *Old Furniture*, May 1928

Jones, 1928b
E. Alfred Jones, *Old Silver of Europe and America from Earlier Times to the Nineteenth Century*, London, 1928

London, 1902
Catalogue of the Exhibition of Silversmith's Work of European Origin in Aid of the Funds for the Great Ormond Street Hospital for Sick Children, exh. cat., St. James's Court, London, July, 1902

London, 1929a
A Loan Exhibition of Old English Plate and Decorations and Orders, exh. cat., London, 1929

London, 1929b
Queen Charlotte's Loan Exhibition of Old Silver, exh. cat., London, 1929

London, 1978
Touching Gold & Silver: 500 Year of Hallmarking, exh. cat., Goldsmiths' Hall, London, 1978

Minneapolis
Francis J. Puig et al. *English and American Silver the Collection of the Minneapolis Institute of Art*, Minneapolis, 1989

Moss, 1966
Mr. and Mrs. Morrie A. Moss Collection of Paul Storr Silver, 1771–1843, exh. cat., Brooks Memorial Art Gallery, Memphis, Tennessee, 1966

Moss, 1968
Mr. and Mrs. Morrie A. Moss Collection of Paul Storr Silver, 1771–1843, exh. cat., supplement, Brooks Memorial Art Gallery, Memphis, Tennessee, 1968

Moss, 1971
Mr. and Mrs. Morrie A. Moss Collection of Paul Storr Silver, 1771–1843, exh. cat., second supplement, Brooks Memorial Art Gallery, Memphis, Tennessee, 1972

Moss, 1972
Morrie A. Moss, *The Lillian and Morrie Moss Collection of Paul Storr Silver*, Miami, 1972

Müller
Hannelore Müller, *European Silver: The Thyssen-Bornemisza Collection*, London, 1986

Newman
Harold Newman, *An Illustrated Dictionary of Silverware*, London, 1987

North
A.R.E. North, "Royal Goldsmiths, the Heritage of the House of Garrards," *Apollo*, vol. 133, May 1991, pp. 353–54

Ogilvy
Julia Ogilvy ed., *Royal Goldsmiths: The Garrard Heritage*, exh. cat., Garrard, London, 1991

Penzer
Norman Mosley Penzer, *Paul Storr, the Last of the Goldsmiths*, London, 1954; reissued as Norman Mosley Penzer, *Paul Storr, 1771–1844: Silversmith and Goldsmith*, London, 1971

Phillips
Philip A.S. Phillips, *Paul de Lamerie: Citizen and Goldsmith of London: A Study of His Life and Work A.D. 1688–1751*, London, 1935; facsimile reprint, 1968

Princeton
English Silver, exh. cat., Princeton University Art Museum, Princeton, New Jersey, 1966

Rabinovitch
Benton Seymour Rabinovitch, *Antique Silver Servers for the Dining Table: Style, Function, Foods and Social History*, Concord, Massachusetts, 1991

Rococo
Rococo: Art and Design in Hogarth's England, exh. cat., Victoria & Albert Museum, London, 1984

Rococo Silver
Rococo Silver in England and Its Colonies: Papers from a Symposium at Virginia Museum of Fine Arts, Richmond, in 2004, London, 2006

Schroder, 1983
Timothy Schroder, *The Dowty Collection of Silver by Paul de Lamerie*. exh. cat., Cheltenham, 1983

Schroder, 1988a
Timothy Schroder, *The Gilbert Collection of Gold and Silver*, Los Angeles, 1988

Schroder, 1988b
Timothy Schroder, *The National Trust Book of English Domestic Silver, 1500–1900*, London, 1988

Schwartz
Marvin D. Schwartz, "Treasures in English Silver from the Morrison Collection," *Antiques*, vol. 85, May 1964, pp. 570–74

Skerry
Janine E. Skerry, "Paul Storr Silver and the Yale University Art Gallery," *Yale University Art Gallery Bulletin*, vol. 38, Fall, 1988, pp. 16–25

Truman, 1989
Charles Truman, ed., *The Glory of the Goldsmith: Magnificent Gold and Silver from the Al-Tajir Collection*, exh. cat., London, 1989

Waldron
Peter Waldron, *The Price Guide to Antique Silver*, rev. ed., London 1982

Wees
Beth Carver Wees, *English, Irish & Scottish Silver at the Sterling and Francine Clark Art Institute*, New York, 1997

Wenham
Edward Wenham, *Domestic Silver of Great Britain and Ireland*, New York, 1931

Wyatt
Digby M. Wyatt, *Industrial arts of the Nineteenth Century, at the Great Exhibition*, 2 vols., London, 1851/1852

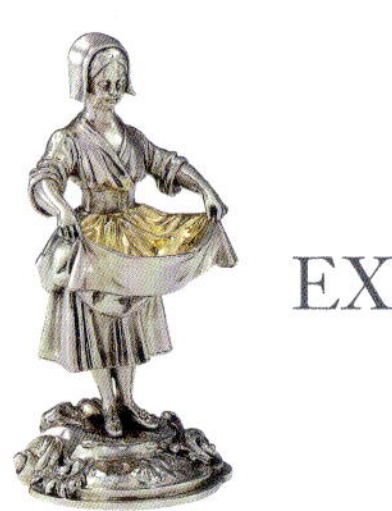

EXHIBITIONS

Bristol, 1965
English Silver, 1650–1800, City Art Gallery, Bristol, England, 1965

Cheltenham, 1983
The Dowty Collection of Silver by Paul de Lamerie, Cheltenham, England, 1983

Dayton, 1972
Silver by Paul Storr in American Collections, the Dayton Art Institute, Dayton, Ohio, March 24–April 30, 1972

Houston, 1956
Silver by Paul de Lamerie in America, Museum of Fine Arts, Houston, Texas, 1956

Indianapolis, 1972
Silver by Paul Storr in American Collections, Indianapolis Museum of Art, Indianapolis, Indiana, February 7–March 12, 1972

London, 1851
The Great Exhibition, Crystal Palace, Hyde Park, London, 1851

London, 1862
The Great International Exhibition, South Kensington Museum, London, June 1862

London, 1902
Exhibition of Silversmith's Work of European Origin in Aid of the Funds for the Great Ormond Street Hospital for Sick Children, St. James's Court, London, July 1902

London, 1928
The Daily Telegraph Art Treasures Exhibition, Olympia, London, 1928

London, 1929a
A Loan Exhibition of Old English Plate and Decorations and Orders, 25 Park Lane, London, March 1929

London, 1929b
Queen Charlotte's Loan Exhibition of Old Silver, Seaford House, Belgrave Square, London, May 1–June 8, 1929

London, 1973
Christie's, *Fanfare for Europe*, Christie's, London, January 1973

London, 1978
Touching Gold & Silver: 500 Year of Hallmarking, Goldsmiths' Hall, London, 1978

London, 1984
Rococo: Art and Design in Hogarth's England, Victoria and Albert Museum, London, May 16–September 30, 1984

London, 1989a
Grosvenor House Antiques Fair, London, June 15–24 , 1989

London, 1989b
The Glory of the Goldsmith: Magnificent Gold and Silver from the Al- Tajir Collection, Christie's, London, 1989

London, 1990
Paul de Lamerie: At the Sign of the Golden Ball: An Exhibition of the Work of England's Master Silversmith (1688–1751), Goldsmiths' Hall (London, May 16–June 22, 1990

London, 1991
Royal Goldsmiths: The Garrard Heritage, Garrard, London, May 14–June 8, 1991

Memphis, 1966
Mr. and Mrs. Morrie A. Moss Collection of Paul Storr Silver, 1771–1843, Brooks Memorial Art Gallery, Memphis, Tennessee, March 6–27, 1966

Memphis, 1968
Mr. and Mrs. Morrie A. Moss Collection of Paul Storr Silver, 1771–1843, Brooks Memorial Art Gallery, Memphis, Tennessee, March–April, 1968

Memphis, 1971
Mr. and Mrs. Morrie A. Moss Collection of Paul Storr Silver, 1771–1843, Brooks Memorial Art Gallery, Memphis, Tennessee, December 3, 1971–January 16, 1972

New Haven, 2001
Myer Myers: Jewish Silversmith in Colonial New York, exh. cat., Yale University Art Gallery, New Haven, 2001 and on tour

Princeton, 1966
English Silver, Princeton University Art Museum, Princeton, 1966

PHOTOGRAPHIC CREDITS

All images of items in the Jerome and Rita Gans Collection are by Katherine Wetzel with the exception of the following photographs by Steve Tucker: figures 3, 5–6, 13, 17, 31, 34, 36–37, 40, 48, 50–51, 61, 66; catalogue numbers 1–3, 6, 15, 29, 34, 39, 41, 52, 57–58, 70, 85, 100–102.

COVER PICTURES

Front cover:
Pair of livery pots, silver gilt, London, 1602/03, maker's mark *TE in monogram, pellet below*. Cat. no. 2

Front flap:
Fish serving slice, silver, London, 1746/47, maker's mark of Paul de Lamerie. Cat. no. 29

Dutch girl, one of a pair of figural salts, silver and silver gilt, London, 1866/67, maker's mark of Robert Garrard II (image repeated throughout the book). Cat. no. 98

Back cover:
***Pot à oille*, or soup tureen, silver, London, 1736/37, maker's mark of Paul de Lamerie (detail of a handle).** Cat. no. 15

Back flap:
Pair of wine coolers, silver gilt, London, 1814/15, maker's mark of Benjamin Smith II. Cat. no. 57